SOUTH-WEST OF EDEN

Other books by C. K. Stead

Poetry

Whether the Will is Free
Crossing the Bar
Quesada
Walking Westward
Geographies
Poems of a Decade
Paris
Between
Voices
Straw into Gold
The Right Thing
Dog
The Red Tram
The Black River
Collected Poems, 1951–2006

Fiction

Smith's Dream
Five for the Symbol (stories)
All Visitors Ashore
The Death of the Body
Sister Hollywood
The End of the Century at the End of the World
The Singing Whakapapa
Villa Vittoria
The Blind Blonde with Candles in her Hair (stories)
Talking about O'Dwyer
The Secret History of Modernism
Mansfield
My Name was Judas

Criticism

The New Poetic
In the Glass Case
Pound, Yeats, Eliot and the Modernist Movement
Answering to the Language
The Writer at Work
Kin of Place: Essays on 20 New Zealand Writers
Book Self: The Reader as Writer and the Writer as Critic

Edited

Oxford New Zealand Short Stories (second series)
Measure for Measure, a Casebook
Letters and Journals of Katherine Mansfield
Collected Stories of Maurice Duggan
Faber Book of Contemporary South Pacific Stories
Werner Forman's New Zealand

SOUTH-WEST OF EDEN

A MEMOIR 1932–1956

C. K. STEAD

AUCKLAND UNIVERSITY PRESS

First published 2010

Auckland University Press
University of Auckland
Private Bag 92019
Auckland 1142
New Zealand
www.auckland.ac.nz/aup

ISBN 978 1 86940 454 3

Publication is assisted by

National Library of New Zealand Cataloguing-in-Publication Data
Stead, C. K. (Christian Karlson), 1932-
South-west of Eden : a memoir 1932-1956 / C.K. Stead.
ISBN 978-1-86940-454-3
1. Stead, C. K. (Christian Karlson), 1932-
—Childhood and youth.
2. Authors, New Zealand—20th century—Biography.
I. Title.
NZ823.2—dc 22

Front cover and flap: The author and his sister Norma, c. 1940
Back cover: The author, photographed by Fred Foulds, 1953
Back flap: Kay Stead (née Roberts), 1955
Cover design: Sarah Maxey

Printed in China by 1010 Printing International Ltd

CONTENTS

FOREWORD

I said many times I would not write autobiography – partly because it might signal, either to my inner self, or to others, a 'signing off' as a writer; and partly because I did not want to mark off areas that were fact in my life from those that might yet be invented. Fiction likes to move, disguised and without a passport, back and forth across that border, and prefers it should be unmarked and without check-points.

But age and the lack of a compelling idea for a new novel have combined, with a very positive response to my most recent non-fiction book, to change my mind. *Book Self: The Reader as Writer and the Writer as Critic* was intended to be just another selection of essays, public lectures and reviews; but the autobiographical elements that got into it seemed to add greatly to the interest and the warmth (apart from small predictable areas of deep-freeze) of response. This means, however, that in the later chapters of the present book there are a few small overlaps with *Book Self*. That was unavoidable, because of the way memory frames and edits the distant past: two or three stories had to be repeated, and I think bear repeating.

The other fact that made the present book possible was that it was conceived, right from the beginning, as a self-contained narrative that would begin at birth, or as soon afterwards as memory set in, and go up to my first departure from New Zealand at the age of 23. I suspect there are grand precedents: Goethe? Wagner? Certainly Yeats, in his *Reveries over Childhood and Youth*. But with or without the back-up of big guns, I wanted to do it this way because I felt that whatever has followed, whether in the way of achievement or misdemeanour, was inherent in what I had been, and had done, in those first 23 years. I was, for good and ill, and for ever, a product of my genes in concord and combat with mid-century Auckland, New Zealand; and to tell this story was, or ought to be if I got it right, a way – one way – of telling the story of my time and my place.

I owe acknowledgements and thanks to old friends who helped me: in particular (taking them in the order in which they figure in the story) Barry Catton, Rob Dyer, Diane McKegg, Jill and Don Smith – and of course Kay Stead. One or two I would like to have talked to have vanished without trace; many, alas, are dead. Jock Upton's daughter, Shirley, kindly gave me information which confirmed my recollection of him. Margaret Scott helped me with relevant extracts from the Charles Brasch journals which she is transcribing.

I received great help and co-operation from my old school, Mount Albert Grammar, and particularly from Brian Murphy, the school archivist, and Chris Long, its development director. Similarly, Ruth Taylor at the University of Auckland helped me with facts about myself and others. Balmoral Intermediate School had no records that went back so far, or none that could be found. New Zealand Army Archives supplied me with my own undistinguished military history. David Verran at the Auckland Central City Library and Dr Michael Bassett provided me with useful records and information in support of my recollection of my father's role in the Labour Party, and subsequently on the Land Sales Court. The Hocken Library supplied me with copies of my correspondence with Charles Brasch, and the Alexander Turnbull Library with copies of letters to Frank Sargeson. Jeny Curnow gave permission to quote two stanzas of 'Spectacular Blossom' by Allen Curnow and Margaret Edgcumbe gave permission to reproduce lines by Kendrick Smithyman.

The rest is memory, which I have relied on, and have found no reason not to trust.

I completed final revisions, additions, subtractions and polishing while holding the Seresin Landfall Residency at Gaiole in Chianti during August–September 2009. My grateful thanks go to Michael Seresin and Otago University Press for that opportunity.

When I was about half way through a first draft, and thinking of calling it *63 Kensington Avenue*, I received a broad envelope from the present occupant of that address, Mrs Sue Donnell, whom I had never met and knew nothing of, enclosing a University of New Zealand Certificate of Entrance Qualification dated 1949, showing that Christian Karlson Stead had been accredited in English, history and chemistry. It had been found under the house, and looked as foxed, torn and dog-eared as a document that has lain about in the dust for sixty years should. Difficult to describe what a strange feeling it produced in me, that this should have come, especially at that moment, as if to confirm that I was not inventing myself, but had in truth existed in a past real enough to leave such precise evidence.

C.K.S.

I
CLOSE TO THE SKY

and I am there still, close to the sky
listening to housewives talk about the War,
watching the pole flash and the red tram
clank off into the future.

ONE
TAMAKI OF MANY LOVERS, AND JACK

From the windows of 63 Kensington Avenue you could see three of Auckland's many volcanic cones: to the south-east, One Tree Hill; north-east, Mt Eden; westward, Mt Albert. I knew the Maori name of Mt Eden was Maungawhau, because it was also the name of my school, only a few hundred yards away, in sight of our house. In those days the wh was pronounced by Pakeha as a w; and even now it takes an effort of will for me to give it the required f – Maungafau. Matters of language learned so early in childhood are almost immovable. I feel, pronouncing it Maungafau, as if I'm making a mistake, a solecism, but I do it, understanding why it is required, and despite the fact that the scholar in me has to be checked from giving support to the child.

Of those three hills only the English names were used by Pakeha; but I knew the Maori name of One Tree Hill was Maungakiekie; and Owairaka, the Maori name for Mt Albert, was also the name of its surrounding suburb.

Mt Eden was grass-covered, with clumps of trees around its base. I used to climb there with other boys during school holidays, and we rode sledges down into the crater. The crater-sides, dangerously steep, got stonier as you sped to the bottom, and no one ever went right from the top. Many arms were broken there, I'm sure, and how far up from the scoria-filled vent you dared make your start was a test of courage, or a measure of folly.

I liked to stand at the summit and look out in all directions. One way you saw the city centre, the port almost at your feet, and beyond it the North Shore and the islands of the Hauraki Gulf. The other way lay the great empty reaches of the Manukau Harbour. Turning half-left from that view you could pick out the main highway running away south towards the Bombay Hills, Auckland's southern gateway. From up there I could pick out Maungawhau School and, using the school as a marker, the red iron roof, one among so many, of 63 Kensington Avenue. Asked once in my middle years to write some sort of autobiographical summary, and trying to imagine how I might give it focus, it occurred to me that most things of real significance in my life and the life of my family had happened somewhere in sight from the summit of Mt Eden.

Mt Albert, visible from that summit and from our kitchen windows, and different from the other two in that it appeared to be smoky blue-grey, was the one I would not get to know well until I enrolled at Mt Albert Grammar, ran the annual round-the-mountain race and played soccer on the field that had been constructed inside its crater, sheltered by Australian eucalypts which accounted for the distinctive colour.

One Tree Hill's visual feature was the single tree that gave it its name, standing out against the sky, an exceptionally large Monterey pine with a wide canopy, a landmark second only to Rangitoto Island as a topographical brand for Auckland. Right beside the tree, softened and partly concealed, stood a monument to 'the achievements of the Maori people', a 30-metre obelisk, designed and bequeathed by John Logan Campbell in 1904, when it was still being said that the Maori were 'a dying race', but not begun until 1939, by which time it was clear they were going to flourish. It is an example of the kind of irony which always besets protest action that when, many decades later again, in the 1990s, two chain-saw attacks by Maori activists made the tree dangerous and caused it, in the end, to be cut down, the obelisk, that clumsy, well-meaning, foolish Pakeha tribute to the tangata whenua, was left starkly exposed. For the activists, the tree had been 'a symbol of colonial oppression'. But what was the monument, which remains?

Everyone in Auckland, Maori and Pakeha, seemed to lament the tree's passing. Without it, the hill looked stripped and the monument ugly. A young Maori poet wrote a lament for it. Angry Pakeha words were written in the newspapers and spoken on radio. A Maori taxi driver told me how, when he first came to Auckland, he had taken his general bearings around the city from his position in relation to the tree, and now he missed it as a friend. Ngati Whatua told Ngapuhi (the northern tribe from which the activists came) that the attack was an invasion of their tribal area, one which, in the old times, would have led to war. Consultations with local iwi went on (and at the time of writing have continued over years) about how, and with what, the tree should be replaced.

Maori myth has it that the original, pre-European, tree on the top of that hill was a giant totara (Te Totara-i-ahua), grown from the sharp stake that cut the umbilical cord of a great chief, probably in the seventeenth century; but nineteenth-century accounts show that the totara, if it was ever more than myth, had not survived, and that time had replaced it with a self-sown pohutukawa, a tree which in its turn fell, probably to the axes of early settlers in need of firewood. When John Logan Campbell, owner of the hill and surrounding land, decided to grow a replacement pohutukawa there, neither the chosen tree nor any but two, and finally one, of the pines intended only as a temporary shelter for the replanting survived. That was the pine of the One Tree Hill of my childhood; and its story, involving myth and misinformation, inter-tribal rivalry, Maori–Pakeha disagreement, cross-cultural misunderstanding and the accidents of horticultural survival on a windy hilltop, catches the complexity, passion and absurdity of our (and every) history.*

In addition to tree-planting and monument-designing, that excellent Scottish settler and 'father of Auckland' John Logan Campbell gifted to the city One Tree Hill and the surrounding 500 acres as public land, named Cornwall Park after some visiting royal. In my childhood it was much as it is now, open grassland, gardens and trees, including many fine olives, though my recollection is that, unlike the olives that have sprung up all over Auckland in recent decades, Campbell's grew large but produced no fruit. There were scoria stone walls, grazing sheep and a tea rooms. Once (and probably more than once) when I was very small, my parents, sister and I walked from Kensington Avenue up Ellerton Road and Watling Street to Manukau and Greenlane Roads, to picnic in the park and climb to the summit. I remember it because the park seemed so beautiful that day; and because getting there in the heat I felt a single bead of sweat run down my brow. My father sweated in the heat, and this one salty trickle, my first, seemed a manly and memorable accomplishment.

Later, I used to stay with a boy, and he in turn with me, called Jack Aitken whose house in Wheturangi Road (also pronounced at that time with a w, not an f)† had a gate in its back garden fence which opened on to Cornwall Park. Jack's father was a senior administrator in the Auckland Central Post Office; and I had the impression (possibly mistaken) that he wished me to understand that his status was superior to my father's, an accountant in the Stores branch of

---

* Details about the tree come from my colleague and fellow-Albertian Professor Russell Stone. See R. C. J. Stone, *Logan Campbell's Auckland*, Auckland University Press, Auckland, 2007, pp. 52–62.

† If f was what the missionaries, who were first to transcribe the Maori language into written form, had heard, they would have used that letter. What they heard was the sound between f and w that was traditionally represented by wh. In other words, the pure f Maori now insist upon (and that is their right – it is their language) is not quite the pronunciation of their forebears.

the same employer, and that he was exhibiting not inconsiderable social flexibility in admitting me to their household. Jack owned a bow and arrow, not the kind I and my Maungawhau School friends made for ourselves of bamboo, but a bought one, the real thing, of varnished wood with steel-tipped and feather-shafted arrows.

Cornwall Park was wonderful boy-territory and we tended to run wild there, or if wild is an exaggeration, then free. A neighbouring tennis court, owned by the parents of a sort of Hubert Lane-ite (we were keen readers of the *William* books), was blitzed with dirt bombs in paper bags. Potatoes were dug up unlawfully from Mr Aitken's garden and boiled in a billy over an unlawful fire. Coming home from the Victory Cinema at night we set fire to a hedge. I was generally blamed for any decline in Jack's behaviour; and I suppose that was not unfair, in the sense that two boys together are usually more trouble than one alone. Fortunately the hedge fire was never traced to us or visits either way would have come to an end.

As it happened one of my favourite books at that time, borrowed at intervals from school, was *Young Jack* by Herbert Strang.[*] The story takes place in, I think, the eighteenth century, and begins with its boy hero, Jack, and his friend Oliver up in the branches of an enormous oak in a village square in rural England, listening to soldiers enlisting, or perhaps pressing, new recruits for war in France. This fictional Jack, together with Jack Hawkins of Stevenson's *Treasure Island* (a novel my father had read to me before I could read it myself), gave the name a special resonance and made it only a short step, in my mind, from fiction to reality and back again. Equally, I identified effortlessly with Richmal Crompton's lawless William, despite the fact that his household mysteriously included a cook and a maid. It was William who seemed to sanction those dirt bombs on the Hubert Lane-ite's tennis court.

---

[*] Many years later, in an idle moment in the old British Museum Reading Room, I looked up Herbert Strang and found it was the joint pseudonym of two authors, one of whom was surnamed Stead.

The war in the Pacific had begun and an American Army hospital (a cluster of prefabricated huts) was being constructed in Cornwall Park; and somewhere else nearby, possibly on land belonging to the Ellerslie Racecourse, was an American military base. Jack and I sometimes hung about the gates of the base and were given chewing gum by friendly GIs, the flat, stick kind, much superior to our own; and occasionally a nickel or dime as a souvenir. When I wrote my novel *My Name was Judas* and had the boys Jesus and Judas hanging about the gates of the Roman camp, I had in mind myself and Jack and those American soldiers. There was a place called the New American Milk Bar in Newmarket, where you could buy new drinks and confections, milk shakes and ice-cream sodas, and listen to GIs talking 'like the movies', playing jazz, and singing 'Deep in the heart of Texas' and 'New York, New York is a wonderful town'.

This was the time when almost the whole of New Zealand's armed forces had been sent far away to fight in the Middle East, Greece and Crete; but now the Japanese had come into the war, attacking Pearl Harbour and sweeping down through the Pacific. Jack's sister Verona, about the age of William's sister Ethel, was old enough to have American soldier-boyfriends, who gave her silk stockings, chocolates and flowers, took her dancing and taught her to jitterbug. One of Jack's and my crimes, productive of sisterly shrieks and reproaches, was reading her love letters. It was chocolates we were after, not gossip (she had hidden the letters in an Adams Bruce chocolate box), but that was not believed.

The connection between the Aitkens and the Steads must have come through the fathers' workplace, but it was the two mothers and the two sons who were friends. Recently I found from my mother's old address book that Mrs Aitken's first name was Alice, but I don't think that first names were used. She was from a family of South Island racehorse breeders and trainers, and had a noticeable head of red-brown hair. She once 'took a holiday' by herself, renting a flat across the harbour in Devonport, and wrote (neither we nor the Aitkens had a phone – few people did at that time) inviting my mother for lunch. Although Jack was not with his mother, I persuaded mine to take me along. She dressed herself (as always when 'going to town') in good dress, coat, hat and shoes, gloves as well probably, and me in jacket, cap and tie, shorts and knee-length socks, and we made the trip by tram and ferry. I loved the ferry crossing, the eerie green sun-shafts and shifty green water under the wharf and around the piles, the grinding of ropes on bollards, the beat of pistons and the sudden freshness of wind and swish of waves as you swung out into open harbour.

It was a first-floor flat Mrs Aitken had taken, close to the bottom of Church Street where my father and his brothers had grown up, and we sat having lunch looking out across the street past the public clock to the sea lane off North Head where shipping passed in and out of the harbour. There was an air of something brewing between the two women, something they wanted to talk about that must have been touched upon already in Mrs Aitken's letter; and when the meal was done it was suggested I might like to go and amuse myself on the little beach across the road – something I was keen to do. It must be that atmosphere of secrets between the women that accounts for my quite particular memory of a day when nothing memorable happened; and it is only now, so many decades later, I stop to ask myself what it was Mrs Aitken wished to confide, and what it meant to say she was 'taking a holiday' in her home town. The fiction writer would speculate and invent; the author of this memoir will allow himself only to record.

Mrs Aitken was soon back at Wheturangi Road, but I'm not able to say whether it was before or after her Devonport 'holiday' that I was staying with the family and came into the parental bedroom on a Sunday morning to find her and her husband sleeping late. Neither stirred and I retreated unnoticed, taking with me the image of her striking red-brown coiffure fitted over a head-shaped wooden stand beside the bed, and her bald head shining and pink on the pillow.

ALL THREE OF THOSE VOLCANIC HILLS, Mt Eden, One Tree Hill and Mt Albert, are deeply indented with what were once pa defences and garden terraces around the base, the most elaborate in the whole country; and Tamaki, as Maori called the Auckland isthmus, was often referred to as Tamaki-makau-rau, which over time seems to have been adopted as its official Maori name. It means Tamaki-of-many-lovers, suggesting a beautiful woman much desired and fought over. The climate, the fertile soil, the two harbours only a few miles apart on opposite coasts, and the abundance of fish and shellfish in both – all of this had the same appeal for Maori that it has since had for Pakeha; and the story I heard at school from a teacher called Mr Robinson (teachers had no given names in those days) was that fierce inter-tribal wars had been fought across the isthmus, and that one battle in particular, on the slopes of the hill our school was named after, was so terrible, a tapu had been placed on its slopes which persisted at the time of the arrival of the first European settlers. So the pa sites on Mt Eden, and also the ones on One Tree Hill, had been long-since abandoned, and were covered in bush when the first settler-purchases of Tamaki land were made. Only when those trees had been cleared was the extent of the terracing of pre-Pakeha times apparent.

The young Pakeha consciousness, as it grew during the years of my childhood (I was born in October 1932) was, without knowing it, the ground of a contest between two cultures – Maori and British. In every significant way the British was winning, because the dominant language, the social conventions, the political constitution, the international allegiances, the literature – all were British. But so many of the place-names and the stories belonging to them, and much else yet to be (in the literal sense) dis-covered during the next half century, were Maori, invisible but alive beneath the surface, and a subtle rebalancing was bound to occur.

And the British heritage was itself complicated, because it brought with it its own contradictory loyalties and antagonisms – Scots and Welsh, and especially Irish, against English; Catholic against Protestant Irish; and working class against everyone. These very evidently faded with time and distance; but they meant that New Zealand manifestations of loyalty to Britain and the Crown, though genuine and at times apparently fervent, were cross-hatched with qualification and contradiction, so that everything said on this subject seemed, to the intelligent child, consulting his own feelings and observing the behaviour of adults, to consist of half-truths, approximations and, often, nonsense.

Meanwhile most Maori lived outside the towns. There were some few among the children at our school (one of them my own cousin, who lived with us while his father, my Uncle Don, was away at the war); and a few kuia were to be seen in our suburb, old enough to have the faded blue moko on chin and lower lip. But when Maori figured in my consciousness it was mainly in place-names, in stories about our colonial past, in Maori folklore (my sister and I owned a book called *Maoriland Fairytales*), and, most vividly and topically, in news about the Maori Battalion, New Zealand's fiercest infantry force, fighting in Greece and Crete, the Middle East and later in Italy. We were told we had the best race relations in the world, and believed it because there was nothing at the time to contradict it. It might even have been true, but, if so, we would slowly have to learn, and learn to accept, that that was only in the sense that everyone else's race relations were worse.

Yet if the British was far and away the dominant culture, and if European New Zealand was not yet out of its colonial sailor suit, the new identity, when it emerged, would be neither British nor Maori. It's for that reason I have always accepted the self-identification of 'Pakeha', because there is no other word that covers the case of what we are. There is even a sense in which it could be argued that most Maori in the twenty-first century are, or will be, Pakeha also; that they embody the same mix, having come to it from the other side. That, it might be argued, is a description which leaves out too much, and especially the social and psychological damage done to colonised by coloniser. But there is no honest way of making the history kinder than it has been; and not many ways, none anyway that are quick, of correcting it after it has happened. Time and goodwill must be allowed to do their work. 'The world', as the poet Andrew Marvell said long ago, 'will not go the faster for our driving'; and like Auckland itself (the only one of New Zealand's major cities that was not planned in advance, and by far its most flourishing) the outcome will not look as it was meant to.

> But as the children grew
> It was something different, something
> Nobody counted on.[*]

So I lived without any sense of absurdity or contradiction as a child whose home address was 63 Kensington Avenue, whose school was Maungawhau, whose nearest suburban shopping centre was Balmoral, and favourite place on earth, Kaiwaka. Neither Kensington nor Balmoral suggested anything remotely English, Scottish or royal to my infant ear. Those words invoked nothing more than the local street and suburb they named. Nor did I think of Maungawhau as hill of the whau tree, nor Kaiwaka as a food-bearing canoe. Those, too, were proper names. Was I living in a condition of colonialism? I would say that already I was becoming Pakeha.

THERE WAS A VOLCANIC CONE – or rather three, known as Three Kings – nearer than the three I have described, not quite in sight from the back of our house, but in easy walking distance. Two of the three cones had been largely destroyed, the scoria removed for roads and building sites. The third was still intact, with much of the surrounding land yet to be built over as the suburb extended in that direction. The rolling fields were neglected, covered with weedy

* Allen Curnow, 'The Unhistoric Story'.

grasses, gorse and blackberry, and here and there some of the original (or, more accurately, previous, since the pre-European tribes had burned off much of the forest from the isthmus) fern, bracken and manuka. This was a place where children ranged about, played games, made huts, fought wars, gathered blackberries in summer and ventured, challenging one another, into the dark of the caves.

The whole area was full of subterranean caves, caused, as it was explained to me, by lava from the volcanoes cooling on the outer side to form a skin, or rock tube, while still flowing on internally, as if blood should form its own vein simply by flowing. Our house was said to be built over a cave; and further down the street, where an alley ran between Kensington and Marsden Avenues, access was dug into it in the back garden of a house during the war, and an official sign put up to say this was our local public air-raid shelter.

It was a typically makeshift arrangement, which I don't think anyone took entirely seriously. No one liked to venture into the private garden broached to provide this facility; and if the time had ever come to use it, those who did would have had to sit in the cold stone dripping dark, because no means of lighting had been provided. Some people had small private shelters, often hardly more than a slit trench, dug in their gardens. I dug one in ours, not much bigger than a single shallow grave, over the top of which I arranged an old fire-screen interlaced with foliage for camouflage. My father kindly ignored it, saying if we had to shelter we would do it under our house, which, though built of wood, had strong stone foundations.

Down there, in a sort of basement accessed from outside, was my grandfather's workbench, a bin for firewood, a sack or two of coal and an ancient cabin trunk which housed carbonettes; there were also garden tools (including an old cutlass, used as a slasher) and the lawnmower. My grandfather's medicine chest from his time as manager on Nauru was there, still smelling of chemicals, and for a time it was used for the tinned food and bottled water we might need during raids. The floor was the scoria rock that formed the foundation the house was built on. It was always dry, but there was no electric light, only a kerosene lantern and a torch or two; and I found it hard to imagine the five of us sitting down there on boxes, bins and coal sacks while bombs hurtled from the skies.

My father was the local air-raid warden, issued with a steel helmet, a flat canvas bag and a gas mask, as if dressed for a movie about the London Blitz. Since there were not enough gas masks in the country to go around, they were issued only to air-raid wardens, policemen and the Home Guard who, I suppose, in the event of a gas attack, would have been useful in counting the dead and reporting to HQ. The warden's job was to walk around the street each night, wearing his steel helmet and making sure curtains were closed, no chink of light showing. Riding my bike at speed to Scouts in the blackout I ran into the back of a car that had not been removed, as required, from the street. I flew face-first into its rear window, which was glass, and gouged very large pieces out of my chin and forehead, then set off to walk home before collapsing. The scars from the stitching are still visible.

At Maungawhau School a kind of rampart was constructed of wood and soil under a line of thick macrocarpa trees, and in air-raid drills we were marched out and required to huddle there in classroom groups. Each child had to bring to school a small cloth bag, worn around the neck, containing a cork to bite on (some kind of protection against the damage bomb-blast could do), ear plugs and a few other items including ID.

This was a time when it seemed the 'real' war was going on in the Northern Hemisphere, when 'our boys' (represented for me by Dad's brother Don) sailed away, and the whole unfolding drama of it was exciting and enjoyable, like a very good adventure story, one we all followed in newspapers and on radio, in newsreels and movies, and even strip cartoons (comics, we called them), most of it centring on 'the Resistance' (France) and 'the Blitz' (England). This was 1940, the period of Dunkirk and Mrs Miniver, when our own mimic preparations at home did not suggest that real bombs would ever fall on us or real enemies invade. 'Our boys' were there but the rest of us were not; and it was as if, in some subterranean way, I felt that the very fact of its high value as 'story' confirmed our New Zealand insignificance. We could supply manpower, submit to rationing of food and clothing, export food to Britain collectively, and individually send food parcels to friends and family. We could listen to the BBC news (on short-wave 'from Daventry' – where was that?) every evening. We could be stirred, as those who were there were stirred, by those magnificent speeches Mr Churchill made, about fighting on the beaches, and fighting on the landing fields, and never surrendering. We could read the poster that said CARE-LESS TALK COSTS LIVES, with its picture of a gabby woman and a ship going down, and wonder what secrets we possessed that might have such dire consequences. We could DIG FOR VICTORY – and my father, who already had an extensive vegetable garden, in fact dug up a piece of lawn and put me in charge of it. My mother kept a notebook in which the value of vegetables I supplied to her kitchen was entered to my credit; and this became a cause of mild friction between us when I reminded her of her mounting debt and she accused me of exploiting the war for personal gain. We could make patriotic gifts and sacrifices, and pretend (even the adults were pretending) that the bombs might fall on us at any minute. But we could not be there, where the bombs were falling *really*; could not experience the danger; could not be, or fail to be, heroic.

Soon the school had a new game for playtime and lunch hours. The children had discovered that the soil brought in to make our protective rampart was full of small smooth chips of marble. Following a recent popular movie about gold mining (set, I think, in Alaska) we began to 'stake out claims' and dig for these chips, and even trade them – marbles, or lollies, spinning tops or other prized things in exchange for our takings from the 'mines'. By the time the teachers discovered what was going on the protective structures were in ruins. We were commanded to stop; the 'mines' were closed down, but I don't recall that our defences were ever repaired. In the playground consciousness, which perhaps reflected the popular mind, the war had faded.

Then came Pearl Harbour and the Japanese surge down into the Pacific, and once again there was a change of mood. Darwin was bombed. A Japanese submarine was seen in Sydney Harbour. A ship, the *Niagara*, carrying gold bullion, was sunk off the coast just north of Auckland. Out in the countryside 'tank traps' were erected over roads that ran up from the sea, enormous logs suspended on steel cables and meant to be dropped across the path of the invaders. Some of Auckland's North Shore beaches were staked and laid out with barbed wire. Now the war was less an exciting story, more like something that was real and might have a bad end.

I remember the fear, which our parents tried unsuccessfully to hide from us. It didn't last long. Soon New Zealand had become a staging post for American forces in the Pacific, a place for R and R, and for nursing the wounded. This was a new kind of excitement, like an invasion of the ubiquitous Hollywood that was in our heads already. Britain was our history, our 'serious' side, our 'class' and our mana – all of which we simultaneously saluted, embraced, resented and even, almost, despised. The impregnable fortress of Singapore, its guns pointing seaward while the Japanese marched in from behind (or so it was said), had fallen. Our shield and promise of safety, the Royal Navy, had proved a pompous fraud. The Americans came as rescuers, and as the deliverers of silk stockings and chocolates, jitterbug and jazz. These were gifts, and a rescue, which would have consequences throughout the succeeding decades of New Zealand's history, right down to the end of the twentieth century.

In the shelter shed in the new 'Centennial Park' established between Marsden Avenue and Peary Road I saw my first used condom. I think I knew what it was and more or less what it was for, but I'm not sure how I knew. I crouched down and inspected it closely without touching it. In the bulb at one end was the gob of semen; on the haft at the other, printed in small blue letters, was the message, 'US Armed Forces. To be used for disease prevention only.'

TWO
DIGGING FOR VICTORY

L ooking west from our kitchen windows, beyond Mt Albert you saw the Waitakere Range – 'the Ranges', as they were called, or 'the Waitaks', always plural. In good weather they stood out, blue, distant and beautiful on the far skyline. Since the prevailing wind was westerly, that was where you looked to see whether it was safe to hang out the washing. When they vanished in grey cloud, rain was on its way. That was also where the sun went down, and where spectacular cloud colours and formations were often seen in the evening.

Our house seemed to sit on a solid slab of scoria. The loose rocks from the two sections, heavy but not too large for a strong seafaring man to heave into place, had been formed into walls and terracing. The soil that remained when the rocks had been removed was light and wonderfully fertile, dark when wet, light brown and almost dusty in dry summer weather. Vegetables and fruit trees flourished; so did flowers and flowering trees.

Some time around 1920 my Swedish master-mariner grandfather, Christian Karlson, after whom I am named, had announced (not for the first time) his retirement from the sea, and had bought the two quarter-acre sections. These he landscaped, laying out lawns, gardens and paths, and designed the house which he named 'Vallamont', a neologism of his own, I suppose, in which the double l might have been a concession to the English language. This name, inscribed on white marble in black lettering, a sort of swirling Gothic-italic, was fixed over the front door throughout my childhood. I was given to understand that it was something to be admired, though my feelings about it were uneasy and tending to the negative.

The whole layout and building of the house had been his work. He insisted on the very best timber, the most exact workmanship, and was pleased to hear one of the builders asking another whether the old bugger was planning to live for ever. Once the house was done and the family had moved in, he must have laboured over the landscaping and planting for two or three years. But then his wife and daughter noticed he was making more frequent trips into town, wandering about the wharves, talking to other seamen. It was a restlessness that could lead to only one thing, his signing on to a new ship, another commission, an adventure. Not for the first time it was to be prospecting for guano (accumulations over millennia of seabird droppings, mined as fertiliser) along the coasts of the New Hebrides (now Vanuatu). The story as I heard it was that he suffered a particularly bad attack of his recurring malaria, brought his ship back to Noumea and died there. My grandmother received the news of his death by telegram in Wellington where she had gone to take a ship to be with him in his illness.

So she returned to Auckland, he was buried in Noumea, and arrangements were made for a headstone to be inscribed with lines from R. L. Stevenson's 'Requiem':

> Home is the sailor, home from sea,
> And the hunter home from the hill.

Stevenson figured in the family mythology, and my grandfather had felt an affinity with 'Tusitala of Vailima in the South Seas'. No one in the family ever saw the grave, nor even a photograph of it; and when, recently, I asked friends visiting Noumea to look for it, they hunted without success. He had come out of nowhere, and returned there.

Christian Karlson was dead before I was born, but the house was full of photographs of tall ships, of sailors high in the rigging or out on the bowsprit, of European men in pith helmets and white suits surrounded by powerful brown men bare to the waist; of such islands as Nauru, Malden, Makatea, Walpole and Ocean Island while they were still idyllic, with flourishing palm trees and beautifully thatched fales; of my grandmother in the latticed shade of verandas with German and French women. Our kitchen table (which I still have) was from the captain's cabin of a ship, the *Salamis*, wrecked on a reef off Malden Island; and I knew the story of how the captain had paced my grandparents' veranda for two days and nights, praying the weather would abate, while the crew salvaged what they could and the ship slowly broke up and at last disappeared. We had a heavy serving dish decorated with the name *Salamis* and the flag of its shipping line, an item which, as the years went by, was downgraded from a treasured memento until it became the feeding bowl for my dog, Skipper.

The polished shell of a giant tortoise from the islands was the fireguard in the room where my mother had her grand piano and my father his desk; and I knew that the 'natives' used to turn these poor animals over and let them cook to death in the sun before turning them into soups or stews. No fires were ever lit in that fireplace, and behind the shell my father stored preserved eggs. On the mantelpiece above it there was a photograph of Christian Karlson, a boat in a bottle, an opium pipe, a Japanese fan and a satsuma vase, all of which had belonged to him. In the lower, out-of-sight shelves of a glass-fronted cupboard that displayed egg-shell china, there was his doctor's book (from which, later, I learned in brief terror, until common sense told me it was nonsense, that 'self-abuse' caused blindness), a six-shooter worthy of the Wild West and, in a polished wooden box, an elegant pair of duelling pistols. These weapons were handed over by my father to the police (but only after an argument with my mother, in which I sided with her protest) when a boy, Billy Turner, who lived in Marsden Avenue, demonstrated once too often that a dysfunctional revolver he had found could be loaded, the muzzle put to his head and the trigger pulled, without the gun going off. The last time he did this demonstration was in the Auckland Domain where, surrounded by a group of his school friends from Seddon Memorial Technical College, he shot himself dead. The police used this as a newsworthy occasion to offer an amnesty for unlicensed firearms; and my father, in the name of social and paternal responsibility, took it, I think, as an opportunity to diminish by a few spectacular items the household's hoard of mementoes of the ubiquitous dead Swede.

Because my grandmother had often sailed with her husband, and sometimes my mother too, their stories of him, and of ships and islands, remained alive in the house, often repeated. I knew about the death of my great-grandmother Annie McDermott, who had sailed with them on one of their adventures and was buried on the island of Makatea. I knew about the time they were becalmed for days – or was it weeks? – until a shark was caught, which the sailors said would break the curse; and how, sure enough, the wind soon appeared, first in the far distance, a brilliant ripple of light on the glassy sea, coming rapidly on, filling the sails and setting them on their way. I knew about the time of the waterspout, of the 50-foot shark, of the deadliest storm when there was nothing to be done but reef sails and pray. I had the image, bright and clear as if I been there to see it, of my mother as a small child on deck in rough weather, tied to the mast on a length of rope for safety, and washed into the scuppers when a big wave went over.

At the grandfather's death my parents' plan to build a house of their own had been abandoned and an agreement reached that they should stay on with the Grandmother. It must have been a relief in a way. Those were hard times; my father earned £2 15s a week. My mother could supplement their income by continuing to teach the piano; but they had no capital and would have needed a mortgage. And my mother was an only child, closely attached to her mother. I'm sure it was an arrangement that grew, later, to seem to Dad a trap from which there was no escape; yet he loved the house and the garden, and made them (almost, but not quite) his own.

So for the first seventeen years of my life, until a younger sister, Frances Caroline, was born, there were five of us – widowed grandmother Caroline Karlson, mother Olive and father Jim, older sister Norma Nellie (named after Bellini's opera and perhaps also the diva who sang the role) and myself, Christian Karlson, always called (until at secondary school I shortened it to Karl) Karlson. That group was at intervals turbulent, sad, combative, hysterical; but it was also full of jokes, music, good talk, caring and love. During our mimic Blitz period I sometimes imagined a bomb wiping out mother, father, sister, grandmother. That would be the end of the world. It was what one understood by tragedy. But the same four deaths at intervals, in an orderly, almost expected, manner over time (1954, 1970, 1975 and 1999) is simply history. History is the tragedy in slow motion; it is the tragedy, but 'given time'.

There was, however, throughout those seventeen years a sixth family member, Christian Karlson my namesake who, I felt, subtly, invisibly, ruled the roost.

MY FATHER HAD TAKEN OVER THE revered Swede's garden, and worked hard at weekends and even, sometimes, on summer evenings; while my grandmother, who was said to have 'green fingers', and who was given, or 'borrowed' without asking, cuttings from gardens all around the suburb, was in charge of the beds of flowers and shrubs. My mother had a succession of piano pupils in the afternoons and on Saturday mornings. Her framed sign on the front of the house annoyed my father because she had kept her professional maiden name:

Unfit for war service, he was living in his mother-in-law's house, and I was sure he felt diminished by that sign, his role as husband-provider compromised.

His vegetable garden, down in the lower, sheltered part of the second section, was well kept, re-dug and replanted annually, and always had a look of good order and fruitfulness without seeming regimented or entirely predictable. There were strings marking rows of planted seeds (the seed packet on a spike at one end to tell you what was there in the ground), staked runner beans, peas, silver beet, white turnips (I loved their earthy taste eaten raw), staked tomatoes, pumpkins and marrows, an asparagus patch and, growing mysteriously out of the compost heap, artichokes, which were fed to the hens.

The hens were an addition to the lower garden, possibly thought of first as a contribution to the war effort, since my father's severely damaged arm, shot in a hunting accident when he was eighteen, meant he was not eligible to be 'called up', even for the Home Guard. I remember the building of the hen house by Dad's friend Tom Paton, himself a professional gardener. It was constructed on a flat concrete floor under a corrugated-iron roof, with creosoted rough-sawn timber walls and door, a single wire-netting window, a hen-sized entrance from the run, three manuka perches and two nests, one containing a china egg, *pour encourager*. Rain from the roof ran, via guttering, down into a wooden barrel, from which water was taken for the hens and the garden. There was something dreamy about the water in that barrel, clear all the way down, alive in summer with flicking mosquito larvae struggling up to put their tails out for air. Just occasionally, on the very coldest winter mornings, the barrel water was covered with a thin sheet of ice.

The scrapings from under the perches in the hen house were used to make liquid manure for Dad's garden. And sometimes, when a passing horse had dropped its bran muffins on the street, Mum would send me out, embarrassed and complaining with bucket and shovel, to collect them. The milkman and the baker each had a horse-drawn delivery van; and there were rag-and-bone men too, collecting scrap. I liked to watch those animals drinking from the troughs that were distributed around the suburbs, snuffing at the surface first, as if to check that it was really water and not a hard surface. Or while a delivery was made they would dip into the nose-bag hung over their heads, taking a snack of chaff. The big draughts had a way of standing square on three legs with the fourth (rear) leg up on the blade of the hoof, like a dancer up on points.

When I was old enough (I suppose seven or eight), looking after the hens became my responsibility. I got to know them well, but was never accepted by the rooster, who saw me as his rival. So did the hens. If I put the palm of my hand lightly on a hen's back she would crouch, ready to be mounted, as she did when the rooster approached her sidelong, insinuating, his wing spread down his leg like a bullfighter's cape, the sun picking out greens and blues in his shiny black feathers. Sometimes I was attacked by the rooster, only once successfully, when he did his kung fu leap with such speed (both dextrous and sinister) he got a spur into each side of my calf in a single strike, leaving two small round deep painful holes.

I liked to sit propped on one of the perches in the hen house, looking out at the patch of feathery asparagus fern just outside the wire, and beyond that to the lemon tree, the biggest I have ever seen, big enough to be climbed (though the thorns made it hazardous); and beyond that again to the differently feathered grey-green foliage of the acacias (wattles, we called them), with their nitrogenous-smelling roots, that sprang up uninvited on the steep, terraced bank beyond the lemon.

Being essentially an ear person, I was quick to learn the hens' language and could do their sounds – the cluck, the cackle, the crow and that curious cawing lamentation suggesting boredom or surfeit – like a native. Later, when I came to learn French, I was taught it first, and fatally, by the eye, off the page, with the result that my hen-speak, or lay language, though I have had no occasion to use it for years, is still much better than my French.

Every year one of the hens that went 'broody' was selected (the others were locked up alone in a dark box until they 'got over it') to sit on a baker's dozen, thirteen eggs. Twenty-one days later cheeping and stirrings under her fluffed-out feathers indicated that they were hatched, or hatching; and soon she would have them out of the nest, following her around the separate coop kept for this purpose. W. B. Yeats has lines

> I count those feathered balls of soot
> The moor-hen guides upon the stream . . .

This is a perfect observation, marred by a wrong adjective – 'feathered'. They look like 'balls of soot' precisely because they are not yet fledged. The charm of Black Orpington chicks is their busyness and assertiveness, which seems absurd in such small vulnerable creatures, while the mother appears full of pride and clucky concern.

Collecting eggs, along with picking fruit – passion fruit (we had two large vines), tree tomatoes, grapefruit, plums (two kinds, damson for jam, the others for eating), apples (Cox's Orange), nectarines, peaches, guavas, lemons – was my responsibility; and then there were my own additions to the vegetables grown by Dad as the DIG FOR VICTORY campaign gathered momentum. Hens were eaten from time to time; and I have the common New Zealand child-memory, or common among mine and earlier generations, and caught perfectly in Katherine Mansfield's story 'Prelude', of the first sight of an avian execution. I also recognise, with the mixture of fondness and mockery that is Mansfield's own, Stanley Burnell's pride at the dinner table as he confirms (it's a kind of grace – 'Thanks to *ME*') that 'what we are about to receive' is composed entirely of 'home products'.

The 'chooks' were part of my life for years, until I was late into my time at Mt Albert Grammar when, going down as usual one morning to feed them, I found them all, twenty hens and a rooster, dead. There was a period during the winter when nothing valuable or vulnerable was growing in the vegetable garden and the gate to the run was left open, the birds released to roam at large. Because that garden area was down in a hollow, enclosed on two sides by typical Mt Eden free-stone walls and on the other two by terraces up to the higher section, it needed only a gate on the path down from the house, and one wing clipped, to keep the birds from roaming away. So at this season they were free to fossick, scratch and pick all through the vegetable garden. It was their favourite time of year, their holiday season. What had not occurred to me was that they were safe while enclosed in the run and hen house, but that once the gate to the run was open, a dog could find its way down there and make sport of hunting them. Perhaps having a dog myself, an amiable harmless cocker spaniel called Skipper who knew that 'down there' was not part of his territory and would never go there, had prevented me from thinking what a stray or neighbour dog might do.

They were scattered about the run, the hen house and the garden beds, their necks stretched and scarlet. This was not history; it was tragedy – or perhaps tragi-comedy. It should at least have meant a feast of chicken for us and our neighbours, friends and relations; but neither I nor anyone in the family had the heart for it, it was too depressing. I dug a communal grave and buried them.

Nor were they replaced. They had become a chore, a habit, no longer a necessary supplement to the cost of feeding the family. There was no longer the war for motivation. The extra garden, the DIG FOR VICTORY one, was already replanted in grass. So the hen house remained, but silent; the netting-fenced run was visible, but unoccupied.

At times in my life I have dreamed about the hens, the hen house, the garden. Sometimes my father is working, crouching down weeding or planting. I speak to him but he doesn't hear me, doesn't turn, and I feel I have failed or offended him in some way. And there is a dream that has come when I seemed to have nothing at all to write, when I have wanted very much to begin something new and the cupboard has seemed bare. In this dream I am seized with the terrible realisation that it is my job to see the hens fed and given water, and that I have neglected them for many years, so long they must surely be dead. I hurry to get there, which is always a struggle. I make my way, between the rosemary on one side and the lavender on the other at the top of the path, past my own vegetable garden with the guava bush in the corner and the pussy willow beyond, down past the tree tomato and the bean-covered netting fence. I am full of anxiety, expecting the worst, when I see them running to meet me, necks stretched forward, expecting to be fed, but alive and well, their feathers glossy in the sun.

Twice that dream has been followed by the breaking of a drought in my writing, like the catching of the shark that preceded the onset of wind and the end of being becalmed in mid-Pacific.

COMPARED TO DAD'S VEGETABLE garden my grandmother's flowerbeds were spasmodically planted, mostly unweeded, but full of flashes of colour and outpourings of scent that came and went with the seasons. She had often forgotten her own plantings before they sprang into life and 'took the winds of [September] with beauty'. But lavender and rosemary were permanent, as were flowering mimosa, daphne, lemon-scented verbena, and 'jessamine', an older word for jasmine found in Shakespeare, and which she perhaps had from her gardener grandfather, John Flatt. A feature of that front garden was a rose-smothered pergola made of curved and twisted logs over the path to the front door. A seat made of the same logs, probably at the same time, was for a time on the back lawn, and I have a large photograph of my grandparents as a young couple, seated on what must have been an earlier version of it, dressed in their best, she in a large white hat, with pearls, lace and leather gloves, he in three-piece tweed suit and soft bow tie, with George V beard and piercing intelligent eyes.

Some years ago, after overdosing on Proust, I tried the experiment of writing, as I imagined Proust had done, in the first person, as if I were a character in a novel, but one with exactly my life, friends, family and experiences. The experiment was not a success and was soon abandoned; there was something false about that blurring of the distinction between fact and fiction. But what emerged first, when I tried to force, and then to float, my consciousness back into my fictional-but-real infant self, was the sense that I must somehow have come to consciousness, not among people, but among rocks and flowers. I knew there was a sense in which this was quite untrue; but if, to the infant sensibility, the animal surround of the family, its physicality, its mothering and fathering warmth, comfort, security – if all of that comes first, it comes perhaps as an *un*-consciousness, from which we emerge into what must be the first sense of *difference*; and in my case, that earliest memory, as of coming to life, was of the garden, the grass, flowers, ivy-covered wall; the scent of lemon flowers and lilac; and the sound of a piano overhead, my mother playing Chopin perhaps, or Beethoven's Waldstein sonata, the bell-like notes cascading down.

This memory represents for me an infant period when everything was idyllic, after which comes a sharp sense of the idyll ending, to be recovered but never completely, never again secure.

There were other early memories, of course, equally fragmentary and uncertain, usually with my mother:

I am with her in the cowshed at the Kaiwaka farm, she sitting on a three-legged stool holding me, and I can see the cows' giant back-sides and their swishing tails held down by the rope that keeps them from backing out of the bail . . .

She is reading me a story that begins (she must have read it many times) 'Mrs Green was a fat duck. She lived in a house on the farm' and ends, 'My, how they *ran!*' . . .

In my infant-size wooden wheelbarrow, painted red and blue, I have collected small centres out of many blue flowers picked from a creeper that grows wild in parts of the garden. These centres are shaped exactly like minute ice-creams, with an orange cone and a white ice-cream top, and I am pretending to offer them for sale . . .

I am asking her to play 'Man at the door' with me (a Depression child's game) and she is saying, 'Not just now, darling' and I am disappointed because I have a suitcase ready, full of 'things' to offer for sale . . .

I have wandered into the house of our next-door neighbours, the Salvation Army couple, Adjutant and Mrs Arnold. They have visitors, also in Sally Army uniform, and the two couples are kneeling in a circle on the floor, praying. This seems strange and frightening, and I run back out of the house, and home to my mother . . .

THREE
TUSITALA TO STANDARD TWO

I turned five on the 17th of October 1937 but my mother, who at that time had no younger child on whom to lavish affection, wanted to keep me at home until the new school year began at the end of January. I didn't want that and we argued. In the end she gave in, I could start school on or immediately after my birthday. We were standing under the Australian flowering wattle on which I had my Tarzan rope, and beside a wooden plank I used sometimes as a bridge, sometimes for making people 'walk the plank', sometimes for practice hammering nails. I suppose my memory of the place and the moment is so clear because I wanted so much to start school, and because I didn't expect at that time (or ever) to win an argument with my mother.

I remember my first day, as one does. I was put in the charge of a red-haired freckle-faced 'older' Primer One boy, Hector George, who lived in Ellerton Road. His mother, Hazel, and mine were friends and his father owned the Blue Boats down on Auckland Harbour. He showed me where you hung your school bag. The curved metal pegs in the wood-panelled corridor figured for years afterwards (and sometimes still do) in a dream: the wall goes up for ever, and I am climbing the pegs, as if going up a mountain rock-face. It's effortless and I feel liberated.

Hector showed me the ornate concrete sand-tray that looked like a warrior's tomb or a war memorial, the wooden climbing frame under the pepper trees, the tennis court, the swimming pool (25 yards), the dental clinic, the smelly urinal and boys' WCs. He told me there was a competition to see who could pee furthest up the wall, each attempt leaving for a few minutes, until it dried a curving trace, your signature up the concrete. He said there was a boy in Primer Four who had peed right over the wall. Behind the urinal was the school incinerator.

My first teacher, Mrs Crawford, had a large comfortable bosom and I liked standing close to her. I remember learning to read only because you did it by sounding out the letters, and for a few days I had trouble with 'th'. At the third time of my taking the word 'the' in my reading book to my mother to ask what it meant she spoke snappishly. That ensured it was committed to memory. Reading came easily and I recall no further problems.

There were tables in Primer One, with primer-size painted wooden chairs. By Primer Four, the desks were flat-topped with lifting lids. In the Standards (begun in year three) they were what Janet Frame mis-heard as 'jewel desks', looking as if they were sledges on dual runners. If you wanted to speak to your neighbour in the Primers you lifted your lid as if searching for something, and whispered behind it. In the Standards, you turned your torso sideways and down, pretending to get out your pencil case or exercise book from the lower compartment. That downward movement, diving for cover from the teacher's machine-gun gaze, is something every veteran of the school rooms of that period will remember.

In the Standards the desks had white china ink-wells, and one favoured child was appointed 'ink monitor' and kept them filled. You wrote sometimes with pencil, sometimes with nib-pen, and there were ink-stains everywhere. The desks were spattered blue-black; so was the work of all but a very few exceptionally tidy and dextrous children. The desk-tops were scarred with small chips, holes made with compass-points, minor indentations, and in Standard Two the pale, freckled girl, Beverley Melrose, with whom I shared my 'jewel-desk', invented the game of 'dentists', which consisted of quietly, unseen by the marksman at the front, filling and smoothing over those holes with plasticine. It was not thrilling but better than nothing, and passed the time.

Each classroom had a wood- and/or coal-burning stove for winter. I don't remember being cold but we probably were in those high-ceilinged airy rooms, their sash windows pulled down or pushed up by a pole with a brass hook at the end. Maungawhau School's two buildings, Primers and Standards, were of concrete, grey and grim-looking from the outside, but not unpleasant within. They are gone now, replaced, earthquake hazards that might have shaken down on us. I think of their taking with them, into the great silence of the Past, certain sounds, remembered as if heard from a distance as they drifted across the football field – the chanting of times tables, the children's singing echoing in the rafters, the shouts and screams from the two shelter sheds (girls' and boys') at playtime. When you look now at ground level through windows of the new school you see computer screens.

Primary school was not exciting. I don't think I knew I was bored, but I know it now, looking back. There was some freedom in the Primers, but not much; and in the Standards it was like the slow enclosing of a brace. I think I was lively, outgoing, optimistic, energetic, interested; but also, and equally, I was easily embarrassed and shy. What happens to such a child if he is required by a fairly strictly enforced discipline (including corporal punishment) to sit for five hours a day, often with arms folded, or hands clasped on the desk in front, silent except when spoken to? Either he gets into hot water, or he turns inward and lives in imagination. I did a little of the former and a great deal of the latter. When I hear

Maori veterans of those years tell sad stories about how they were strapped for speaking Maori I always want to ask, do they think it was only te reo Maori that was forbidden? I was strapped for talking te reo Pakeha.

But learning went on at a certain level. I could say, as W. B. Yeats does in his grand, dreamily arrogant way, 'Because I found it hard to attend to anything less interesting than my thoughts, I was hard to teach.' But I can be more precise than that. It would not be right to say I was a failure at primary school, but certainly I didn't shine. Arithmetic average to poor. Painting and drawing awful. Handwriting clumsy. And spelling? The best you could say was that it was erratic. 'Rotten' would be more truthful. I had the words, could read them in books and could put them together to make fluent sentences of my own. But ear predominated over eye, and my visual recollection of words on the page was always approximate. Over many years I have improved but I am still not quite a secure speller. I was a professor of English in my late thirties before I heard a minion in the university mail room comment to another how often he saw accommodation misspelled with a single m. Oh, I thought, so there are *two*! It was a mistake I ought not to have made, because I knew from a very early age that there were two in committee. That was because my father was a member (often chairman or secretary) of so many, I seemed to see the word almost daily.

It was to be a comfort, when I came to do graduate research in England, to see manuscripts by Yeats and recognise how bad, how much worse than my own had ever been, his spelling was; and to learn that even the formidable T. S. Eliot, Harvard and Oxford educated, was not strong in that area. Much later I learned the same was true of Ted Hughes. They were poets. Words existed for them, not in the mind's eye, but in the mind's ear, and in the mind's capacity to make of them elegant and complex grammatical sequences. The same is true of Shakespeare, who spells his name differently on each of the few surviving documents he signed, and, in the only manuscript play-script surviving in what is thought to be his hand, spells the word 'sheriff' in five different ways. Even allowing for the fact that spelling was not standardised in Elizabethan times, this seems extreme and suggests words existed for him as aural, not as visual, items.

I was quick to learn reading, and also to read aloud at sight which many children found difficult. I was a fluent talker too, but that was not considered a virtue, except for a brief period in Standard Two when the teacher discovered I could tell the class stories. They were invented on the spot, and when, after some weeks of these performances, he asked me where I got them, I blushed and lied that they came out of books, after which my enjoyment of the limelight lapsed, and my fluency with it. It was in that year I won the Thrift Essay Prize – always a book.* I chose *Mr Midshipman Easy* by Captain Marryat, thinking, perhaps, that it might be as exciting as *Treasure Island*. I don't recall that it was.

At end-of-year examination time I came somewhere in the middle of the class, in a school that was itself somewhere in the middle.† I thought of myself as an ordinary pupil, competent at best, not clever as my sister was considered to be. But on the other hand there were moments in the classroom when, all at once, it would seem that something was quite clear to me which everyone else was struggling to understand – everyone, I should say, except Joan Allaway. Joan always came top of the class, top in everything. She went on to Auckland Girls' Grammar where she continued to come top, until she reached the minimum school-leaving age of fifteen and was taken away by her Closed Brethren parents and never heard of again. I name her here to record the waste, and to lay the blame.

---

* Thrift Essay Prizes were competed for each year throughout the Auckland region. I don't think I won one again until 6A at Mt Albert Grammar, when I chose a collection of prize-winning short stories from an international competition I had myself entered unsuccessfully.
† Maungawhau School polling station was seen for many years as a dependable predictor of the national result.

It was perhaps because I seemed to be a dull pupil (an impression, as I will explain, reinforced for my mother by my incompetence at the piano), that my parents bought a complete set of Arthur Mee's *Children's Encyclopaedia*, which I imagine was touted around the suburbs as a costly but infallible way to convert your child's dull bronze into the gold of examination success. Whenever I appeared to be at a loss, or underemployed, my attention was directed to the twelve deep-blue volumes in their own varnished wooden bookcase. I remember disconsolate Sunday evenings turning the shiny white pages with their black and white illustrations – great paintings, great portraits, great people; items retrieved from ancient tombs; broken marble, bones. There was a famous work of art represented there, possibly Pre-Raphaelite (of which the Auckland Art Gallery had a musty collection) – *Hope*, a semi-naked woman in some uncomfortable place, possibly (and if so inappropriately) on top of the world, swathed in draperies, blind, or wearing a blindfold. I stared at her. It was how I felt browsing Arthur Mee's *Children's Encyclopaedia*. I never read more than a sentence or two of the text, and an occasional caption. It was a form of slow torture, which I inflicted on myself, when asked to, out of a sense of guilt and obligation to my parents, who had gone to so much expense in the hope of making me a better, a more successful, scholar.

We were not a literary household. Music and politics pre-dominated; and there was a lot of listening to what was then called 'the wireless' (as movies were 'the pictures'). Our wireless had a plywood cut-out figure of Peter Pan playing a pipe, fixed over filmy fabric through which came the sound, and when you looked behind, as I did when very small, hunting for the speaking person or the musicians, you saw magic 'valves' that dimly glowed.

My father, when he wasn't out in the evenings at committee meetings, read constantly, but it was seldom fiction. He subscribed to the *New Statesman and Nation* (as it then was); also to Victor Gollancz's Left Book Club, and read each new publication as it appeared, with encouraging titles like *The Socialist Sixth of the*

World. He owned and had read Marx's *Das Kapital*, Spengler's *Decline of the West*, Bernard Shaw's *The Intelligent Woman's Guide to Socialism and Capitalism* – and strange studies like *The Glands of Destiny*, which purported to explain medically the behaviour of famous people in history. I remember browsing in it and finding a discussion about whether the tumour on Henry VIII's leg would have been syphilitic or varicose, and what effects each might have had on his behaviour.

Dad liked political biographies, and had also an appetite for Pepys and eighteenth-century British naval history. I see him slumped in his chair, always smoking, the ash getting longer and longer until it fell on his shirt or cardigan, to be brushed away accompanied by a fit of coughing. Mum read fiction, but spasmodically. What she liked best, I suspect, were romances of the sea. Daphne du Maurier's *Rebecca*, the novel before it was a movie, but the movie too, was the dream-world into which she could make happy escape. But her reading was also influenced by the politics of the Left – the novels of Theodore Dreiser, for example. My parents were both members of, and regular attenders at, the Fabian Society, which had its meeting rooms at the bottom of Queen Street over the road from the Central Post Office, Dad's workplace.

No one in the house read poetry, though my grandmother, who, being of her generation, pronounced it poitry, could quote passages of sentimental Victorian verse:

> The cottage was a thatch'd one,
> The outside old and mean,
> Yet everything within that cot
> Was wondrous neat and clean.

> The night was dark and stormy,
> The wind was howling wild;
> A patient mother knelt beside
> The death bed of her child.

A little worn-out creature –
His once bright eyes grown dim,
It was a collier's only child –
They called him Little Jim.

Often, like this one, and Wordsworth's 'We are Seven', which she also had by heart, they were about graveyards and the deaths of children.

Though she had these scraps and fragments from her childhood, the Grandmother's reading was only, and constantly, what she called her 'books', which were in fact magazines. She had her 'books' on regular order from a shop on Dominion Road across the road from Potter's Park. She was a fan of Hollywood movies. We all were, but the 'fan' in her case was short for fanatic, and a lot of her reading was about the lives of the stars.

My own reading was a reflection of the family culture. There were the *William* books and *Young Jack*; there was *Alice in Wonderland* and R. M. Ballantyne's *Coral Island*; and there were a lot of comics. I read *The Wind in the Willows*, not once but often, loving Ratty and Moley, Badger and Toad of Toad Hall, but always balking at the same point, somewhere towards the end of a chapter called 'The Piper at the Gates of Dawn'. When I read it as an adult I decided this balking (from which I must have recovered and pushed on) was simply an early manifestation of what I would learn to call discrimination. Then as now I loved story; I loved character; I loved place, scene, what I have since called 'the poetry of fact'; but I had no ability to focus on the kind of writing that became misty with capitalised nouns such as Presence and Nature and Awe and Him.

Sometimes, when I was at home from school with a cold or other bogus ailment (once established, I usually managed to spin an illness out for a week) my grandmother would buy me a book when she was collecting her magazines. She chose these always by title, without more than a glance at the jacket description. They were usually, as she supposed them to be, children's books, but not always. I recall, for example, a rather florid adult romance called *Friday's Child*, in which the lovely heroine was described as having 'small breasts like apples'. It was probably in this way I acquired my first books set in New Zealand, by romance writers Nelle Scanlan and Mary Scott. Later, but still at primary school, I read R. L. Stevenson, Rider Haggard, Conan Doyle. I don't suppose it could be said, given what came later, that I was intellectually lazy. Unfocused, would be more accurate. The focus would come at Mt Albert Grammar. In the meantime I liked best what happened out of doors, and what I perceived with my senses.

OUR APPROACH TO MAUNGAWHAU School from Ellerton Road was really the back entrance, and took you past the toilet blocks and shelter sheds. The front of the school faced Wairiki Road, with wide wooden gates and a wide path down to double rose-covered pergolas flanking a circular garden with a sundial at its centre. Over to the right there was a small area of carefully nurtured native trees, as if something from the past was being preserved against 'the March of Time'. Between the pergolas and the main building there was a paved space for outdoor assemblies, which was also the girls' basketball court. Three or four steps led up to the big front doors, painted dark green. Directly above was a concrete balcony that opened off the upstairs staffroom. The bell hung there and, incised into the balcony front, like a prison tatt on the school's brow, was its motto, 'It is tone that makes music'. One might have expected my mother to approve, but she didn't. She called it 'sniffy' and 'snobbish' and said it had nothing to do with music.

The headmaster was Mr Woods, a small grey man in an even smaller grey suit. When I read in a history book about someone being 'clapped in irons' I thought of him in his suit. There was a red fire extinguisher outside his office, and I remember, when writing an essay about a fire engine, pretending I 'needed to go' (you had to ask to be released from the classroom) so I could check how it was spelled and use the rather flash word 'extinguish' rather than just 'put out'. This sort of thing was encouraged. One teacher even advised, 'Don't say "The man was tall." Say, "Tall was the man."' But I rebelled at that suggestion.

The school caretaker, Mr Watson, was a retired merchant seaman with a British regional accent, crippled legs and misshapen feet. Mr Watson had a murky lair at the side of the main building, under the classrooms, and liked to engage us in conversation there, speaking in an instructional and sometimes admonitory tone copied, I thought, from the teachers. He told us he had been in a ship that sank in the North Sea in the First World War and that he had spent eighteen hours in the icy water. Prayer had saved his life but not his legs. Like the Adjutant Arnold next door, and Mr Honeycomb at the Shackleton Road Baptist Sunday school, he described himself as 'God-fearing'.

One day (this was when I was aged about seven) I was in a group of boys at playtime when David Baggot hit Lindsay Weaver, who cried and said no one should hit him because when he was hit he 'swelled up'. I looked, expecting him to inflate like a balloon but could see no change. David (not really a rough or bullying boy) laughed at Lindsay's whining, and Lindsay called him a bugger.

At this moment Mr Watson emerged like Barnardine from his lair, saying he had heard a boy say bugger.

We were silent, suppressing grins and giggles.

Didn't we know it was a very bad word?

Silence.

Did we know what it meant?

Four or five heads were shaken.

'It means . . .' But having begun he didn't know how to go on, what it meant was clearly so awful.

'It means,' he resumed, 'a man who has to do with other men . . .' There was a pause, until he added, 'Or animals.'

A farmer, I thought.

There was a broad square of playground outside Mr Watson's lair – when I arrived in Primer One, a slightly sloping area of grass bordered by a path, but very soon all sealed in asphalt with fine loose gravel scattered over its surface as if for the purpose of skinning the knees of small boys. One playtime a rat emerged from the area of the incinerator and, taking fright, ran in the wrong direction, as if to cross the square instead of retreating to safety. A cry went up and soon a pack of children, boys and girls, were in shrieking pursuit. I watched, wanting it to escape, knowing it wouldn't. The fastest runner had soon caught up and kicked it. The animal flew into the air, landed, facing the wrong way, turned and hobbled on, was kicked again, booted about like a football, squealing, kicked, finally, to death. The memory remains with me, the pity for the creature, the feeling of sick horror, my hatred at that moment of the pack, my recognition that there are those who will join it whatever it does and that they are different from, and more numerous than, those who will not.

Regular visitors to the school included Mr Bernard, who taught swimming, a Salvation Army officer who taught us 'Bible', and 'the Fun Doctor', who came at the end of each year and put on a show of juggling, disappearing eggs, expanding handkerchiefs, a white rabbit out of his hat, and balancing chairs on his nose – a routine which never changed from one year to the next.

From the weekly visits by the Sally Army person I remember only a few stories – Shadrach, Meshach and Abednego in the fiery furnace, for example – and that we were asked to learn the books of the Bible. I didn't bother, but memorised them just from hearing those who had taken the trouble repeating them in class. I can still get through to Job (we pronounced it 'job', not 'jobe') without faltering.

It was said Mr Bernard had seen a child drown and so had set himself the task of teaching schoolchildren to swim – and what school, given such motivation, could refuse him? I remember noticing, but without understanding it, that a strange expression crossed Mum's face when I told her how the boys hurried to get dry because Mr Bernard came into our bathing shed and used to help rub us down, always hard, so it hurt.

JOAN ALLAWAY, WHO, IF SHE HAD BEEN offered Arthur Mee's *Children's Encyclopaedia*, would probably have read it through in a matter of weeks or months, and committed large parts of it to memory – Joan with her pale skin and long, never-to-be-cut Closed Brethren hair, did not interest me in the way Merle Whalen did. My feelings for Merle were not sexual – it was much too early for that; nor could they have been described as sociable, since I don't think we ever talked – no more than the usual uninflected exchanges between two children in the same classroom. She might in fact have been a very dull girl, with little personality, since I have no memory of her at all except her appearance. My feeling for her was aesthetic. I took great pleasure in her face, her enigmatic half-smile, her beautiful eyes, and in the way a big bow of ribbon drew your attention to her thick wavy hair. I told my mother she was my girlfriend, but for two or three years I didn't tell Merle. Then it must have seemed the time had come to declare myself, and an idea of how to do it.

My sister Norma, two years ahead of me at school, had a boyfriend, older again, Leo Parker, a Samoan who was doing metal-work at Seddon Tech. The Parkers were very religious, and so, briefly, was Norma, who had gone through the process of 'giving her heart to Jesus', for which she received a certificate, a kind of receipt from the Above. This was just one stage short of the full Baptismal business – total immersion in the tank under the floor-boards of the Shackleton Road Baptist Church, where she and Leo were fellow-worshippers. From time to time he would give her a polished copper heart, shaped on the school lathe out of a penny. Repetition must have diminished the store she set by these tokens of his regard, and I was able to bargain for one with the idea that I would give it to Merle.

Choosing my moment when the teacher was gone from the classroom, I went down the row to where Merle was sitting and gave her the heart, with some kind of clumsy declaration. She blushed scarlet and looked so angry I retreated to my seat, my own embarrassment the equal at least of hers. A few moments later, when she had recovered from the shock, she slammed my finely polished heart back on my desk. I'm sure we never spoke again.

If what happened during school was boring, so was a good deal that happened in the afternoons when it was over. I was sometimes sent to play with a boy called Billy Hibbert who was said to resemble the child movie star Bobby Breen. Billy's sisters, a good deal older, used to dress him in a bow tie and jacket, swish his hair in an upward curly-curve in the Bobby Breen style, and sing their own variant of Bobby's best-known song, 'When there's a rainbow on the river'. Theirs went, 'When there's a rainbow on his liver'. Billy pretended to hate this, but I noticed he never tore off the bow tie or ruffled the carefully swished-up hair. Apart from this resemblance, Billy was an unremarkable boy, and I wasted many hours with him waiting for something to happen. Once only, something did. As Billy and I mooched about on Kensington Avenue in the half-light of a winter evening, a sash window was flung violently up and a coffin pushed out, to be slid quickly into a hearse and rushed away by two sinister black-suited men lurking in the drive. There was at the time a fashion for *noir* movies in which just such things happened, and my imagination went to work on it at once. It might indeed have been the basis for one of the stories I told during my brief period as the Tusitala to Standard Two.

Across the road from Billy Hibbert lived Don Cater, another classmate, who had a movie projector and real Walt Disney cartoons – Popeye, Mickey Mouse, Donald Duck. The projector was only a child's toy, but it worked. You closed the curtains, put a light globe on a lead into it, wound the films through by hand and the moving pictures were projected jerkily on to the wall. I was deeply envious.

Don's mother was very thin, and I secretly thought of her (perhaps because his father was so strongly built) as Popeye's girlfriend, Olive Oyl. The Caters' sitting room contained a mantelpiece clock. Below the clock-face three golden balls swung back and forth, and the whole was contained inside an inverted glass vase. It seemed to me to impose a strange mesmeric silence on the room, disturbed, but also created, by the faint rhythmic breathing of the mechanism. In that room in the evenings Don's father, in the daytime a cabinet maker, played and taught the flute. Walking to work, rugged, athletic (as were his two sons), a tuft of pale hair projecting out of the top of his open-necked shirt, Victor Cater looked every inch the Kiwi working man, and it was hard to fit his flute to that image. Some years later, however, after the war, he was appointed flautist in the newly formed National Orchestra, and the white tuft became a black propeller.

Nearer to home on our street were the Surridges. They were Catholic and John, my age, went to the Good Shepherd convent school on the other side of Dominion Road. He showed me holes in their back lawn, about as wide as a knitting needle, which he said were made by an insect called a penny doctor. You were supposed to put a straw down the hole and you would catch one. I tried, and watched him try, but never saw a penny doctor. John's father, very dapper with slicked-down Brylcreemed hair and a dead-straight parting, was a guard in the Japanese POW camp at Featherstone, where some sort of prisoner revolt, whether real, or imagined by the guards, led to an 'incident' in which fifty prisoners were shot dead and as many more wounded. On leave from the camp, Mr Surridge taught me to box (straight left and right cross), and to count to ten in Japanese, a sequence I still remember. When the war ended he left home with 'another woman' and never returned.

Next door to the Surridges were the Cranches. My memory of Mr Cranch, which may not be accurate, is that he was a taxi driver always at home from work on his front veranda, seriously ill, possibly dying of TB, but shouting full-voiced to, or at, his children from his terminal perch. Among the Cranch children were twins, Nancy and Jean, one of whom was to be among the 151 killed in the Tangiwai disaster of Christmas Eve 1953, when a lahar from the crater lake on Mt Ruapehu swept down the mountain in the night destroying a bridge just as the Auckland–Wellington express was due to pass over it.

The Cranches were at number 55. At 57 were Mrs Holmes and her only child, Victor. She was a stout solo mother, and used to call her boy in a voice he could hear even from the next street, with a curious rising note on the second syllable – 'Vic-*TOR*. Vic-*TOR*.' Vic-TOR was older than the rest of us, and joined the RNZAF as soon as he reached the minimum age.

At number 59 were Mr and Mrs Candy and their only daughter, whose name, I think, was June; and at 61, Adjutant and Mrs Arnold, the Salvationists. Mrs Arnold was supposed to have saved my life when, as a baby, I went into a 'convulsion'. The adjutant's funeral was the first I ever attended, and I remember trying to believe, while the Sally band played and the congregation sang about gathering at the river, that he was really inside that polished wooden box, wearing his uniform, the toes of his shiny black shoes pointing heavenward, and that he would never come out.

Across the road were the Willetts family whose miniature son, Gary, my junior by a few years, would one day be top jockey in New Zealand and Australia. Their neighbours on one side were two women, so private I never heard their names, and imagined (not what I would imagine now) they must be unmarried sisters. On the other side was a bachelor, Mr McLaren, who ran over to tell us, when he heard on the radio that the 'aviatrix', Jean Batten, was just now arriving at the end of her record-breaking solo flight from Europe. We all rushed out and saw her single-engine plane doing its overflight of Auckland before landing at Mangere.

Another Kensington Avenue boy, Bruce Tabb, a few years ahead of me at school, was always a picture of anxiety. He went everywhere at a half run, as if feeling it would be decorous and proper to walk, or at least to appear to, but quite impossible in these times of urgency and danger. I thought of him as *Alice in Wonderland*'s White Rabbit. He muttered to himself as he went. Whether he was hurrying himself on, or urging himself to slow down, there appeared to be always a conflict going on between one Bruce Tabb and the other. He became a good Labour Party man and my fellow-professor at the University of Auckland, head of the Department of Accountancy.

BRITAIN DECLARED WAR ON GERMANY in September 1939 and New Zealand followed immediately. 'Where Britain goes, we go,' our politicians liked to say. I would have been in Primer Four at the time and I have what I believe to be a memory of the day: Dad is sitting in his armchair tying his shoe-laces and Mum and the Grandmother are standing by, watching him. He has been called unexpectedly to work and there is an air of drama. When I ask what is happening I am told we are at war. On the wall behind Dad's chair is the finely engraved brass plaque, mounted in a circular wooden frame, which the Grandmother's family received when her half-brother was killed in France in the 1914–18 war. A bosomy helmeted Britannia, accompanied by a lion, holds out a laurel wreath over the name of the dead soldier, Owen Vincent Freeman,[*] and around the outside of the plaque are the words, 'He died for Freedom and Honour'. It was to have been 'the war to end wars'; now it was to have a sequel, as if the 1919 Treaty of Versailles had not written 'the end' but only 'to be continued'.

My grandmother always felt a profound guilt about the death of the only one of her siblings to survive childhood. She had been deeply attached to him, his protector against teachers at school, and at home against the brutality of his father, her stepfather. Owen

---

[*] His name was Freeman, not Flatt, because my great-grandmother's first husband had died and she had married a second time.

had asked her should he 'join up', and she had encouraged him. She saw herself as the dupe of patriotism and of the capitalists who engineered wars for profit. Her expression now was one of anxiety. My parents looked worried too, but with them there was perhaps also a hint of excitement.

Three months later, December 1939, a Royal Navy cruiser, HMS *Achilles*, crewed almost entirely by New Zealanders, was engaged off the coast of Uruguay in a gun battle with a German pocket battleship, the *Admiral Graf Spee*. The German ship was cornered and driven back into the port of Montevideo, where its captain scuttled it rather than let it be taken by the enemy. When the *Achilles*, victor of what was now known as the Battle of the River Plate, returned to port there was a march of the crew up Queen Street to a civic reception, and my mother took me to watch, and pushed me forward to the front of the crowd so I could see. It was my first experience of a really big crowd in a state of patriotic fervour. It might have been a British ship, but these were 'our boys' and they had 'done the job'. It proved too much for my hypersensitive mother, who came under sustained migraine attack, retreated into a chemist shop, and called for aspirin-relief and a chair.

Soon, in the window of the shop where my grandmother had her 'books' on order, there appeared a wooden, grey-painted model of the *Achilles* made by some local handyman. It was for sale for thirty shillings, not a small price if you think of that as about half an average weekly wage. I coveted it for a long time and at last my grandmother, who seemed in those days still to have a small leftover hoard from her husband's legacy, bought it for me.

I don't think it can have been long after the parade that Dad's youngest brother, my Uncle Don, enlisted for the army and was posted overseas. He came to say goodbye, wearing his battledress uniform. He sat me on his knee, and I was surprised by the roughness of the khaki, something which, when the war was over, I would myself wear once a week at Mt Albert Grammar and, later again, doing compulsory military training in the 1950s. He gave me a pocket knife to play with, and when he was leaving (an emotional moment for the adults) told me it was mine. Some days or weeks later I was practising throwing it at a tree in the garden, trying to make it stick there as a real knife-thrower would, when a throw missed and the knife vanished inexplicably into the ivy-covered rock wall. I felt that to lose the knife might be bad luck for my soldier uncle. I hunted unsuccessfully until dark, and went back next day and often to hunt again, but it was gone.

When a letter came from him at last it spoke of the uselessness of .303s against tanks. And then, after another long silence, came the news that he had been captured, I think in the Battle of Crete, and was in an Italian POW camp. Was I in any way to blame? I didn't think so, and took comfort that he wasn't dead. Like the knife, he was just lost somewhere, vanished into the black hole of 'her Hitler's' war.[*]

* Hitler was always 'Herr Hitler' which was mispronounced 'her' – puzzling to the ear of the child, except that so many things were unexplained and mysterious.

FOUR
TWO AND TWO
HALVES TO TOWN

By the time I was in Standard Three Germany had effectively overrun all of Europe except Britain, the worst of the Blitz had happened, Russia was well and truly invaded and fighting for its life, the Japanese had bombed Pearl Harbour and the United States was winding itself up to enter the war on all fronts. At this time there was a large classroom map of the world hung over one of the blackboards on a wooden pole. It was a Mercator's projection, and because of the way the world was laid out, with the international date line to the far left and far right, New Zealand appeared twice, once in the lower left-hand corner and again at the lower right. I don't remember that this repetition was ever pointed out or commented on, but I was struck by it. It seemed to me to suggest our insignificance. We were so unimportant we could appear twice and it didn't matter, made no difference. It was something which, many years later, got into a poem I called 'You Have a Lot to Lose', commissioned for the Commonwealth Arts Festival in London in

1965, which I read in the Royal Court Theatre in Sloane Square. They were just a few lines in a longish poem, and were self-fulfilling in the sense that they passed, I'm sure, quite unnoticed:

> And if at the lower reaches of flat maps
> We repeat ourselves
> We repeat ourselves
> Unnoticed.

When I looked at us on that map it seemed that all the world's significant events, and everyone of importance in it, were remote from us, away mostly *up there*, or if not, then *over there*, to our left and to our right.

I remember learning that our population was one and a half million, and that we were part of the Empire on which the Sun Never Set. You could see this great British empire marked in red on the world map, and how, beginning with Britain (not bigger than we were, but so much better placed!), the sun, moving east to west, would track right across Canada lighting also some small splashes of red in the Caribbean, then across the Pacific – Samoa, Fiji and other British island territories – to New Zealand, right across Australia, onward to Malaya and Burma, then the Indian sub-continent and finally Africa with its many red splashes, coming home again to Britain, to bombed but enduring London, Buckingham Palace, the Houses of Parliament.

A history book through several years of the Standards was called *Our Nation's Story*, with a picture of Captain Cook on the front, so we did learn a good deal of our own New Zealand history, including something of its turbulence, though mostly from the settler perspective. But somehow we also learned British history, hero tales often, which were sometimes heroine (a serviceable word, entirely acceptable at the time) tales – 55 BC and Julius Caesar; Boadicea and her chariots of resistance; the Norman conquest; Joan of Arc (France creeping in there, with the English as villains); Henry VIII, the break with Rome and the subsequent wives; Elizabeth I, the Spanish Armada and Drake's game of bowls; the Stuarts and the execution of Charles I (beheadings and burnings were always of interest); Clive of India; Livingstone in Africa; Scott at the Pole . . . They came as *our* stories, no less than the specifically New Zealand ones were ours, so we were prepared, a little later, to 'get' all those jokes in *1066 and All That* ('One in the eye for Harold') when it was discovered in the grammar school library.

We were receiving, in other words, a British education of its time, with local trimmings. It has become an unfashionable historical narrative, probably in Britain no less than in New Zealand. But I'm not sure that, as historical narratives go, it was seriously worse than any of the alternatives that have replaced it. None is without partiality; each has its 'point of view'. It's true we were, in effect (though the word was no longer acceptable) colonials; and that was a condition which had to end. There was no choice about the direction New Zealand would take; any more than there is the least possibility that we will not sooner or later become a republic. We must go there, and complete the process of severance – which, it should be said, Britain itself, joining the European Community, has done at least as much as we have to bring about. But that recognition doesn't prevent me from reflecting that the colonial condition had benefits as well as deficiencies. It was not (I speak as a Pakeha) subservience; and it did direct our attention outward to a larger framework, a bigger world, saving us from the excesses of introspection which have beset us in recent years.

IN THE SOMNAMBULISTIC WAY ONE does when writing something that is taking its own course at its own pace I find I have gone to a box that once belonged to my mother and extracted from it three Candid Camera shots (street photos) of myself and my mother, one of us with my sister Norma. I have spent so many of my waking hours, especially in the 25 years since I began easing myself out of my role as university professor, writing fiction, that it is easy for me to forget that I am not still doing it; to forget that fiction and autobiography spring from quite different intentions and play by quite different rules. Fiction draws a great deal on real life; but what is taken, and how it is altered, and what, essential in reality, is nonetheless cast aside in favour of invention (or nothing) – all such matters are determined solely by what the novel requires in order to achieve shape and narrative interest. Autobiography, on the other hand, does not permit of invention. Fiction may choose to make use of facts; autobiography requires them. The truth of fiction is exemplary, not literal; the truth of autobiography comes of the effort to make a record that will stand against the facts.

So I look at photographs at this moment, first I think to reassure myself that the people I write of, so many of them now dead, so many gone from my life and from any easily accessible record, did indeed exist; also as a reminder that one among those that have vanished into the smoke of memory is the boy I suppose myself to have been.

What interests, perhaps surprises, me in the three street photographs is how well-dressed we are. They were more formal times; and in black and white I can only guess at colours. But Mum has dressed us up for town, and herself too. Her three hats in the three photos are, or seem to me, each of them quite stylish. She wears three good sets of shoes. We look happy together, and quite prosperous.

In the earliest picture it is summer. I am wearing a white floppy sun-hat, a tie, a summer shirt, no jacket, dark shorts and shoes with short socks. Norma has a gauzy summer hat, floral dress and beads, girly shoes of the round-toed shiny kind and white socks. Mum has a broad-brimmed hat with some kind of white floral arrangement at the front, a summer dress that goes half way between knee and ankle (the same length in all these photos, though they are a few years apart), a loose, open coat-length jacket and white shoes.

In the next two pictures, which are just mother and son (holding hands as they stride along), the weather is cooler, cold in the last.

I appear to be about seven in the second. In the third, aged nine or ten, I'm wearing a winter overcoat, long dark socks, a white scarf (rather flash) and cap.

Yes, we are real – it's us; but it's history too. That car in the background, and the homburg that man is wearing – they belong to another age. Is it possible to write of these people we once were without invention?

I take another photograph from the box. This is Maungawhau School, 1941, the very Standard Two that for a brief time listened to my improvised stories. The smallest boy, cross-legged at the front holding the sign, has bare feet. I remember now, prompted by those feet, that his family were said to be 'poor'. In a time when by present standards of affluence everyone was poor, 'poor' meant deprived, even possibly hungry. They lived in the smallest house in Ellerton Road, straight across from the school gates, and my father, as chairman or secretary of the school committee, insisted they were to receive several bottles each day from the crates containing the school's Government-supplied free milk.

There in the middle row is Beverley Melrose in a spotted dress, which I'm sure I remember was blue (the spots white) – the girl who invented the game of dentists. There is Ian Lamont, my friend later on, who will die at eighteen; Don Cater, the flautist's son; Margaret Buseau, the child of Jewish refugees; John Hornibrook, who will marry my wife's brother-in-law's sister; Betty Speed, whose brother will become a dentist and, one day so far in the future it is unimaginable, do an emergency repair on one of my teeth; Lois Johnson, one of six sisters born in succession, to be followed by six brothers . . . Or so the story would go.

Lawson Sinclair, John Wood, June Friend, Glenys Green, Stanley Goldstein, David Baggot, Ailsa . . . ? After close on seventy years I find I can still name most of them without more than a moment's hesitation. That is reassuring. Karlson Stead is there, huge eyes and a buttoned-up shirt.

And here is Standard One, 1940. Billy Hibbert has a tie with a tie-pin. Bobby Breen without his bow. Joan Allaway's long hair hangs forward over her shoulders, fetchingly. Ray Goodall, Barry Catton, George Pollock, Lindsay Weaver. Brown Kani Panapa is there, and blond Karl Marx Robinson. Kani has just laughed and moved, and is slightly blurred. Holding the sign at the front in this one is a freckled round-cheeked boy called Everard. I can't remember his surname; but I recall that when we talked about how babies were made, and what the father did to the mother, he said it wasn't true, and that his mother had said if he listened to such talk she would 'give him a thrashing'. I was impressed by the word. A 'thrashing' – it sounded so comprehensive.

And Merle Whalen, there she is in the Standard Two picture – no great beauty I suppose, but still with something of the remembered radiance – yet to receive her copper tribute; yet to reject an author's heart.

THE LIFE STORY MY MOTHER HEARD from her father was brief and simple. Christian Karlson had been born in southern Sweden in 1870, and was brought up by a foster-mother, a poor widow, Amalia Becker, in the port of Malmö. Amalia Becker had children of her own, so he grew up in a family. While he was still very small, a well-dressed woman used to come for him from Helsingborg. She was kind, affectionate, brought him presents, took him for drives in her carriage. He soon came to understand, though it was not said, that she was his real mother, but she never took him away with her, always left him in poverty, with the foster-mother and her children. When he was (he thought) about five he decided he would not speak to this mystery woman, because he knew he belonged with her and she had abandoned him. He would punish her. He went with her on those drives because he was required to, but remained obstinately silent. After a time she stopped coming, and he never saw her again. Did he, later, regret his pride, his intransigence? That question and its answer were not part of the story he chose to tell.

He received minimal schooling and then was sent to work minding sheep on the hills outside the town. As he grew into his teens he spent more and more time visiting the port, learning about the foreign ships that came and went. At the age of seventeen, when he would soon be due for military service, and probably to avoid it, he signed on to a German ship, left his homeland and never returned.

Not a lot is known about the next decade, except assumptions and guesses that can be made from photographs and letters he had kept. He seems to have sailed out of English ports, studying there to qualify as mate, and then as captain. He told his daughter he was considered by his English shipmates to be serious, reserved, late to join in a party and early to leave.

No doubt he was ambitious. By the time he reached New Zealand at the age of thirty he had already his certificate, issued by the British Board of Trade, to be 'master of a foreign-going ship'. Apart from the Scandinavian languages he was now fluent in English and could get by quite well in French and German. In Auckland he met my grandmother, ten years his junior, and proposed to her in what she always called '*the* Albert Park'. In 1901 he received his letters of naturalisation as a subject of the United Kingdom (New Zealand was still constitutionally a colony), and for the remainder of his life Auckland was his home port, and the South Pacific the region he made his own.

Sometimes he commanded ships, often sailing vessels. As he grew older, he took jobs overseeing work in the islands. Guano, used as phosphate fertiliser, was the gold he went after on behalf of the companies he worked for. I have a small piece, kept in the family, on my desk where I write – smooth as polished marble to the touch, and cream coloured. There is a passage in Joseph Conrad's *Lord Jim* in which an Australian called Chester is describing how he has discovered 'a guano island somewhere, but its approaches were dangerous, and the anchorage, such as it was, could not be considered safe'. 'As good as a gold mine – better!' but he can't persuade anyone to take the risk.

'Once I talked for three hours to a man in Auckland. "Send a ship," I said, "send a ship. I'll give you half of the first cargo for yourself, free gratis for nothing [. . . .] Damn rocks and hurricanes. Look at it as it is. There's guano there Queensland sugar-planters would fight for – fight for on the quay, I tell you."'*

Chester gets his ship but he and it vanish without trace, emphasising the difficulty and danger of retrieving guano in usable quantities. Christian Karlson supervised the laying of deep-sea moorings and the building of roads – particularly on Nauru, but elsewhere as well – that made retrieval of this 'gold' possible.

He died on 29 July 1930, a few months short of his sixtieth birthday, as a result of what was meant to be 'one last' search for new guano deposits up the New Hebridean coast. Smitten with a particularly bad bout of malaria, he got his ship back into the port of Noumea, and lingered there, between life and death, not properly cared for. The death certificate, a strange mix of inaccuracy, uncertainty and Franglais, says he suffered 'paludre fever' (malaria) over a period of some weeks, complicated by pneumonia, and died in the Station Hotel, rue de Rivoli, Noumea. Details given include, 'domicile Auckland, New Zealand; aged 65; Capitaine of Trading Vessel; born in Norwegia; Father and Mother names not known; married; name of Wife not known; no other renseignements or informations declared.' It is signed 'Edouard Dalmayrac, second adjoint of the Mayor of Noumea.'

Long after the period I am writing about, my mother saw an advertisement in a magazine, in which a Swedish bank offered to conduct enquiries about matters of concern to potential customers abroad. She wrote, sending what information she had about her father and, after a lapse of time and an official application to the Swedish Crown, she received a copy of the contents of a sealed envelope held in the Maria parish of the city of Helsingborg. This, and follow-up material gathered by the bank, established that

* *Lord Jim*, 1900, chapter 14.

Christian Karlson's mother had been a widow with three children, Cecilia Rosenström, who became pregnant to an army officer (unidentified except by the name Karl) and bore a son given only the name Christian. This pregnancy had been concealed and an arrangement made (it must be assumed for money) that the child would be fostered. Cecilia then married again, a maker of shoes, Carl Axel Löfqvist, and had three further children.

So my grandfather had died without knowing anything of his blood family, his officer father, his middle-class mother, his six surviving half-brothers and -sisters. He knew only that there was something to know and that he could not know it. He turned his back on them, his phantom family, and made New Zealand, as far away as it was possible to go, his home. It is not an uncommon story, but sad – for the woman no less than for the child.

My mother made contact by letter with the younger members of what were now her Swedish family, who were welcoming, and even, briefly, with her father's one surviving half-sister, who was not pleased to learn, or to be reminded of, her mother's inter-marital adventure with the military. Letters and photographs went back and forth for a few years, shrank to cards at Christmas, and gradually lapsed altogether. My mother died, and the severance was complete.

IT IS DIFFICULT FOR ME TO WRITE ABOUT my grandfather without an occasional feeling of falseness. Insincerity threatens, as if from behind a curtain, though I am uncertain why, or what form it might be taking moment by moment. I bear his name, of course, which might be one reason. But more than that there is the sense of an almost excessive family reverence. I shared this, grew up inside it, learned, without being taught, that Swedes were special people, rational, orderly, civilised; that they were peace-loving (history is always skimped in these mythologies); that they had been able to do, and retain, socialism (always a positive in my family) with democracy, without enforcement. This was patriotism, a love of country, worthy of a loyal Swede, but only likely from one who had not spent his life there. Not that the myth did not, like most myths, contain a good deal of truth; but no one intelligent and alert who lives a lifetime at home (wherever the home, and however worthy) is likely to have anything but mixed feelings about it. And weren't Christian Karlson, the abandoned child, and Cecilia Rosenström, the mother who abandoned him, both victims of Swedish puritanism?

But perhaps the reverence came less from what the grandfather had taught his wife and only child to believe about his country, and more from something abstracted from the character and force of the man himself. There is an Ingmar Bergman movie, *Saraband*, in which a dead woman who never appears except four or five times as a photograph seems to dominate all the characters and most of the action. My grandfather's presence was of that kind. Like everything that comes from the culture of a family, that presence was indelible in me at the same time that some part of me questioned it, wondered what this important person I would never meet had been like, *really*.

Did my father perhaps resent another head of the house, absent, but more potent because unseen? And did my awareness of his silence on the subject provide a small dash of lemon on the sweet torte of Mum's filial and the Grandmother's conjugal piety? Yet Dad had allowed me to be named after my grandfather; and the only time I remember hearing him mention Christian Karlson it was to say, with some satisfaction, that the Swede had seemed to approve of him as a husband for his daughter.

In my adult life I was to travel overseas often, but I was middle-aged before I set foot in Scandinavia. First it was Denmark, to a university in Aarhus. A year or so later I went back with a Danish friend, Ulla Amsinck. I gave a poetry reading at Kiel, Ulla met me there, and we drove, in heavy snow, catching glimpses of a frozen river and shore-line, to Nyborg where we boarded a ferry. The sea was frozen, but cracked into great jig-saw fragments, and the ship heaved and crunched and shuddered its way through. Then it was the road again, all the way to Copenhagen.

I had intended to take the hydrofoil from Copenhagen across to Malmö, but the ice had become so thick all crossings were cancelled. There is a bridge across the Öresund now, but not then. Each day I went down to the waterfront and looked through the grey haze across the misty-white sea, and imagined Malmö where my grandfather had been a boy. I might have been the Anglophile Frenchman, Des Esseintes, in the Joris-Karl Huysman novel *À Rebours*, who makes plans to go to England but decides the reality could never match his imagining, and so contents himself with dining on roast beef in Calais and looking across the Channel.

In the years since, I have been to Sweden a number of times, but always further north. I have seen it in summer, when the mysterious demi-daylight, or twilight, goes on and on, each day touching fingertips with the next. I have experienced the Swedish formality (which the Danes mock), the Swedish style, charm and high-bourgeois seriousness. Kay and I have been to Stockholm in midwinter, the city at night like a star-filled sky, with pyramids of tiny lights in a million windows, and even the dressmakers' dummies St Lucy figures, with candle-crowns and blinded eyes. We have swum in the Baltic in summer off the island of Gotland, where I gathered wild strawberries, threading them on a straw as Swedish children do, while Kay submitted her naked self to the extreme unction of the village sauna. We have had lunch there, out of doors with Swedish writer friends (Ingmar Bergman's daughter among them) while a house martin came and went overhead, feeding lunch of a different kind into three small yellow gaping beaks . . .

Fleeting visits, always, but with each one the myth retreats a little. It is not that there is disappointment; only that myth and reality can never be the same. Normality has a way of asserting itself, even in the most extraordinary places. Roast beef and distant imagining must always in some mysterious way exceed real England.

So the part of me that is 'Swedish' has been 'home'. But still Malmö, where Christian Karlson spent the years when one becomes what one is, and for ever, and where, if shadows of our living selves were allowed to return after death, I think his would be wandering – that unvisited city still floats for me beyond a pale haze across a frozen Öresund; and I think probably that is how it should remain.

I WONDER WHERE MUM AND I WERE going in that earlier of two photographs in which we walk purposefully hand in hand down lower Queen Street. It could have been to the ferry, could even have been the day we visited Mrs Aitken who had 'taken a flat' at Devonport. We must have come into town by tram. The family owned no car. I can think of no one who did in our street, except the mean old Scot who parked his, against the rule, in the road during the blackout, and who charged my father thirty shillings for the repair of the smashed rear window that left these scars still visible in my forehead and chin. The local policeman thought we should have laid a complaint so he could take the Scot to court; but because my first child-feeling, when there was an accident, was always guilt, and my first thought how to talk my way out of it, I had made up a story that I had seen the car but that my front wheel had slid on a loose stone as I went to go around it. It was only later, too late, I realised it was not my fault, but the car-owner's, that I had not seen it. I felt committed to my untruth, couldn't take it back, and so there was only weak ground for a complaint.

The tram fare was twopence for the first section (each about a mile), and a penny for each succeeding. From Balmoral shopping centre to the bottom of Queen Street was three sections – so fourpence. Half price for children. 'Two and two halves to town', which is what you said to the conductor if you were allowed to be the one buying the tickets, was a shilling (ten cents). The tram had 26 reversible double seats, and (the notice on the platform at each end said) 'seven standing if full inside'. So with seven at each end, and at least twenty standing inside, a tram at rush-hour held about ninety officially, but in reality more like a hundred. Men and boys liked to show their athleticism by jumping off before it had stopped. If you faced the way the tram was moving you hit the ground running. A poster at the back showed how, if you jumped facing the wrong way, you hit the road hard and fell, probably breaking a leg or arm, or cracking your head on the paving. There was no notice saying don't jump; it just told you how to jump so you would be less likely to be hurt.

And it was the men, and the boys aspiring to be men who, arriving at the stop just as the tram moved away, sprinted to jump on to the back platform. The driver, watching you in his rear-vision mirror, often sped up just for sport, the tram's acceleration was rapid and it could be an exciting race. Once on board you might choose to stand out on the platform even if there were seats vacant inside. It was good to be out there in the wind, especially by the time you reached smoking age. The tram, keeping up a good pace between stops, swayed and clanked and ground its way along the iron tracks, its pole to the overhead wire sparking at the junctions. It took about half an hour to get into town.

On the ferries too it was a sign of manhood to jump for the wharf as the vessel came in; and even (though this was more dangerous, and happened less often) some hero, arriving after the gangway was up, the engine getting up steam, and the last straining rope just about to be released, might make a leap to get on board. I never heard of anyone missing and falling into the harbour, but it must have happened from time to time.

The Grandmother called the Balmoral shopping centre 'the Terminus', because the tram terminus was what it had been when she first moved to 63 Kensington Avenue. So for me as a child 'the Terminus' was a place, a place-name; just as 'the Duration', which was spoken of constantly (we would do this, or have that, 'after the Duration') was the war itself.

But in fact the trams now ran on past Balmoral, another complete section to Mt Roskill, the real terminus. And beyond Mt Roskill, Dominion Road extension was laid out in two strips of concrete, with an unpaved section between on which it was intended further tracks would be laid down. Then the line would go all the way to Waikowhai, and you would be able to take a tram from one harbour to the other, Waitemata to Manukau (a second such route because there was already one from the Quay Street wharves to Onehunga). But buses replaced trams before that had happened, and the line was never completed. Today if you wanted to make that journey on public transport, it would have to be by bus.

It was when we were teenagers, and while Dominion Road extension was still laid out for tram-tracks, that Ian Lamont, the merry-faced little boy in the Standard Two class photograph, would take me roaring out there at high speed on his lethal Norton motor-cycle. The fact that there were two strips of concrete with a gap between made speed seem less dangerous. At least you could never hit anything coming the other way.

It might have been while I was still in Standard Two, or a little later, there was a radio programme in which claims for unusual or extraordinary doings by New Zealanders were made and explained. One such was of a man who could claim to have crossed New Zealand . . . I have forgotten the details, but let's say it was forty thousand times. He was a tram driver whose route was the one that went from the bottom of Queen Street all the way to the Onehunga wharves – from one harbour to the other. The journey took (I am inventing the numbers, but they were of this order) an hour, so in a forty-hour week he did it forty times – two thousand times in a year. In twenty years of driving trams he had crossed New Zealand from coast to coast forty thousand times.

TAMAKI OF MANY LOVERS, PORTAGE for ancient Maori waka, wasp-waist of the fish of Maui, site of a Pakeha-planned and never built coast-to-coast canal, and of a harbour-to-harbour ghost-tram (52 seats and seven-standing-if-full-inside) no longer running except in the head of a writer at his laptop: these are no more than ways of describing, of laying claim to, and a hold on, his own whenua, his place and its history.

FIVE
WITH THE TONGUES
OF MEN AND OF ANGELS

When I was five I broke my right forearm, both bones, and the scar, caused, I suppose, by the bone pressing outward against the skin, is still there. While I was still learning left from right and uncertain, I always felt for the scar.

I was on my way home after school and showing off to a little girl called Irene with a pale freckly face and soft ginger hair. She was a strange child, silent and shy. Once she arrived at school late and was stopped by the teacher as she crept into the classroom. In front of us all she was asked why she was late. Her whispered reply was inaudible, and she was told to speak up. Still very quietly, in an agony of shyness, she said, 'I had to put on my shoes.' I don't think anyone laughed. Miss Crawford seemed surprised. 'Don't you always have to put on your shoes?' I don't know whether the answer was yes or no. Irene was allowed to go to her desk, and the day went on as usual.

Across Ellerton Road from the Primers building there was a

house with a low hedge. I threw myself forward on to it, hitting it with my stomach and rolling forward in a somersault, landing on the lawn. Irene, obliging I suppose, because that was her nature, pretended to be impressed, so I came through the gate to the public footpath and did it again. She was still interested, so a third demonstration seemed called for. This time something went wrong. The pain was extraordinary and the horror worse. On the injured arm I seemed now to have two wrists. I bellowed my way home, only a few hundred yards, accompanied by Irene, who wept in sympathy. When we got to the (as it seemed then) very wide and tall gate of 63 Kensington Avenue she tried to open it for me but couldn't; and each time I tried with my left arm the right, unsupported, sagged so unbearably I had to hold it again. At last my mother, hearing the cries, came down the path and took me in.

This memory has revived the logistics of those times. We had no phone; nor did any of the neighbours. I know the doctor was called and came quite late in the afternoon, so he must have been summoned from the public phone box at the top of Ellerton Road.

Dr Dreadon used to make home visits in the mornings in his car and take patients in his room in the afternoons; but this was an emergency. Why, then, no ambulance? I guess one had to be nearer death than I was to qualify for that.

Dr Dreadon confirmed a break, put a temporary splint and a sling on the arm, prescribed aspirin for pain, and instructed my mother to take me to the hospital next day where an X-ray would confirm his diagnosis and the bone would be set.

We went to the hospital next morning by tram. I remember the bare hard wooden forms of the waiting room at Auckland Hospital's Accident and Emergency because the wait went on so long and I was in pain. At last I was called for X-ray and then, after another wait, given a general anaesthetic while the bones were set. The plaster went across forefinger and thumb and up all the way, with a right-angle turn at the elbow, to the underarm. I believe I was kept in hospital two nights.

The plaster remained for some weeks. My skin itched under it, and school friends wrote their names on it. When it came off the arm was shrivelled and there was a big scar half way between elbow and wrist, but the doctor was satisfied. He told me to punch him in the stomach, hard as I could, but I didn't dare. The arm seemed so weak I thought it would break again.

MOST OF THE NIGHT BEFORE I WAS taken to hospital Dad spent with me, lying alongside me on the bed, catching sleep when he could, talking to me when pain and the discomfort of the splint kept me awake. It was the only time I remember him talking to me about his life and telling me, in particular, the story of his own, much more serious, accident. It was as if he was making me feel he knew about pain and was keeping me company in mine. Men had to be brave together.

His right hand was paralysed, the skin discoloured and blotchy (probably from inadequate blood supply), the arm withered and hideously marked with deep scars, especially in the area of the biceps. When I was very small and used to climb on his lap in the evenings I sometimes tried to force his fingers, locked half-closed, to open. But it was impossible. He could not move them, either to open or close, and neither could I. The wrist was also locked, but there was mobility in the elbow.

At the age of eighteen, shooting rabbits on his uncle's farm at Kaiwaka, he had pushed the shotgun ahead of him through scrub. He always claimed he had put the safety-catch on. If that was so, it failed. The trigger caught on twigs, the gun went off and blasted through his arm. He was some way from the farmhouse, tried to make his way back, and collapsed unconscious from shock and loss of blood. It was evening and he would have died there if a neighbouring farmer, hunting for a sick cow, had not seen him in the half light. He was brought back to the house like a dead soldier, face-down across the neighbour's horse. A tourniquet was put on the arm and he was taken through the night, first on a horse-drawn dray over rough back-country roads to the railhead, then in the guards' van of a freight train to Auckland.

At Auckland Hospital it was decided the arm must be amputated, but by that time he was too weak to survive the operation. Pneumonia set in, and for some days he was close to death. When he recovered it was decided the arm might be kept; but the paralysis of the hand was irreversible and he set about becoming left-handed. He was in hospital many months. One day a friend, reading the newspaper in the next bed, noticed the name Stead in the death notices and asked was it a relation. It was his mother. He had not seen much of his family lately, had known his mother was ill, but had had no idea her life was threatened.

You have to live with someone disabled to know how many daily difficulties and adjustments the lack of a limb, or of its full use, entails. At the table he could hold only fork or knife, not both at once, so if the meat needed cutting my mother would do that for him before serving the meal. He did most of his gardening one-handed; but he could dig a good straight furrow, left hand gripping the handle, right foot pushing in the blade, and frozen right hand somehow guiding the spade ahead and to the side. He could chop wood, holding the axe firmly with his left hand and sliding the handle into the half-closed right. He often tucked an object under the right upper arm, gripping it there (as you see people do who have an amputation just above the elbow) while doing something to it with his good hand – unscrewing a jar, for example, or pulling out a cork. His left hand and arm had become very strong.

But he could not hold a nail with one hand while driving it in with a hammer in the other; couldn't use a brace-and-bit, or a chisel and hammer. 'Jim's not a handyman,' Mum used to explain, with no special emphasis. It was only a statement of fact. But in the suburbs of those days it was like the lack of another qualification. His friend Tom Paton did the 'handyman' things for him (building the hen house; erecting a double clothes-line in the back yard); and then, in the evening, Mum cooked a meal for everyone, and the two couples, the Patons and the Steads, settled down to play bridge.

Dad's handwriting had an extreme left-leaning tilt, the capital letters of his signature, J. W. A. Stead, appearing to be standing tall but not unbowed in a strong wind blowing across the page from the east. The most surprising thing was to see him tie firm bows in his shoe-laces with one hand. So in that memory of what I think was the day war was declared, he is leaning forward in his chair, concentrating, watched by Mum and the Grandmother, and that deft, improbable finger work is part of the image.

If the injury had been done in war and he could have worn an RSA badge, his life might have been a fraction easier, the disability a fraction more tolerable. As things were, in those days when the word 'cripple' had not been replaced by 'disabled', he felt it was simply a disfigurement, a source of shame for which he lacked an excuse. He felt it especially when strangers referred to it in a tone of patriotic gratitude, thinking it was a war wound, and he felt he had to explain that it was not.

DESPITE THEIR VERY ENGLISH-SOUNDING name the Steads were Catholic Irish, perhaps the descendants of settlers 'planted' before the Reformation. But at some recent time they must have moved back to England, and my grandfather, James Bond Read Stead, was born there. His father, it was said (something I heard more than once in my childhood), had attended Oxford University, and there was supposed to be a pewter mug in the family recording that he had rowed in the annual Oxford–Cambridge boat-race. The family must have fallen on bad times. Two brothers with wives and children moved to the United States, and from there one set went to Canada, the other to New Zealand. On his New Zealand certificate of marriage to Elizabeth Ellen Abrams, my grandfather's occupation is given as 'storeman'. They lived in Church Road, Devonport, and my father and his siblings went to the local Catholic convent school, St Leo's.

There is nothing to suggest my grandfather James flourished in the new country, but nor did he fail, or not while Nellie (as she was known) lived. After her death his two youngest children, Don and Joyce, still school-age, were sent to Kaiwaka to be cared for by Nellie's sister, Lily Bowmar, who was on her way to having nine children of her own. His three older boys, Jim, Joe and Leo, were already working. He himself was by now working on the wharves and, for a time at least, he drank to excess. There were stories about the horse-drawn dray that picked up drunks off the last ferry and plodded around Devonport rolling each one off at the appropriate gate. Grandfather James, pining for Nellie, was from time to time delivered home in this way. Later he consoled himself with a woman referred to in family legend only as 'Biddy the Housekeeper'.

I only ever saw my English/Irish grandfather at Christmas. He always came, very tall, well-groomed with a rather posh accent, bringing chocolates for the festivities, and for me and my sister, each a half-crown. By that time he owned nothing, neither property nor investments nor money in the bank, and was living in what was called in those days 'a rooming house' in Mt Eden. He died there of a heart attack, at the age of 66; and I remember my father explaining *sotto voce* to Mum that he would probably not have made confession nor taken communion for a long time, and the fact that he was found with arms crossed over his chest meant he had tried to make 'an act of contrition'. To my child ear, overhearing this, the idea of a man, alone and in pain, attempting to perform a last-minute ritual that might just save him from Hell, had something ghastly about it. Did he believe at that moment that his future in eternity, blessed or in torment, was hanging in the balance? Or did he do it as you might cross your fingers when telling a lie, or touch wood when something you hoped to escape from was talked about? But the worst part of it, I thought, the part that my imagination dwelt on, was that he was dying, and that he knew he was.

All four of his sons, brought up Catholic, lapsed. Only the daughter, Joyce, youngest of the five, retained the faith. Aged Catholic aunts were disapproving but not surprised. Nellie, the boys' mother, had been Protestant and had not converted – so what could you expect? In Dad's case the lapse was complete. He never went near a Catholic church for the rest of his life, and never expressed any kind of religious sentiment. But there were, nonetheless, shreds of Catholic loyalty. On the very few occasions when Norma or I heard and repeated anti-Catholic jokes, he made his disapproval clear. Once the whole family went to a French movie about a Catholic saint, which ended with a deeply felt soprano voice-over of 'Ave Maria'. Catholics in the audience stood, Dad with them. Mum remained seated. What were the children to do? In perfect illustration of where the first loyalties of sons and daughters most often lie, Norma stood, I remained in my seat.

When, close to death, Dad began to compose a personal memoir, handwritten and looking like a field of wheat in that brisk wind from the east, his opening observation was what a different society New Zealand had become in his lifetime, in that, now, the election of a new Pope could be the major item on national television news. Clearly he had grown up feeling he was part of a minority in a country that discriminated against it.

He wrote four or five pages, and stopped. A few years later Mum embarked on hers, also handwritten, and kept it up for twelve or fifteen before giving up. She chose a title that suggested a sense of style and a talent for the dramatic: 'Venus on the Wane'. It came from an observation of the midwife as my mother emerged from the womb into the darkness of very early morning. But 'on the wane' seems more like bad news than good, and I can imagine delicate negotiations with editors if it had ever gone the distance.

Sometimes, when urged to write autobiography, I have wondered about the ethics of committing to print knowledge derived from having had – through the accidents of love, friendship or family connection – admission to another person's private reserve.

Versions of both my parents have appeared in my fiction – Mum, for example, with an absurd Katzenjammer German accent in *All Visitors Ashore*, Dad as a failed Irish businessman in *The Singing Whakapapa*. In fiction there is, for the reader, no way of being certain whether there is fact as well as invention, and if there is, where one slides into the other. But a memoir plays to different rules. How would my parents have felt if they had known that the eyes and ears of their infant son had been a sort of video recorder tracking them on their daily paths between bedroom and bathroom, garden and gate? But don't I have those pages – his four or five, her twelve or fifteen – as a sort of licence? *They wanted to go on record*, and failed only through lack of stamina, talent or (more likely) hope.

Can they rely on me, then, 'never to speak ill of the dead'? Possibly not. Can they hope for the benefit of the doubt, which is the blessing of charity? I think so.

'Though I speak with the tongues of men and of angels and have not charity, I am become as sounding brass or a tinkling cymbal.'

OF THE PLACES MY IMAGINATION occupied as escapes from the extreme boredom of primary school by far the favourite was that Kaiwaka farm where my father did himself such damage. I went there often, at first with my family, later alone. It was only 60 miles from Auckland, but the trains were slow and it could take, sometimes, five hours.

My memories of the farm fall into three phases. In the first, indistinct, with a few vivid moments, my great-uncle Bill, a bearded old widower in a felt hat, was the farmer, assisted by young Bill, the eighth of his nine children and his only son. I remember horses – many horses on the lower paddocks as you came in on the long drive from the road; and I'm sure I heard later that horses were old Bill's folly, because they wasted pasture (it was a dairy farm), cost time and money, and the market for them had vanished. In my memory the horses are streaming – cantering, trotting, tossing their manes – along a fence-line, keeping pace with my uncle Joe's small car (the family's first) as it bumped its way in from the road. Horses had a glamour that cows lacked and they made a fine picture; but they were like art for art's sake, unserious.

Another image from that time is one of Mum on a milking stool, holding me between her knees while someone nearby ties the leg-rope, washes the teats and applies the cups. There is the sound of the cows' hooves stamping and sliding on the wet concrete of the shed floor, the clatter of a bail being opened, the chuff and hiss of the machine and the clap of the belting.

In the second phase, Great-Uncle Bill is dead, the horses (all but the two working animals, Bosun and Rusty) are gone, young Bill is overseas with the RNZAF and, in the classic pattern of the Second World War, the farm is run by three daughters, Jo, Mac and Gwen. Jo cooks and keeps house. She has a lovely voice, with a crack in it, and a dreamy charm. She is married, but her husband, like her brother, is overseas with the New Zealand forces. Mac also has a fine voice, but big and loud, good for calling out orders to the dogs – and to me. She does the milking, takes the cream to the gate on the horse-drawn konaki, and runs the farm. She is up before first light, sleeps naked after lunch and comes in late from the milking shed for the evening meal. She and I have an ongoing battle about the dogs, which I think she treats cruelly. Typical farm dogs, thin and nervous, fed only skim from the milking shed and bones from the table, they spend all day and night chained to their kennels under the pines, released morning and night to bring in the herd. When one of the dogs shows the least sign of wanting to stray, his front paw is tucked into the collar so he must make his way on three legs. When Mac is out of sight I release the paw – something she will remember, and berate me for, half a century later. 'I've had to wait all these years,' she will say at a family funeral, 'to tell you what a bugger of a little kid you were.'

Mac is being courted by her cousin Wallace Hastie, who sometimes rides over from Mangawhai to help her with the milking, and I come upon them kissing between cows, his brown leather hand kneading the big breast-mound under her dungarees, both wearing gumboots, he still in the black oilskin and sou'wester he was wearing when I saw his stately progress across the fields, as if he disdained the public road.

Gwen, the third sister, who has lost two fingers of (I think) her right hand to the belt that drives the cream separator, seems to have no particular duties except to be around to help when needed. In the meantime she entertains me, and makes me a redskin headdress of sacking and pheasant feathers. She even repairs the leather harness and oils the moving parts of the two-horse buggy so she can put Bosun and Rusty in the shafts and take me with her on a drive to the post office and Jacques Store. But the up-and-down motion makes me sick and she has to drop me off at the house of Kath Lebourne, one of her married sisters, half way on our journey, and pick me up again on the return.

Every morning I ride with Mac on the konaki to and from the farm gate where we leave the full cream-can for collection and take back the empty from the day before. Along the way we stop off at the sty to feed the pigs, tipping a can of skim, and food scraps from the house, into their trough. They are noisy feeders, slurpers, grunting, shouldering one another for a better position. But there is something attractive about them too, as if they are apologising, explaining that the mess they live in is a product of circumstance and they would prefer it otherwise; and the deep, unstable note, more like a chord, somewhere in that characteristic oink-sound, can be strangely beautiful.

I ride Bosun, always bareback, ranging all over the farm. From time to time, when he breaks into a trot, I slide slowly to one side, fight to regain balance, and fall off. He stands for me, but it usually takes more than one leap to get back up there, and sometimes I slide right over and land on the other side. Best is to find a deep rut, lead him there to stand in it, and make my jump from the higher ground.

In all of this I love the proximity of the animals – the smell of the horse's hair as you hold tight, hugging his neck when he breaks into a canter; the soft bristle of the cow's neck-ridge; the rough wet lick of the dog's tongue on your face when you let his trapped foot free of the collar. At night, when the candle has been put out, I lie in a big brass bedstead listening to the silence and the sounds that break it, a morepork calling and receiving an answer from far off, the distant warning bark of a dog on a neighbouring farm, and an occasional high shriek from the bush that I think must be a kiwi.

One day I was sent to collect a parcel of meat that would be delivered to the box at the gate. I think it would have been a share of the kill of an animal sent to the works; but since there was no electricity on the farm, and consequently no refrigeration, it could only be received in moderate-sized lots. I rode Bosun, singing. The horse would have determined the pace, usually pretty slow on the outward journey, though he was always good for a canter on the way back. The box, facing the road, was on top of a gnarled fence-post beside the five-barred farm gate and close to the cream stand. Still astride the horse, I reached around to get the parcel, not notic-ing, or noticing but not alert to it as a warning, an intense hum that came from within, and the whirr and bustle of wings round about. Bees had swarmed there and, as I wrote much later in a poem, 'they came at me, stinging'. Bosun was stung too. He took off without waiting for instructions, and I managed to stay on his back, and even to hold on to the meat, tucked against my stomach, though my hair was full of bees and there were stings on my face and arms. I have thought about that moment often, and I seem to see it as if from the outside, Bosun racing along the green and brown ridge against a blue sky stacked with white cloud, his rider just holding on, trailing behind his head a plume of angry bees. Next day my face was swollen to moon-shape out of which my eyes seemed to peer as if through two holes.

The Bowmars had preserved one extensive section of the origi-nal bush, which included a giant kauri; and there were several other gullies and ridges where the grassland had been allowed to revert. I still have in my head the layout of the farm and the near-neighbour properties, like a map; but once, in the past decade or so, after that family funeral where Mac's remembered irritation about the dogs was unleashed on me, I walked over the farm trying to find my way back to remembered places, and found everything so altered, the map became confused, overborne by the present reality. As soon as I was on the road back to Auckland, however, the map reformed; and I possess it still.

So I can lead you now, without hesitation and with no possibility of being lost, out of the big farm kitchen with, at one end, its wood-burning range where all the cooking is done and at the other its handle-winding party-line telephone where naughty children listen in on neighbours' conversations; through the porch where oilskins and gumboots are shed on entry; through the back garden with its vegetable beds protected by a brush fence; out the small gate and past (not through) the eucalypt-shaded five-barred gate on the drive; down a slope into an area of swampy grassland; on around the edge of the original bush; over or through two fences and on again into manuka and taller trees which I suppose must be regenerating natives . . .

James K. Baxter says somewhere that there is for him (and I think he implies it must be true for every poet) a place from childhood where poetry has its origin, or its roots; and it is there you must return, in imagination or in fact, to recover the source of your inspiration. For him, it was a cave above the sea somewhere near where he grew up in St Kilda. For W. H. Auden it was 'the murmur of underground streams' in 'a limestone landscape'. For me, it is the place I am leading you to now. We make our way down through trees to a stream that widens out, stalled, over a clear shingle pool where small brown fish, themselves almost transparent, dart in and out from the shadowy banks, and sometimes, caught a moment, transfixed, hang suspended like mobiles in sun shafts that come through the overhanging trees. Under the banks are eels; and if we crouch here and remain still we may see one come nosing out, turning, rolling and showing for a moment its white belly, elegant in movement, never urgent.

Upstream, the flow spills over smoothed stone, welling out of a deep hole worn in the rock by a small waterfall. The hole has been drilled, and its edges smoothed, over many centuries, and the water is crystal, clean and clear.

When I told Jo of this place I had discovered she recognised it from my description and said that, long before, she and her sisters had found it and given it a name taken from a famous children's book (I've forgotten which) – 'the Naiad's Bubble'. But at the time I am writing of I was the only person who went there or had any interest in it. It was mine; and though, on my ramble over the farm after that family funeral, I could no longer find it, and even wondered whether the modern talent for shifting landscapes about had perhaps eliminated it altogether, it is mine still.

SIX
KARLSON
THE RECORDER

K aiwaka was not only my escape, in reality and in imagination, from the disciplined *longeurs* of primary school; it was also a rest from the fraught, and sometimes turbulent, atmosphere of home, where Dad's resentment of his mother-in-law became more apparent with the years, and where my parents' vacillations between affection and animosity grew more extreme, producing in me a more or less continuous state of anxiety.

I don't believe that, before embarking on this memoir, I have ever given my father and his life quite the focused thought I am giving it now; and reflecting how few memories I retain of him at Kaiwaka, it occurs to me that, at least while he remained in the Post Office, his holiday times were brief compared to those of the rest of his family. I remember, for example, a holiday in a rented bach on Waiheke when he, after some days with us, had to go back to work during the week, but came down to the island at weekends. Then I think by contrast of Mum and the Grandmother having coffee in the mornings (coffee and chicory essence out of a bottle, because of the war) while listening to their favourite radio serial; and of the leisurely ladies' morning teas the pre-school, or home-from-school, child was silent witness to in Smith and Caughey's tea room, with laundered napkins and cakes on silver stands, while Dad, taking his cut lunch in a brown-paper bag, worked eight-hour days. I think also of the atmosphere in the house with the 'breadwinner', 'head of the house', sent on his way, the lifting of pressure the women felt, so brilliantly recorded in Katherine Mansfield's 'At the Bay'.

> Yes, she was thankful. Into the living-room she ran and called 'He's gone!' Linda cried from her room: 'Beryl! Has Stanley gone?' Old Mrs Fairfield appeared, carrying the boy in his little flannel coatee.
>   'Gone?'
>   'Gone!'
> Oh, the relief, the difference it made to have the man out of the house. Their very voices were changed as they called to one another; they sounded warm and loving and as if they shared a secret. Beryl went over to the table. 'Have another cup of tea, mother. It's still hot.' She wanted, somehow, to celebrate the fact that they could do what they liked now. There was no man to disturb them; the whole perfect day was theirs.

Mansfield is a brilliant recorder of what a heavy presence these males exerted. She is not entirely without sympathy for Stanley, the father figure; but it is comic, teetering on the brink of contempt. There is sympathy for Jonathan Trout, the potential artist/actor, trapped in an office world of 'three stools, three desks, three ink-pots and a wire blind'; but no thought that Stanley might be seen as similarly trapped by the obligation to support and sustain the women (wife, sister-in-law, mother-in-law) and children.

It was against this background of female leisure (but also female under-employment and boredom) that the three sisters running the Kaiwaka farm became, or have become in current historical narratives, prototypes, World War II's female heroes, forerunners of what was to follow. They were marvellous women, I loved them and I salute them. They did well, as well as the men had ever done; but *they were only doing what the men had done*, and only so their men could be released into situations of violence, deprivation, danger and often death. It is not that the new narratives are wrong; only that they are one truth replacing another; that they are aspects of fashion, even of manners, of what it is *proper* to say at a given time, rather than having the finality of intellectual truth.

I wonder also whether what was my Paradiso had, for Dad, too many reminders of the trauma that had left him with the ugly and visible burden of a withered arm and paralysed hand. Those disabilities were scarcely ever mentioned – either by him (he didn't complain) or by us (we took them for granted).

So here is a further reflection: when, over-riding protest from Mum and from us all, he handed in my grandfather's revolver and duelling pistols, was he, as I have always imagined, and as I have suggested in this narrative, taking advantage of the law and a police amnesty to rid the house of one more set of mementos of the Swedish ghost? Or was he demonstrating a horror and fear of firearms that sprang from direct knowledge of what they could do?

WE STAYED WITH THE BOWMARS MUCH more than they did with us, but the traffic between Kaiwaka and 63 Kensington Avenue was not all one way. Colleen had town holidays with us, and there are photos of her on the beach with Norma, her exact contemporary. Her brother Bill, the only male among the nine Bowmar children, stayed with us while he was completing air-force training before being deployed overseas. Among the interlocking families, 'staying with' was what we all did. Cousins Peter and Bruce Stead, sons of Dad's brother Leo, came up from Christchurch for holidays. Cousin Donny (son of Dad's brother Don) lived with us for at least two of the years his father was a prisoner of war, and went to

Maungawhau School; and when Don returned, he too lived with us for a time.

There were also Stead cousins in Auckland, Ngaire and June, daughters of Dad's brother Joe; and one or another set of cousins would drift together in school holidays for swimming and 'going to the pictures'.

At Cheltenham another of Dad's aunts, Ruby, lived with her health-crank husband, Bill Webb. He had a canoe called *Topsy* on which he paddled to work each day across the harbour, even in the foulest weather, bare to the waist and only putting on his working clothes on the town side. He slept in a hammock with silken tassels and ropes like dressing-gown cords that hung inconveniently in their sitting room, blocking the view, the only adult male in the family at that time who would have lived up to Field Marshal Montgomery's much-publicised example: 'I neither smoke nor drink and am one hundred per cent fit.' But he let Norma and me borrow *Topsy*, and there is a photograph of us, both in bathing suits, she standing, paddling, I kneeling, pointing forward, heading out as if for Rangitoto.

Kipling wrote of Auckland (after a stay of four days in October 1891),

> Last, loneliest, loveliest, exquisite, apart,
> On us, on us, the unswerving season smiles.

So much of my life as a child was lived out of doors, and with a freedom to roam and explore, to take risks – in the water, on bikes, on horseback. The weather, in recollection, never seems to have been a significant obstacle to any of this; and it's true that Auckland's climate is mild. I was 25, a postgraduate student living in Bristol, before I saw snow fall. On the other hand, and despite Kipling, there were times in Auckland when it seemed indeed 'the rain it raineth every day'; and winter mornings when we woke to frost on lawns and gardens, and on the roofs. Timber houses in those days were hardly insulated; the conventional wisdom was that winter heating was only necessary in the evenings when wood and coal fires were lit; and because of wartime austerity, permits were needed for the use of any additional electrical heating. People wore more clothing then, but children certainly felt the winter cold.

Despite the lack of a car, my parents were good at holidays, using public transport (the ferry to Waiheke, the bus to Maraetai), leaving the Grandmother in charge of the fowls and the dog, setting aside their daily differences and making the most of the moment, however brief and infrequent. Maraetai, where they rented or borrowed a bach, and where I swam, fished off the wharf, went out with a local fisherman called Dinty Moore (and threw up, over the side of his boat), was the scene of my near drowning. Although I can't have been much more than five at the time, I remember vividly the relief of being rescued, picked up, carried ashore and set down on the sand by a very large youth. Recently, in the *Guardian Weekly* Notes and Queries column, I saw a discussion among people who had heard it said that drowning was a very comfortable way to commit suicide. Remembering the horror of that battle between the will to hold one's breath and the compulsion to suck in whatever element is out there, even one that will kill you, I wanted to contribute (but didn't) by asking why, if it was such a comfortable way to die, the CIA had found water-boarding such a quick and convenient method of extracting false confessions.

After the war, when my father bought his first car, a second-hand Austin that boiled and fumed and had to be rested as we climbed the Brynderwyns on the way to Waipu for the New Year Highland Games, our holidays ranged further afield, particularly to Ngongotaha on Lake Rotorua, where I learned trout fishing, the old technique no longer used, winding the line in over the spread fingers of the left hand (if the cast is with the right), and suggested by W. B. Yeats in his poem 'The Fisherman': 'And the down-turn of his wrist / When the flies drop in the stream.'

Until I was a university student I never went further south than

Rotorua, nor further north than the Bay of Islands. It is in the social and political climate of those eighteen years, and in the compass of that magically rich space, with its kauri bush and cabbage trees, its tidal inlets and mangroves, its many beaches and harbours, creeks and streams, that my sensibility was formed, my friendships, loves and family attachments cemented, my loyalties, and what Wordsworth would call 'my moral being', created.

IN THE THIRD PHASE OF MY KAIWAKA visits, the war was over, Mac and Gwen were married and had left the farm which was now run by Jo and her husband, Hamlyn Worsfold* – Ham – back from the war. I went up on the train alone, and ranged about as ever on the immortal Bosun. The pigsty had been moved from the ridge above the cowshed to a place half way along the drive to the road; and on the other side of that drive Ham had had a dam bulldozed to provide extra drinking water for the cows in summer. There was still no electricity; but there were long-term plans for a new house close to the road that would make it possible. There was a baby now, Jane; and soon a sister, Elizabeth. I remember them, first, as beautiful blonde toddlers, then small children, so my post-war visits must have gone on for a few years.

Ham set me tasks, such as burning off patches of gorse and scrub to give better access to the dam, and left me to do them unsupervised. He showed me how to set rabbit-traps, and how to kill the rabbit with a single blow to the back of the head. It was brutal, and the traps were cruel, but it was necessary, and, though I felt pity, I did it like one of her Hitler's 'good Germans' without the qualms I would have had later in life. He taught me to skin the rabbit and hang the skin out to dry, turned inside-out and scraped clean, on a

---

* I discovered much later a literary connection in addition to the family one. Ham's father was F. H. Worsfold, to whom A. R. D. Fairburn dedicated his comic poem 'The Rakehelly Man'.

bent piece of number 8. He showed me how to make a brushwood eel-trap. Some of the rabbits were eaten, some, I think, boiled in a huge vat along with eels and fed to the pigs; but there were too many (still no refrigeration) and much waste.

Ham was lively, keen, intelligent, funny and engaged me in talk around the table at night under the hissing lamp. He was the first person to suggest I should go to university. I asked, did you have to be very intelligent to get in? and when he said probably not, I thought, though unlikely, it might just be possible.

There was a boy, a visitor on a neighbouring farm, with the (as I, burdened with Karlson, thought) wonderful name of Bob Smith, and together we ranged over ploughed and harrowed fields picking up pieces of kauri gum turned up by the blades. I would take a sack of this back to Auckland on the train and sell it for one and six a pound. Fifteen shillings for ten pounds weight – that was good money in those days for a boy.

I remember one (or it may have been several, compressed in memory) day of classic haymaking on a nearby farm, the call made on the party line to neighbours that the cut was to be made tomorrow, and everyone rallying. There was no bailer, and for a good part of the day I was on top of the stack helping to distribute the hay evenly and pack it down as it was delivered from the field. Everyone came with food and cold drinks, everyone worked up a huge appetite, the billy was boiled at intervals for tea, large amounts were eaten, and work went on even after the sun had gone down. That summer I arrived home no less the skinny whippet I always was, but with a few new muscles, and very brown.

Cousin Mac's marriage to her cousin Wallace Hastie must have led to visits to the Hastie homestead at Mangawhai, which have left fragmented but vivid memories. I had been there before, as an infant. There is a photograph of me aged possibly five or six, rather formally dressed in grey jacket and shorts, tie, shiny shoes and long black socks, sitting astride a grey saddled pony that has about its neck ribbons that must have been won at a fair. And I remember, at about that age, casting myself off in a dinghy and getting caught in the flow of the outgoing tide, only rescued from being swept out to sea by someone wading and pulling me in at the mouth of the estuary.

But my memory of the old Hastie homestead must come from a later visit, or visits. The two brothers, Wallace and Nelson, had lived there as bachelor-farmers since their sister had gone off to med school in Dunedin and qualified as a doctor, and the house showed all the signs of their having simplified living to the basics. Some of the rooms were no longer used, and were even left open to wind and weather. Old split saddles and broken harness, rusty axes, spades and gum spears, discarded boots, hats and smelly oilskins, lay about on verandas. In the fields there were disks and harrows and other equipment disappearing under infestations of blackberry. When a sash window jammed in the neglected part of the house, it went unrepaired; and if you wanted an egg for breakfast you might as well look into one of the unused rooms as out in the garden, since the hens came and went at will, and laid where the fancy took them. In one of those rooms I found a silver cup, splendid in size but tarnished by neglect, inscribed 'Wallace Hastie, Nelson Hastie, Australasian Champions, Cross-Cut Saw' – and a date. All this may explain the decision that a new house had to be built for the new couple. Mac would marry Wallace, but she would have a new house separate from Nelson who could carry on as before, showering occasionally in the waterfall and letting the old homestead decay around him.

High in the large tract of original bush the Hasties retained on their property a huge kauri had been felled to provide the timber, and it was decided Nelson would harness his bullock team and bring the log out to be pit-sawn. Along with neighbours Ham was summoned to help, and took me with him. There were eight bullocks harnessed together in pairs, wearing huge wooden yokes. They were driven (Nelson wearing a red bandanna and cracking a fearsome leather whip) up the hill on a wide track through the bush, and brought as close as possible to where a wooden race remained from the days when serious logging still went on up there. They were then turned downhill in readiness, and a steel cable was run from them directly to the kauri, already stripped of all branches. Using bullock-power, the log was slowly pulled, levered, wedged, manoeuvred, on to, and down, the race; then dragged on from there down the remainder of the hill-slope track to the pit where it would be sawn into timber.

It was a day's work and such a huge task, done without machinery and with such ingenuity, there was a feeling of having for a moment stepped back (even further back!) into New Zealand's pioneer past.

AS TIME PASSED AND MY LIFE AS A grammar school boy became more crowded, I went to Kaiwaka less often. So I will leave my Paradiso with one further scene, which is exemplary only because it is so vivid in memory.

Ham decides we will go eeling at night. Colleen, the youngest of the eight Bowmar sisters, has come on a visit from Dargaville, where she is now living with an older sister. Jo, pregnant, will have to stay with the little girls, Jane and Elizabeth, already asleep. There is a fourth person comes with us, Bob Smith from the neighbouring farm. With a lantern on a stick we walk all the way out to the road, cross it, climb a fence or a gate, and go down into what was also once Bowmar land, to the site of the first Bowmar farmhouse. The creek there is deep and the surface quite still in the light of the lantern.

Ham is buoyant, full of jokes, information, anecdotes. He is descended (as I am) from early settlers who were in the Bay of Islands in the 1830s, and his talk ranges about in a way that might touch down at any moment anywhere in the century just past, though he is fresh from, and doesn't speak of, its most recent and most spectacular conflagration. He is, I begin to see, excited by

83

the presence of his young sister-in-law, Colleen. He teases her, flirts with her, hugs her, and she responds. There is an electricity between them which combines with the stillness of the night and the special effects of lantern light on the creek's bronze mirror; with the dark silhouettes of trees, the call of moreporks and the far barking of dogs; with the sense that we are somewhere very close to the site of the original homestead and that its ghosts are alive and well; and finally with the fact that we are catching eels – many eels – tugging on the line, dragged ashore, and soon turning this way and that, glistening silvery-black, swimming to nowhere through the long grass.

Wordsworth speaks of the intensities of childhood that are lost as the years pass. He is right – but the loss is not always something to be unequivocally regretted. I think there is a warrior in the genes of the male child, and there is also a hunter, and neither quite fits the world we now have to occupy.

But while it lasts, and before the spoilsport intellect enters to cast its shadow over the treasured memory, here we are in the lantern light, four of us together in an atmosphere of sex, death and unconsidered predation – Ham the soldier, farmer, intellectual and good man; Colleen, who will marry, have children, find religion and take it with her as a missionary to Africa; Bob Smith, the shadowy Everyman, as anonymous as his name; and Karlson, the recorder.

SEVEN
A REAL PIG ISLANDER

My grandmother was known to the children as Nana, to her daughter as Mum, to her son-in-law as Mother. As I see her at this great distance (I now three years older than she was at her death), she is very clear to me but also something of a mystery, and none of those designations seems appropriate to the woman as I re-imagine, or re-invent, her. I have therefore, for the purposes of this memoir, re-named her. She is 'the Grandmother'.

Of those five members who made up the family at 63 Kensington Avenue, the Grandmother was the unconsidered one, the one taken for granted. It is only a slight exaggeration to say I grew up with the idea that she was unimportant – loving and generous, but not a person whose opinion you would seek or, if offered, you would need to treat with great respect. And though I don't excuse myself, it seems to me this was something I felt so early in life it must have come from my parents – not just from Dad, who I'm sure resented the economic dependence he could see no way to escape from, but also from Mum, who dominated her mother, yet still exhibited the emotional dependence, and the consequent ruthlessness, of the only child. They were both, Jim and Olive, bound to Caroline Karlson, and both (unconsciously, I think, in the case of Olive) resented it, even though she was the last person to exploit her position of power, or even to recognise that she had a 'position' of any kind, powerful or otherwise.

Yes, she was a very simple woman, uneducated certainly, probably unreflective; but she was more. The love and the generosity were constant and total. She had lost her father in childhood. Her widowed mother had married again for security, and the stepfather, a farmer at Kamo just out of Whangarei whom she called 'Mr Freeman', had been cold, pious, disciplinarian, ungenerous and unkind. Her two sisters, Olive and Ethel, had died of diphtheria in childhood, and her half-brother, Owen, in the Great War. Her attachment to this younger brother was intense, as Katherine Mansfield's was to hers, and there was, it seems to me, something of the same flavour of flamboyant despair in the way Katherine told friends her brother had been 'blown to bits' and the way the Grandmother told me Owen 'had his head blown off'.

Her mother had sailed with her and Christian Karlson on one of their adventures, had died, and was buried, on an island in the remote Pacific, so there was no grave to tend. She had wanted many children of her own and had succeeded in having only one. Finally she had lost her beloved husband, and I don't think there can be any doubt that she saw as a huge stroke of luck, and the only good to have come out of his death, that she now had her daughter and two grandchildren with her, under her own roof, in a house big enough for us all. In her daughter's names, Olive Ethel, and in her grandson's, Christian Karlson, were remembered, and in some slight degree absolved, three of her great griefs.

On my sister and on me she lavished undivided love and attention. She was a source of warmth so dependable one didn't have to do anything to receive it, and therefore enjoyed it like sunshine, giving it no thought and expressing no gratitude. My mother's love was wonderful and rich, but complex; there were times when you had to work for it, earn it, charm it out of her, amuse her, show cleverness or guile. As a child I was conscious every minute of my mother. It has only been in the long retrospect that I have given more than passing thought to the Grandmother.

The deaths of her two sisters, within a few hours on one afternoon, had been the great trauma of her childhood, and she often recounted how, with Olive having died just a few hours before, Ethel, choking on the last minutes of life, had staggered from the bed to the window, fighting to breathe, and collapsed there. There was no doctor at hand to perform the tracheotomies that would have saved them. It was those deaths that explained the Grandmother's readiness with sentimental Victorian poems and ballads about graveyards and the deaths of children.

> The first that died was sister Jane;
> In bed she moaning lay,
> Till God released her of her pain;
> And then she went away.
>
> So in the churchyard she was laid;
> And when the grass was dry,
> Together round her grave we played,
> My brother John and I.
>
> And when the ground was white with snow,
> And I could run and slide,
> My brother John was forced to go,
> And he lies by her side.
>
> 'How many are you, then,' said I,
> 'If they two are in heaven?'
> Quick was the little Maid's reply,
> 'O Master! We are seven.'

On the other side of that appetite for sentimentality there was a certain toughness, resilience and sense of humour. The Grandmother was affectionate, loyal, spontaneous, staunch (even to the point of truculence); uncomplaining, hard-working and redoubtable. She was also loud, picturesque and sometimes embarrassing. Her contributions to political debate (of which there were many in our house) consisted of slogans. Capitalists, in her discourse, were for ever 'grinding the faces of the poor'. They were 'profiteers' and 'warmongers', to whom the common soldier was 'canon fodder'. Religion was 'the opium of the people'. Michael Joseph Savage had 'saved us from the Depression', and Sid Holland had 'a face like a crushed jam tin'. It was a sort of shorthand for what we all thought – background noise, like the cheering of the crowd, and looked on with indulgence rather than respect.

Her sense of humour was strong, wayward and sometimes quite insensitive. I remember occasions when, sitting beside her in the tram, I would become aware of a trembling in her fat shoulder that I knew meant something had (as we said in the family) 'set her off', and that she was fighting to suppress the gales of laughter that were welling up in her. She was not, like the poet George Barker's mother, 'huge as Asia', but she could certainly be 'seismic with laughter'. The object of this hilarity was often something entirely inappropriate. She could appreciate the story of, and even shed a tear for, Wordsworth's 'Idiot Boy'; but if, on the right (or the wrong) day, she had seen him in the street or on a tram, the sight might quite easily have 'set her off'. It was not that she was unkind – not in the least – only unpredictable and irrepressible. I may well do her an injustice, but I do wonder whether, in another age, she might have joined the crowd to see a public hanging, though she would have wept for the victim.

She was a follower of food theories propounded on the wireless by Dr Guy Chapman.[*] So despite free milk in schools Norma and I, on arriving home, were required to drink a glass of milk containing

---

[*] Father of R. McD. Chapman whose student, and later fellow-professor, I was to be.

lime juice, and eat a raw carrot. There were other food supplements, including cod-liver oil. In the mornings she always listened to, and sometimes followed the advice of, the great broadcasting 'personality' of those days, Aunt Daisy, whom in voice and bold articulation she somewhat resembled.

When asked her religion she liked to answer 'Heathen'; but nonetheless, when in charge of Norma and me at bedtime, as she often was if the parents went out to meetings or to the pictures, she made us 'say our prayers'. This may have been from some notion of propriety; or, more likely, a kind of superstitious just-in-case life insurance for us, since I think she feared for our lives every minute. The 'prayers' were in fact just one prayer, which she taught us when we were very small, and had us say, like good little Victorian children, on our knees at the bedside:

> Gentle Jesus Miek'n'mile
> Lookupon a littlechile
> Pity my Sumplucity
> Suffer me to cometothee.

This was followed by 'GodblessMummy'n'Daddy, Norma'n'Nana'. I thought of 'Miek'n'mile' as Jesus' second name; and 'my Sumplucity', which needed to be pitied, was possibly the battered and balding pink rabbit I took to bed every night. The fourth line was unintelligible. The whole process was overseen by Gentle J Himself, who looked out from a framed picture on the wall above my bed. I have a possibly imprecise recollection of this, but I see Jesus wearing a golden crown, a copious blue gown with many folds and, in the dim light of his own halo and of a lantern he carries on a long staff, 'Knocking at the door of the Heart' – the door overgrown with creepers. The feelings that picture gave were more sinister than reassuring (the creepers over the door were spooky); and this was increased by the disquiet I always felt at any mention of the heart. The fact that we all possessed one, that it went on day and night, and that its continuance was necessary to survival, seemed to me very disturbing; and the idea of anyone 'knocking at it' was at least unpleasant and, if dwelt upon, terrifying.*

It was underneath this icon, and overseen by the self-confessed Heathen, that one was required to kneel and repeat a meaningless formula. If the Grandmother had set out to demonstrate to us that 'religion was the opiate of the people', she could not have done it better.

But what was most remarkable about her was her singing. In the weekends, when she was first up and in the kitchen, I always woke to the sound of her voice. She sang anywhere, at any time of day, and in that I took after her, I suppose in imitation, because she made it seem a perfectly normal thing to do, but in temperament too. I also inherited her ear for voices. She might hear only a few words of a voice, or a few notes, and at once identify the speaker or singer. Often she couldn't remember the name. 'It's the fat one with the big moustache.' 'That's the Russian who died last year in Monte Carlo.' Or she would mispronounce: 'That's Jigly', 'That's Gallacoochi'. But she was always right.

She had a good memory and her repertoire was large and catholic – anything from the popular songs of her childhood and youth, through hymns ancient and modern to what she always referred to as 'Grand Opera'. She listened on Sunday evenings to 'Uncle Tom and the Sankey Singers', and often sang along with them. If there was a reason (a wedding, a funeral) to go to church, I could always pick out her voice, however far I removed myself from it, not bellowing or shrieking but clear and true. She was incapable of singing a wrong note. It was, I think, a fine, an exceptional voice, and because she never stopped entertaining herself with song, it

---

* Since writing this I have checked. The painting, by William Holman Hunt, is called *The Light of the World* and represents Christ knocking at a closed and overgrown door with no handle, so it can be opened only from within. I have the blue gown and the gold crown right, and he does hold a lantern, but not on a long staff. Seeing it again gave me the same sinister feeling, and was confirmation that my memories of that time are fairly dependable.

stayed true even into her sixties. Mum, who of course sang in tune, was the pianist and music teacher; but the Grandmother was the Voice. 'Full many a flower is born to blush unseen / And waste its fragrance on the desert air.' I feel I grew up with a great diva, wasting her precious sounds on the desert air of the family kitchen.

When, as people did in those days, on special occasions, or sometimes when there were relatives or friends visiting, we sang around the piano, we were all in tune except Dad, who sang along but was on and off the note like a novice on a bicycle. As a small boy I found it hard to understand why he would sing a wrong note rather than the right one. It was almost as shocking as if he had found it difficult to speak English. Music was the second language of the household, and he was the only one deficient in it.

The Grandmother used to say proudly that she was 'a real Pig Islander', by which she meant that both her parents were born in New Zealand – something that was rare for a person born in 1881. A number of her close relatives, including her father, were buried in the Symonds Street Cemetery, and she looked on the English trees there with a proprietary affection, particularly in September when, as we passed in the tram, she would direct my attention loudly to their 'new spring dresses', embarrassing me not just because it was a cliché (the critic was already incipient) but because she had said it the year before, and the year before that. As we lumbered by, that graveyard would remind her of one or another relative whose story she would tell, and I would listen with half an ear. One, I remember, however: her uncle or great-uncle had accidentally poisoned himself (she was vivid on the subject of his slow and agonising death) by swallowing what he thought, reaching for it in the dark, was medicine, but from the wrong bottle; and it was as a result of his death (or so she said) that bottles containing poison were subsequently made with downward ridges so you could feel and be warned. His funeral procession, she told me, had stretched all the way from Three Lamps in Ponsonby, right down College Hill and all the way up the far side.

Most of those graves are gone now, swept away by the development of a motorway, but that of one of her grandfathers, Martin McDermott, was just a few years ago still to be seen behind the wall on the western side of Symonds Street, across the road from the grave of Governor Hobson.* He died too early for her to have known him, but she used to do an imitation of his widow's Scottish accent – 'Gangaway hame and tull yurr mitherr aim vurramuch obleeged t'hurr'. She also spoke often of her other grandfather, English John Flatt, who, at the age of ninety and without glasses, could sit outside his house in Thames and read the newspaper by the light of the street lamp.

John Flatt, she told me, had been an Anglican missionary (strictly speaking a non-ordained catechist) in 'the early days', but fell foul of his employer, the Church Missionary Society, because he criticised the Anglican community's excessive acquisitions of Maori land. Many years later I stumbled on the fact that this same John Flatt, briefly returned to London in 1837 in order to marry, had given evidence to a select committee of the House of Lords convened to report 'on the State of the Islands of New Zealand'. I looked up this report in the old British Museum and read a forty-page transcript of my great-great-grandfather's evidence; and on the basis of this reading concluded that what the Grandmother had reported to me had been wrong: my forebear, it seemed on that cursory reading, was reporting missionary land purchases and holdings in a tone that made them seem normal, and therefore (I assumed) acceptable – even justifying them as inevitable given the great size of the missionary families, particularly that of the Rev. Henry Williams, who had eleven children.

Many years later again, when I wrote my novel *The Singing Whakapapa*, I looked deeper into the matter and found that what my grandmother had told me had been, in essence, correct (as

* A recent hunt, however, failed to find it. There are two or three heavy headstones that have broken off in recent years and fallen face-down, and I am sure his is one of those.

family myths often prove to be). Although in his evidence to that committee seeming to excuse those acquisitions of land, Flatt was really exposing them and describing their extent in the case of each missionary. These were facts not previously reported, and therefore unknown to the Church Missionary Society in London.

JOHN FLATT'S STORY IS, I THINK, OF GREAT historic interest.[*] He had gone out to New Zealand in 1834, travelling with another lay catechist, the printer William Colenso, who would be famous in our history for the record he was to make in 1840 of the speeches and incidents surrounding the signing of the Treaty of Waitangi, now always referred to, with perhaps undue reverence, as New Zealand's 'founding document'. Flatt had been eager to take up the position he was appointed to as agriculturalist, assistant to the missionary settlement in the Bay of Islands and in particular to the Rev. Richard Davis. Once there, however, he was given little work, made to feel unwelcome and soon sent by Davis and Henry Williams to the missionary settlement at Matamata, headed by the Rev. Alfred Brown under the protection of the chief Waharoa. Here, along with that small community, Flatt became involved in what was to be the last inter-tribal Maori war, that between the local tribe, Ngati Haua, and Te Arawa of Rotorua.

As tension rose between the two tribes and it became clear an attack on Matamata was imminent, it was decided the mission must be closed. On 11 October 1836 Flatt was despatched with two horses and a small group of Maori to drive the mission herd over the Kaimai Range to the more secure mission station at Tauranga. He was back four days later; and on 18 October set off again with the one remaining horse, another group of about twenty mission Maori

---

[*] When *The Singing Whakapapa* was published, my friend and esteemed colleague Professor Raewyn Dalziel (widow of Sir Keith Sinclair) told me crisply, and I suppose understandably, that she had read it, but that she preferred not to get her history from works of fiction.

and some items the Rev. Brown felt should be sent to Tauranga for protection. Flatt called a halt by the Wairere Falls where he and his party camped for the night. In the early morning they came under attack by an Arawa taua. All of his party escaped except Flatt himself, and a young woman or girl (different accounts are given of her age), Tarore. Flatt was stripped of everything including his clothes; but, protected by the tapu Waharoa had put on the missionaries, his life and that of his horse were spared. Tarore, unprotected and a tribal enemy, was murdered in front of his eyes, her heart torn out, as was the custom with the first kill in an engagement.

That death, traumatic for Flatt, has figured in Maori history, not because it was unusual in its brutality, but because a little bag Tarore carried around her neck was among the items the attacking warriors took away with them. That bag contained Colenso's printing of the missionary translation of the Luke gospel into Maori; and it was said it was instrumental in converting the Arawa tribe to Christianity. The message of peace was received and accepted; there was to be an end to the cycle of utu. So when Tarore's grave was rededicated in 1977 by the Maori Queen, Dame Te Atairangikaahu, the inscription recorded that her 'Gospel of St Luke brought peace to the tribes of Aotearoa'.

Meanwhile scandal was brewing among the missionary community. The Rev. William Yate had been caught in sexual engagements with young Maori men, and it was resolved that all unmarried missionaries, ordained or lay, should be sent home to England to acquire wives. Flatt returned to London to marry the woman he was already engaged to. There, however, he was told that his services with the Church Missionary Society were no longer required. If he wished to return to New Zealand (and he did) it would have to be under his own steam, and he would have to find another way of earning a living there.

It was the reasons for this dismissal that I tried to make sense of in the narrative of my novel *The Singing Whakapapa*, and I will not here rehearse the part that is invented and which (though I am convinced of it) may or may not be correct. What I can be sure of, however, is that Flatt deeply resented his dismissal; and that, in revealing to the House of Lords committee the extent of unauthorised land purchases by the Anglican Mission in New Zealand, he was taking revenge on those (in particular Henry Williams and Richard Davis) who had not wanted him as agriculturalist. By not welcoming him and admitting him to the fold, they created exactly the effect they were trying to prevent. In London Flatt gave the information they wished to keep secret, not only to the House of Lords committee, but also to Edward Gibbon Wakefield, the super-colonist whose schemes the missionaries had opposed; and Wakefield (citing Flatt by name) used them in a pamphlet which took the form of an open letter to Lord Glenelg, Secretary of State for the Colonies.

The consequences for both Williams and Davis were, in the long term, dire. Questioned from London, probed and challenged about their land holdings, both men prevaricated. Distance made the process long and slow. But in the end the Rev. Davis was ordered to leave the Bay of Islands mission farm he had made his own, and go to work at Kaikohe. He complained bitterly that he had served the cause faithfully, and that 'to live and die for the benefit of the heathen' had been his sole concern; but the CMS had had enough of the embarrassment caused by these land grabs, and sent him on his way. Archdeacon (as he now was) Henry Williams, whose holding of 22,000 acres had already been halved by the land commissioners after the signing of the Treaty of Waitangi, was instructed by his masters in London to reduce it even further, to a maximum of 2596 acres. He refused; and, as I wrote in my novel, 'On 30 November 1849, eleven years after [John Flatt] had put the London clerical cat among the New Zealand clerical pigeons, Archdeacon Henry Williams was dismissed.'

The ups and downs of historical fashion are a rich source of irony and humour. Wakefield, the colonist and land-grabber supreme, is distinctly unfashionable among New Zealand historians, while the Anglican clergy, who opposed him (including Henry

Williams who recently received a late posthumous reinstatement by the Anglican Church to his archdeacon-hood) are on the whole more acceptable – *because* they opposed him. That the missionaries, while resisting Wakefield's grand imperial designs, were busy making little family empires of their own is overlooked or forgiven. Having, all of us who are Pakeha, profited by what Wakefield did in establishing settlements in New Zealand, we can now deplore the man and his work, make public apologies to this and that Maori tribe, even make token recompense, comfortable in the knowledge that what was done then cannot be undone now.

And John Flatt? He was, and is, a nobody, long since forgotten. For myself, a special irony when I was writing my novel was that I was not able to find his grave, though I believe it must be somewhere in the graveyard near the Te Aroha Racecourse; while Tarore, the obscure young Maori woman whom he may have loved, and who was murdered before his eyes, has come out of the shadows of the past, and has a grave re-dedicated by the Maori Queen.

Flatt returned to New Zealand with his new wife, struggled to earn a living, and in the end made a successful life here and established a family. He was cheeky and resourceful. When James Busby, the British Government's agent in New Zealand before there was a governor, travelled to New South Wales to make a report in person, he suggested Flatt, with his wife and infant, might occupy the back of his house, tend the garden, feed the livestock and see the hens were kept out of the vines. When Busby returned he was slightly miffed to find them occupying the whole house. It pleases me, when I visit the Treaty House, as it now is, a hallowed memorial to the foundation of our nation, to think my forebears occupied it, and that the Grandmother's father took his first infant steps there. [*]

***

[*] Since writing this I have learned that Busby's vines extended out from the house to where the flagpole now stands, that he made his own wine and that it was commended by the French explorer Dumont d'Urville, which adds significance to my forebear's task of protecting the grapes from the domestic fowls.

There is, as far as I could discover, only one recorded encounter between Flatt and Henry Williams after Flatt's return from London. It took place on the seafront at Paihia at a time when Williams was still in charge of the Anglican Mission in New Zealand, but must have been coming under increasing pressure from London to answer allegations about land. Flatt was destitute, and may have made the mistake of asking his former master for help. Williams, registering simultaneously where he considered Flatt belonged in the social scale, and his own bitterness that Flatt had given information to Wakefield, suggested that 'perhaps your rich friends in London might buy you a dray'.

As well as irony there is, looking back, piquancy in the sense of links that bring the past suddenly close. Colenso was one of the figures I read about in that standard schools' history of New Zealand, *Our Nation's Story*. So was Henry Williams. Williams' tough face and steel-rimmed spectacles, the fact that he had been a naval man before he was a man of God and had fought in the Napoleonic Wars – all this was familiar to me as a child at Maungawhau School. Yet I had no idea that the Grandmother whose talk I only listened to with half an ear, who told me of her grandfather reading the newspaper without glasses by the streetlight outside his door in Thames, was speaking of a man who had been Colenso's colleague and travelling companion, Williams' employee, and ultimately the whistle-blower who brought about Williams' dismissal from his post and the loss of his title as archdeacon.

AS TIME WENT BY THE GRANDMOTHER became more eccentric, more independent, more isolated, more herself. Like her pioneer forebears she liked to walk long distances rather than take public transport, but one of her knees became weak and would go 'out'. I never knew quite what this meant except that it was clearly painful, and Mum seemed to know how to put it back 'in' while the grandmother lay on her back groaning and weeping. There were times when she would crash down in the street, and Norma and I would try to give the impression we had nothing whatever to do with her, while Mum applied herself to the task of putting it right. The Grandmother also developed bunions, and her solution (another keen embarrassment) was to cut holes in her shoes to make room for them.

She had friends and a few relatives she liked to visit, but they were old and vanishing as time went by. There were two old ladies, Cousin Cissie and Cousin Amelia, who lived in a shoe-sized house in Mt Eden and asked me, when I was still quite small, to sing for them. I remember this only because, when I had sung and been praised, Cousin Cissie, a tiny woman with round rimless spectacles who had been a schoolteacher, asked me how I beat time, and since I didn't really have an answer but felt politeness required one, I said I did it with my big toe inside my shoe. This produced laughter, and for me, embarrassment. The two sisters had no wireless but listened to radio broadcasts on crystal sets (one each) with headphones.

There was the Quelch family in Devonport, another musical group, he a German sea-captain friend of Christian Karlson. Mum had been left with the Quelches (at that time living in Parnell), for three years from the age of five, while her parents went away on one of my grandfather's extended contracts in the islands; and their daughter, Dolly Quelch, had married my uncle Joe, so there was a feeling of close relationship. The Quelches had an attic in their house with a window looking across the harbour to the central city, and full of musical instruments and music stands. As children we treated it as our studio, creating programmes which we pretended were being broadcast live to the city. Later, Ngaire Stead, daughter of Dolly and Joe, learned the oboe and would one day join Don Cater's father as a member of the National Orchestra.

Among other of the Grandmother's friends were the Simons family, Labour stalwarts, the father a retired miner dying of what was called 'miner's complaint', which I suppose was emphysema if it wasn't lung cancer. Their very handsome daughter, Thelma, who taught 'elocution' and had a clear, at times formidable, articulation and voice, had been crippled by poliomyelitis (known then as 'infantile paralysis'), and was able to walk only with crutches and callipers.

The Grandmother was short (possibly 4 foot 11), overweight and diabetic, and apart from regular injections of insulin, she used to dose herself at intervals, on the recommendation of a friend, or perhaps something read in one of her 'books', with a concoction of boiled prickly pear, a cactus she had planted in a warm corner of the front lawn for that purpose. I think I have heard since that this plant has hallucinogenic effects, but if they did for her we were unaware of it.

By the time Norma and I were at Grammar, if the parents went away overnight, as they did occasionally, the former roles were reversed, and we were watching over the Grandmother. There was an occasion when Mum and Dad were in Christchurch and the Grandmother became ill and was taken to Greenlane Hospital in an ambulance. There she was put on what should have been her regular diet and given her normal doses of insulin. The effect of this was to produce insulin shock, because the diet had never been adhered to. (This, at least, is how it was explained to me, though it may be that the hospital was just excusing a mistake of its own with the dosage.) I was called to the hospital and found her in the happy delusion that she was on board ship again, far out in the Pacific, the nurses and doctors were the crew, the far end of the ward was the galley, and I was her beloved Christian Karlson. The nurses gave me a bowl of sugar and water, and a spoon, and I spent a long afternoon feeding it to her to correct the insulin imbalance.

She recovered, but her mind, never a sharp instrument, seemed afterwards always slightly clouded, though not unhappy. In particular she became even more obsessed with Hollywood. Her 'books' had made her an authority on Tinsel Town gossip, though her pronunciation of what she read was often comic. Nigel Bruce, for example, an actor of those days, was Niggle Bruce.

She took to going to five o'clock movie sessions, and only after the family evening meal was over (avoidance may have been part of her intention) eating the meal left for her in the oven. If she liked a movie very much, especially if it was a musical (there were a great many in the 1940s) she would go to it, the same movie every night for a week.

She took to smoking, but in secret, and would never admit to it. I or Norma would catch her at the back door, puffing on one of Dad's De Reszkes and looking dreamily out at the night sky; but at the sound of a footstep the cigarette would be sent spiralling out and down into the compost heap in the lower garden. Challenged, she would say we were mistaken. She did not smoke, certainly not, never smoked, had not been smoking. To me, when I think of it now, this represents the outward manifestation of an inner life, a life of fantasy, no doubt connected to those classic Hollywood movies that were her 'life of the mind'.

I WILL CONCLUDE THIS CHAPTER WITH a brief anthology representing just a few of the more bizarre and/or sentimental of the Grandmother's songs and lyrics – a selection which the reader may well choose to pass over, and straight on to Chapter 8. (I omit samples of her 'Grand Opera' arias, which are all well known.)

The funniest in retrospect are the popular (I suppose music hall) songs of her youth. For example:

> Waltz me around again, Willie,
> Around, around, around.
> The music it's dreamy, it's peaches and creamy,
> Oh don't let my feet touch the ground.
> I feel like a ship on an ocean of joy,
> I just want to holler out loud, 'Ship ahoy!'
> Waltz me around again, Willie,
> Around, around, around.

That is only the refrain. There was a narrative, most of which I have forgotten, but part of which went

> Each night she'd tag him
> To some dance-hall drag him,
> And when the band started to play,
> She was up like a silly
> And grabbed hold of Willie
> And these were the words that she'd say –

followed by the refrain.

Another with a narrative was from the first days of motoring, the story being told by a young woman whose 'beau' takes her out in his new 'automobile', but every few miles he has to

> Get out and get un-der
> Get out and get un-der
> To fix up his auto-mo-bile.

I learned these things simply by listening. They are all somewhere in my head, music as well as words. Another music hall favourite went

> Down
> In jungle town
> A honeymoon
> Is coming soon
> When you hear a serenade
> To a pretty monkey-maid
> And the chimpanzees
> Sing in the trees
> Sing in the trees
> She'll be true
> To Monkey Doodle-do
> Way down in the jungle town.

The Grandmother was also strong on sentimental lyrics and arias. There was one she sang with great gusto and feeling which I think was called 'Tosti's farewell to his sweetheart' (the sweetheart clearly deceased). I may just possibly be confusing that title with the wrong words and music, but in any case the one I have in mind went,

> Speak, speak, speak to me Thora,
> Speak from your Heaven to me;
> Love of my life, child of my dreams,
> Hope of my world to be;
> Love of my life, child of my dreams,
> Hope of my world to be – e – e – e [each of these a
> separate, rising note]
> Ho-ope of my world to be.

That was sentiment in the first degree, inviting flamboyance, exaggeration and comedy. Not dissimilar was 'The Lost Chord', I think by the Sullivan of Gilbert and Sullivan:

> Seated one day at the organ
> I was lonely and ill at ease,
> And my fingers wandered idly
> Over the noisy keys;
> I know not what I was playing,
> Nor what I was thinking then,
> But I struck one chord of music like
> The sound of a great Amen,
> Like the sound of a gre-e-e-eat Amen.

And it continues at some length about his failure ever to recover this heavenly sound-bite.

There was also a song, 'Jerusalem', not the William Blake one now popular with English football (or is it rugby?) fans, but a very fruity and fulsome one about a vision confirming a beyond-the-grave future in which the biblical promises of 'the Holy City' would come to pass.

> And all who would might enter there
> And no one was denied.
> No need of moon nor stars by night,
> Nor sun to shine by day.
> It was the New Je-ru-sa-lem
> And would not pass away.

For a confessing Heathen the Grandmother had a lot of hymns by heart; and I sang those with her too, most of them, considered either as music or as poetry, utterly, ineffably, inexcusably banal. My sense that there was good and bad, better and worse, among these songs and lyrics, just as among the popular songs of the 1940s I learned from radio and movies and crooned around the house, was keenly developed; and I look back on that as another proof of how wrong late twentieth-century post-modernism has been in insisting there is no such thing as an aesthetic response, and that all such preferences are learned, socially conditioned. Why, if that were so, would I, even as a child, have had such clear positive and negative responses to things, *all* of which were equally parts of my social conditioning? Those responses were aesthetic, and were in fact the beginnings of criticism.

Yes, the hymns were banal; but a very few – 'Come to the church in the wild wood', for example, or 'Softly and tenderly Jesus is call-ing' – were capable of causing a small momentary flutter of response in the unbelieving soul. And in any case, banal or otherwise, sing-ing, like walking or running or swimming, was its own reward and its own pleasure.

> Softly and tenderly Jesus is calling,
> Calling to you and to me.

See by the portals he's watching and waiting,
Waiting for you and for me.
Come home, comehome comehome,
Come ho-o-ome,
Ye who are weary come ho-o-ome . . .

And so on. As a child I was touched by that one; but the critic in me, ashamed of itself, always sang 'portals' as 'portholes', in case the feeling was showing.

There was, however, a song about an Indian brave killed in battle, which was deeply affecting because of the way the music interlocked with the words and seemed to give them a depth they didn't possess on their own. I sang it (and would still if I had any voice left) with emotion:

'Neath the green grass
The brave warrior is sleeping;
Guarding the pass
His long vigil he's keeping.
Where in his pride
He hath roamed in his childhood,
Fought he and died
In the depth of the wildwood;
Where in his pride
He hath roamed in his childhood,
Fought he and died
In the depth of the wildwood.

I sang it possibly imagining myself as the brave and the 'wildwood' as the bush at Kaiwaka; but perhaps for the Grandmother there was a thought of the dead half-brother with the marvellous warrior name, Owen Vincent Freeman, who had (so the brass plaque said) 'died for Freedom and Honour'.

EIGHT

A SHORT HISTORY OF THINGS THAT DIDN'T HAPPEN

I think of Allen Curnow (1911–1991) and James K. Baxter (1926–1972), by far the most distinguished of my New Zealand predecessor poets, as having literary culture. Curnow's father was a clergyman-poet whose work appeared in several anthologies, a man adept in a variety of traditional verse forms, a skill Allen preserved over many years in his satirical role as 'Whim Wham' in the *New Zealand Herald* and the Christchurch *Press*. Baxter's grandfather was University of Canterbury professor J. Macmillan Brown.[*] His mother was a graduate, his father a famous World War I pacifist, who wrote a book about his experiences and whose head was full of poetry

---

[*] Long ago I read somewhere an account of Macmillan Brown, who was something of an anthropologist as well as a classical scholar, being guided around one of the islands in the remote Pacific by a Swedish Captain Karlson.

he could quote from memory. Baxter's family culture opened the door to poetry for him, a door that was always open, so that in a lifespan half the length of Curnow's he wrote, probably, three times as many lines. Curnow's family, on the other hand, exerted a strange pressure, at times inhibiting, something that had to be resisted, and yet profited from too. Ultimately, for both men, that literary culture, absorbed in childhood, can be seen only as an enormous enrichment.

I came to poetry, not by the first door of family culture, but the second, education; or perhaps it would be more accurate to say education combined with accident and appetite. If there was a family culture at 63 Kensington Avenue it was music; but there were two – music and politics. My mother was a very good pianist, and I'm sure I first heard Beethoven and Chopin, Schubert and Brahms, in the womb. Equally I could say that, though nameless and invisible, I was briefly present at one of New Zealand's seminal political events, the Queen Street riots of April 1932. My mother was three months pregnant, and at some point the action following the police baton assault on the socialist orator Jim Edwards, outside the Auckland Town Hall, grew so violent, Dad put her in a taxi and sent her home to safety, where the Grandmother was looking after the infant Norma. What Dad did afterwards he didn't say. Did he join the others, smashing plate-glass windows down Queen Street? That was not his style; but as all of us know who have experienced serious protest getting out of hand, a point is reached at which your 'style' goes, and what remains is collective action, 'us' against 'them'. The Chinese speak of 'a revolutionary situation', meaning that there is a point at which circumstances determine an outcome of violence and change, whether large or small. I suppose the Queen Street riots were one such moment, small but significant in the history of an island nation which repeats itself on those left and right bottom corners of Mercator's projection. Another was the huge protracted series of protests against the Springbok tour of 1981. If in the womb one can be said to have been present, I can say I was present at the first. I was certainly present and active, half a century later, in the second.

I was a Depression child of Labour stalwarts, my father a Party official, and later a trade union secretary, my mother active when and where possible. I must have been just three when Labour won the 1935 election in a landslide, a majority that was to be confirmed and increased three years later. I remember the picture of Michael Joseph Savage, the Labour leader and first Prime Minister, on the kitchen wall close to my infant high chair – and that was so early in my life that Mickey Savage (as he was popularly known) and Mickey Mouse were somewhat mixed and confused in my consciousness. In fact there was something mouse-like about Savage, both in face and in voice. Others in that first Labour team had the kind of oratory the role of Labour leader and the name Savage might have suggested. Savage himself was a quiet-mannered, reasonable old aunty, who began each new explanatory paragraph with, 'Now then . . .' It was hardly stirring stuff, and Jack Lee, who survived him by many years, was to say that Savage never said nor wrote a word that anyone remembered. But he headed the team which, in the teeth of opposition from (as the Grandmother would say, quite rightly) 'vested interests' and the press, ensured for the first time that every New Zealand child had a secondary education, set up a free health-care service, built state houses for the poor, established a state-owned radio network, increased pensions for widows, the old and the infirm, legislated for a forty-hour week, industrial arbitration and a guaranteed price for farmers, nationalised the Reserve Bank, set up a state insurance company to compete with private insurance houses, and in general established the first (at least in the Anglophone world) welfare state. For my parents, I'm sure, and many like them, 'Bliss was it in that dawn to be alive, but to be young was very heaven.' Savage was revered, and that picture close to my high chair was replicated in kitchens throughout the land.

Among my earliest political memories is of being woken in the night by my father and A. S. Richards, MP for Roskill and a member of the first Labour Cabinet, talking, sometimes shouting, through the wall from the bedroom Norma and I shared as infants, in the big loud voices politicians in those days got into the habit of using, as if they were always addressing a crowd without the help of a microphone; getting excited and banging the table with their fists – and then breaking off into fits of smokers' coughing. Dad was chairman or secretary of a local Party branch, and Richards' campaign manager. Later, during one, possibly two, elections, I distributed party pamphlets and was rewarded by Mr Richards (as he was to me – Arthur to my parents) with half a crown, the same present my Stead grandfather always gave me at Christmas. Richards wore three-piece dark suits, of course, with a watch chain across his waistcoat from which hung a small medal that showed he was a Member of Parliament and gave him free access to travel on the railways anywhere in New Zealand and at any time, a right which persists in the currently disputed travel rights of MPs.

At the age of seven (which I think the Catholic Church says is the age of reason and moral responsibility) I asked to join the Party. My parents laughed at first, but then Dad joined me up. I received a membership card on which was printed Labour's objective of those days: 'The socialisation of the means of production, distribution and exchange', a goal which (unlike the Party) I have not forgotten. I also got a lapel badge – a silver fern with a red centre and the letters NZLP.

Labour was into its second term in government and the war had begun when it became known among the faithful that Savage was dying of cancer. John A. Lee (popularly known as Jack), a First World War veteran who had lost an arm and won a DCM, the Party's great orator, pamphleteer and scallywag author of power-ful semi-autobiographical fiction, was ambitious for the top job. He need only have held his fire and it would probably, in time, have been his; but impatient, and feeling Savage had slighted him with Cabinet posts more minor than he deserved, he wrote a thinly veiled attack on the revered leader, 'Psychopathology in Politics'.

I suppose it was the kind of impulsive action that wins medals (posthumous often) in war. This time, more than an arm, he lost his political life – and there was no medal. The Party, already in anticipatory mourning, turned on him. At its annual conference Lee was expelled. My father must have been there. How did he vote? I wish I knew, and that I could say he went against the tide, but that is unlikely. The expulsion seems to me to have been an act of folly equal to Lee's own. The article could have been overlooked; the Party should have behaved as if it had never happened, or had gone unnoticed. Lee's huge potential, his popular appeal, his debating skill, his brilliant pamphleteering – it was all wasted.[*] If his talent had been more purely literary it would not have mattered so much. But there was something about his published fiction, a lack of depth, of reflection, of education, of literary culture, of sensibility, that meant it was always oratory – oratory, but written down.

When Savage died it seemed the whole nation went into mourning. The coffin was brought from Wellington to Auckland by train, stopping at towns along the way. It was to be brought from Auckland Railway Station into Queen Street on a gun-carriage, and Dad took me into town to see history as it happened. He meant me to remember it, and I do. I was seven, too short to see, and the crowd was enormous, so Dad hoisted me up on his shoulders to watch it pass slowly by, accompanied by a military guard and covered with a flag. It was only a few months since I had been with Mum watching the men from the *Achilles* march by. Now the mood was quite different, but equally powerful, with a sense of what Shakespeare calls 'the many-headed monster' becoming one – one consciousness, one voice, and now one silence. The noisy collective rapture of the *Achilles* welcome was replaced by an almost complete stillness,

---

[*] Decades later, in October 1971, when Frank Sargeson, David Ballantyne, Maurice Shadbolt and I went as a delegation of writers to honour Lee on his eightieth birthday, I made the mistake of saying that I had thought of writing a play about his fall from Party grace. For some weeks afterwards I was deluged with letters full of 'the facts', and suggestions about how they might be used.

in which you heard only the slow crisp steps of the marchers, the creaking of the gun-carriage, the slow, muffled beating of a drum, and an occasional audible sob from among the crowd.

Two or three years later when the Savage Memorial (worthy of a Soviet general secretary) was complete, up on Bastion Point overlooking the harbour, I stared in through a glass panel in the iron doors and tried to imagine the great little man, Mickey Mouse-Savage, lying inside the catafalque, dimly lit by a mysterious glow from above, saying 'Now then . . .' to the empty room. I have a photograph, which appeared in the *Auckland Star*, of my parents leading a delegation of Labour worthies that year, carrying a wreath to be laid there on the anniversary of the death. Dad looks very important. Mum is enigmatic, but wearing her best.

As for the other culture of the house, music: compared to what is possible now, I suppose it was insignificant. Tours by overseas performers, or any performers, were over 'for the Duration'. There was no major orchestra, no LPs or CDs. There was radio, singing at home and at school, choirs, the piano, Ngaire's oboe, Victor Cater's flute, and church – and that was all. But it filled a great deal of our waking consciousness; and if for me it was a joy, it was also, and much more significantly, a torment.

Very early I persuaded my mother to begin teaching me the piano. She intended to teach me, but she thought it was too early to start. As with starting school, I persuaded her. She was right – it was too early; but any time, early or late, it would have made no difference. Because I was known, even as an infant, to sing in tune, to have 'a perfect ear', to be musically gifted, she expected piano would come as naturally to me as it must have come to her. *Au contraire*, I was a failure – possibly the worst pupil she ever had; or the worst, anyway, who, having demonstrated a lack of talent, had to go on being taught, whether through her stubbornness or mine, or both, I can't now say. My sister was not brilliant, but she sailed through the grades, passing one exam after another. Mum would never allow me to sit even the first exam, I suppose because

I was her son, and she could not face the thought of others in the profession hearing how bad I was.

What is strange is that I never gave up. For years I dreamed my way through lessons and daily practice. I could play a delicate scale (the simple ones). I could hear its delicacy, its rightness. There were some simple exercises I could do well enough. But as soon as the fingering became fast or complicated, I couldn't do it, couldn't make it sound as I knew it should. I could hear (the ear never failed, and was honest in its reporting) how bad it was, and it was all my own.

My hands were small, but so were my mother's. Some people have said, 'Of course you failed because your teacher was your mother. She should have sent you to another teacher.' And it's true it made it hard having her there in the house, hearing me, so that any practice could turn into an unscheduled lesson. Sometimes she would call from two rooms away, 'Third finger. *Third* finger', knowing, just by the sound, that, though I had struck the right note, I had struck it with the wrong finger. There were times, a very few, when she must have decided she would wake me out of my dream and apply force – not physical force, but moral/mother force. I remember one such which went on and on, ended in tears, hers as well as mine, made me late for school, and got us nowhere.

No. It was not that my teacher was my mother; it was that I lacked something as simple as the digital dexterity the piano requires; or it might have been something more complex, some break, or delay, in the line of communication between hand and brain (though I was to prove, in sport, and later in dancing, very well co-ordinated). A cause scarcely seems to matter. The fact is that I was a failure at the piano; and that affected my own view of myself, and my mother's view of me. She and I were very close and very fond. I suspect her secret thoughts about me would probably have been that I was a darling boy, that she loved me to the absolute limit, but that I was not very bright. How, otherwise, could I fail at what she found so easy? Years later, when I had academic successes, and even an MA with first-class honours, she used to tell people how hard I had worked, as if my success had nothing at all to do with natural talent. Even a PhD from Britain, a professorship and international publication didn't seem to alter her view of me, and she spoke always as if I had triumphed over a handicap.

If there is anything in all this I harbour a late grudge about, it is that she did not say simply, 'Karlson, it's not going to be the piano for you. It must be something else.' Another instrument, perhaps – like cousin Ngaire's oboe. (After seeing a Kirk Douglas movie with the absurdly suggestive title of *Young Man with a Horn*, I harboured a brief wish to become a jazz trumpeter.) But why not the instrument I had in my throat, which she could hear me exercising daily with neither thought nor ambition? For the two years at Mt Albert Grammar that I retained, or could still use, my soprano voice, I sang in the school choir. It was a very good one, conducted by Mr Willmott, known among the boys as 'Itchy'. We sang on Radio 1YC, and in the Auckland Town Hall, where Norma claimed she could distinguish my voice among the sopranos even from the gallery. There, except for a brief re-emergence two years later as a baritone in a secondary-schools music festival, serious singing began and ended for me, though I am described in the school's account of my time there as 'a chorister'. After that it was the shower, carols at Christmas, songs in the car on country roads, and a long silence.

When Kay is asked, by people who hear that her husband is a writer, 'Do you write too?' her answer has always been, 'No, I'm a reader.' If there are writers, she says, there must be readers, and she is one. I can say the same about music. If there are people who make it, there must be those who listen, and I have been one of those all my life. The difference is only that Kay says this of herself as reader without regret. In myself I can't entirely suppress the regret.

So to the boredom of primary school, and at home that of Arthur Mee's *Children's Encyclopaedia*, must be added the unremitting sense of failure our piano – a grand, of course – induced in me. And (since this is painting-in-the-shadows time), in that household of 63 Kensington Avenue, so full of life, affection, music, jokes (my father liked to tease and invent silly names for his children) and political debate, there was also the constant anxiety that a quarrel would blow up between the parents, turn sour and potentially violent, poison the air and 'holler its name to the reverberate hills'. I used to see it coming, like a storm on the horizon. When it got close enough to be beyond doubt, I would go around the house quietly closing the windows so it would not be broadcast to the neighbourhood. I have always had a special talent for shame and embarrassment[*] – the last kind of child who should have had noisy fighters for parents.

And then, after two or three days (the weekends were a dangerous time) of skirmishing and clamour, by a turn of the tide as inexplicable as the one that had brought it about, the row would be over, and I would come into a room and find the two, Mum and Dad, entwined in a keen embrace. Like Shakespeare's schoolboy, I trudged 'unwillingly to school' and, as often as not, trudged unwillingly home again.

When asked did I have a happy childhood I have never known how to answer, because I believe, except in extreme cases (cases more extreme than mine, anyway), an answer must depend more than anything on temperament. Although a shy child, I was temperamentally an optimist, full of bounce, often in minor trouble because not able to repress the inappropriate bright thought, the quick quip, the pun or joke. I enjoyed my life, and there was a lot to be enjoyed, including the natural world which I found always absorbing. The anxiety I suffered constantly was not for myself. In fact I could say it took me out of myself, made me less self-centred than I might otherwise have been. What made me anxious, and often deeply unhappy, was that these two, my parents whom I loved, and who loved me and loved one another, could inflict on one another so much pain.

---

[*] Recent brain research has suggested that at least until the age of twenty we process embarrassment with a different part of the brain, and that it is consequently more intense than in later life – a fact, if it is a fact, which explains a great deal of my behaviour in the years covered in this memoir.

MUM WAS INTELLIGENT, ENQUIRING. She was not strong on phatic communion. When she asked a question, even of one of her children, it was in order to hear the answer, and think about it. She was sensitive; there was a grace about her. If there is a gene that makes an artist, and if I have it, I received it from her. She could be combative. She was firm, capable of a certain toughness. When things went wrong with Dad, and her nerve broke, she could slide effortlessly into hysteria.

From time to time I would find her sitting at the window in their bedroom, staring out at Mt Eden, her cheeks wet, her eyes red and filled with tears. If there was not an immediate and obvious cause, in other words if there had been no quarrel with Dad, I would know the reason: she was sad because of 'the baby'.

I think I was six when 'the baby' came and went, but the sadness continued for many years afterwards. There had been a certain amount of forewarning that 'a new brother or sister was on the way'. Norma, two and a half years older, knew more about it than I did, and was excited. Then there must have been a night when Mum was rushed to the 'nursing home', where babies were born. These were private institutions, run by nurses and amateurs, though the babies were delivered by the woman's GP, usually male. Norma and I were both delivered in a nursing home. I imagine them to have been primitive places, chloroform the painkiller and forceps the instruments in a crisis. (I can still find the forceps indentations in my own skull). When my younger sister, Frances Caroline, arrived, seventeen years after I was born, all this had changed and she was delivered at National Women's Hospital.

The morning after the night of the crisis my father came into the bedroom Norma and I shared to tell us there would be no brother or sister. Norma wept. I felt the rush of an unfamiliar emotion, an excitement. It would be easy to say it was the primitive satisfaction of a child ego that had been anticipating a rival and has just learned that there would not be one after all – and perhaps that is what it was. My belief is that it was something quite different: the rush of adrenalin which word of a significant death always brings. One has felt it often enough since, of family members, of Prime Ministers and presidents. It is why people ask, and answer, the question, 'Do you remember where you were / what you were doing when you heard President Kennedy / Princess Diana / Norman Kirk had died?' It is why I remember the scene so clearly, Dad coming in and pulling up the green wooden Venetian blind, turning, and saying 'I'm afraid there isn't going to be a little brother or sister . . .'

The baby had been born, 'a perfect little girl' he said, and had died less than an hour later. The pregnancy, I learned when I was older, had gone only seven months. In a good hospital such a baby would not have died. Among the papers my mother left when she died, along with the handwritten and prematurely terminated text of her 'Venus on the Wane', there was a small sheet of paper, with no letterhead, no address nor anything official, just torn from a note-pad, on which an unfamiliar but well-formed hand had written

Baby Stead
Anglican. Block H. Section 8.
Plot 70
Waikumete Cemetery

I was told she was to have been named Irene; and perhaps because of the strange little ginger-haired girl who'd been late when she had to put her shoes on, and who had tried to help me open the gate when I broke my arm, I always thought of her as having ginger hair. 'The baby' was a puzzle who came and went without ever having been, and left our mother weeping.

DAD CONTINUED VERY ACTIVE IN THE Labour Party, which was where his most serious ambitions lay. He was always chairman or secretary of the local branch and a campaign organiser at election time. For a time he was chairman of the Auckland LRC – the

Labour Representation Committee. He was also secretary of the Fire Brigades Union – not because he knew anything about fighting fires, but because he knew how to negotiate with employers on behalf of the men. I went with him once or twice to the Auckland Central Fire Station and was shown the polished wooden poles the men slid down, through holes from the upper floors, when the alarm bells rang, and how, beside their beds at night they put the legs of their trousers over their boots so they could be into them at a bound.

Labour had held office since 1935, and the war had meant elections were deferred. But by 1943, as the tide turned in favour of the Allies, Prime Minister Peter Fraser, always conscientious on constitutional matters, decided it was time to go again to the country.

Dad wanted to be in Parliament, though he seldom said so aloud. He was rather shy and reserved, always affectionate with me, kind and full of jokes, but not confiding. Just once, however, in a moment when real feeling showed, he told me that if the day came when he walked up the steps of Parliament Buildings as a Member, it would be the proudest of his life. In that moment I made it my ambition that I, too, would one day be an MP. It was an intention which lingered somewhere in my mind for half a lifetime, never abandoned, merely deferred and never embraced. I look back on it, certainly not with regret, but with curiosity – another one of those lives one might have lead but didn't.

With the calling of an election in 1943, Dad must have seen his chance. Jack Lee was still MP for Grey Lynn but his sacking from the Party meant that someone would have to stand against him as the official Labour candidate. Lee had very strong support in that area, and had formed his own Democratic Soldier Labour Party. There would be divided loyalties, as there were still within the Party itself; but Labour loyalties would almost certainly prevail, and Lee would lose the seat.

There was to be a selection ballot, the aspirants making their case before a team made up partly of local members and partly of members from Party headquarters in Wellington. I remember seeing the speech Dad had written in his tall, left-leaning hand. It was lying on the desk that looked over the front lawn, across the school grounds and towards Mt Eden. I read some of it, but I don't remember what it said.

I was also there to hear him deliver it. Mum too, and Norma. Perhaps he thought it would help to be seen as a family man; or perhaps he wanted us to see him shine, and take his first step on the parliamentary ladder.

His speech was not a success. He was nervous – I could see it in his face and hear it in his voice, right from the start. He began to depart from his script and then, like a bareback rider slipping sideways when his mount goes into a fast trot, couldn't get upright again. The memory of all this is vivid because it was painful, because I felt for him, because I knew it mattered, and because I used to think of it sometimes later, when I had to speak in public. What he needed, I'm sure, and hadn't had, was experience, practice. He had been a backroom Party man, a man for behind-the-scenes negotiations, for smoke-filled rooms. Facing an audience he was suddenly shy, clinging to his script for fear of losing his way, departing from it because it seemed too formal, then unable to return to exactly what he had written because it didn't match the informality he had just allowed himself.

I don't mean that it was a disaster, or a huge embarrassment; but remembering it I think I recognise these things because in the intervening years I have experienced them myself, and have learned ways over, around and through them. That was all he needed – some practice. He was like someone sitting an exam without having first taken the course.

The others took their turns, droned on or ranted in the approved manner, promising killer blows to the vile capitalists of the National Party. One of them, Fred Hackett, got the selection. When it was over I heard some of Dad's supporters commiserating. 'What went wrong?' one of them asked, and I heard him blustering about how it was all 'stacked against him', they were 'wised up from Wellington'. Perhaps it was, and they were, but I winced for him. That phrase 'wised up' was not his normal way of talking. It belonged to Humphrey Bogart, not to my Dad. He was trying to cover his embarrassment while suffering the pain of defeat and a huge disappointment. This was his chance, and it was gone.

Labour won the 1943 election with their massive 1938 majority significantly reduced, but still with a comfortable 45-to-34 advantage. Fred Hackett won Grey Lynn from Jack Lee, and was there for life. I remember him (because one was to see him, or his image, in the years to come) as undistinguished with a lot of teeth. A loyal son speaks there, of course, but I always thought of him as well-named, the hack who got the posts Dad might have had, MP for at least twenty years, Cabinet Minister from '46 to '49 and again from '57 to '60. I never heard Dad mention his name. If there was bitterness, it was silent. Jim Stead had accepted another defeat.*

THE WAR BEGAN BADLY, GOT VERY bad, worse, and then, slowly, went into reverse. There were those moments of fear that the Japanese would reach our shores; but I hardly ever doubted that 'we' – 'the Allies' – would win. By late 1943 the Germans had been defeated in North Africa, were in full retreat in Russia, and were having to enforce their dominance over Italy, which had tried to sack Mussolini and surrender. Meanwhile, the Americans were driving the Japanese back, inch by bloody inch, in the Pacific. Allied landings on the Italian mainland began in January 1944, and the NZ Div (those who had survived, or been drafted after, the campaigns in Greece, Crete and the Middle East) were part of the invading forces fighting their way up the boot. In June the

---

* Keith Sinclair describes Fred Hackett as 'a party hack, but well-liked' (*Walter Nash*, Auckland University Press, 1976, p. 355). Michael Bassett in conversation remembered him as 'a hang-dog old bugger'.

Normandy landings began the liberation of France. The fearful retaliatory bombing of German towns and cities was taking place with increasing intensity, and 'her Hitler' was requiring even greater sacrifices of his people in the name of the Reich. The level of carnage, the acceptance of deaths, civilian as well as military in huge numbers, was extraordinary. We sang 'There'll always be an England' with great confidence now. And when 'God Save the King' was played at the end of the pictures, only very unpatriotic (and daring) persons walked out without waiting for it.

Norma and I, with our parents, followed all of this in the news-papers (two delivered each day except Sunday, the *Herald* in the morning, the *Star* in the evening) and on radio news, local and BBC. So the sketch-map (both in time and in space) of that vast, almost unimaginable war, exists in my head now as clearly, almost, as the map of Mt Eden, or of the Kaiwaka farm. Those events were 'real', in the way so many things in the big world 'overseas' were, seeming to have an intensity which the *real* 'real', the things we could see and touch and listen to at first hand, lacked. The *real* 'real' was ordinary. One had yet, not to discover, because one had discovered it already, but to *recognise*, how marvellous the ordinary was, or could be.

Was Mt Eden real? Was Kaiwaka? Of course they were. They were my whenua. But the significant thing, the important, the *world-scale*, thing, was always, almost by definition, as in a nursery rhyme, 'over the hills and far away'. It was out there with Mrs Miniver and Dunkirk; it was V2s over bombed London; it was in the book-world of *Young Jack*, with thatched cottages and country lanes; it was in occupied Paris, and liberated Paris, and even in the Hollywood 'We'll-always-have-Paris' Paris. As a reader I knew the dense heavy green of England's summer parks and gardens, the tan and gold stillness and steeply angled light-shafts of her autumn days, and the white silence of a snowfall, before I had experienced any of them. We were (I have said it) colonials, suffering from what Allen Curnow would call 'Overseasia'. But perhaps, in our failure to bring to consciousness the marvellous in what was familiar, we were only like human beings everywhere. Being 'colonial', in that case, was being human, but more so.

New Zealand food was going to Britain in ever larger quantities; and we were still encouraged individually to DIG FOR VICTORY at home and to send food parcels abroad. Since our household no longer had family in England, or rather, no longer knew who or where they were, our occasional parcels (stitched in sacking as recommended) went to the family of Norma's pen-friend in Rugby whose name I forget. I think it was about this time that rationing began to be relaxed, and there were commercial promises of things, at present denied, which would soon return.

> After the War is over,
> After old Hitler's through,
> After the Japs are beaten,
> We're coming back to you –
> Dee-licious Tyne-brand herrings
> Famous in days of yore.
> Oh what a tre-eat awaits you
> Af-ter the War!
> [Sung to the tune of 'After the Ball'.]

Standard Five, 1944, was my last year at Maungawhau School. I should have had one further year, but the New Zealand Department of Education had decided there would be a new level of school, between primary and secondary – intermediate schools, where what had been Standards Five and Six would become Forms One and Two. So some primaries lost their Standard Five and Six ('decapitated' was the word used officially – there was a positive French Revolution in the school system) and others were to be all head and no body. Maungawhau Primary and Mt Roskill Primary were 'decapitated'; Brixton Road Primary became Balmoral Intermediate. I would spend one year in Form Two at Balmoral Intermediate before going on to Grammar.

My teacher in Standard Five was a thin grey-haired woman whose name I forget. Miss Someone. She had retired from teaching and come back because of the teacher shortage caused by the war. She was a rather shadowy person, who kept order without being a disciplinarian. I don't remember that she used the strap much – perhaps not at all. Late in the year she told my mother, in a tone of pity and concern, that I appeared to be an unhappy boy, and Mum passed it on to me, as if enquiring whether it was so. It seems somehow unorthodox – of them both. Was I unhappy? I didn't know, didn't think so, and told Mum I was not. Perhaps the deeper anxieties were apparent to an observant and considerate teacher; but it's more likely what she was registering was my boredom, and consequent dreaminess – my inclination to cut off from the world around me and go away somewhere into a space of my own.

There was now a sixth member of the family, my cousin Don, 'Little Don' to distinguish him from 'Big Don', his father the POW in Italy. There is a photograph of him in shorts and jacket with matching cap, which I remember were pale grey, flannel – his 'best clothes'. He was a shy child who had lived for most of his early years in his mother's Maori family up north. Once, early in his stay with us, he got angry and hissed at me, '*Pakeha!*' I realised that, because he was paler than his Maori cousins, 'Pakeha' had been what they had hissed at him when he displeased them. His presence in the house gave me the pleasures of being an older sibling – I could show off to him, 'boss him around', 'double' him places on my bike. I was fond of him and think I was kind – I hope I was.

Little Don's Maori mother, Trixie, by far the best-looking and most interesting of my aunts, was full of bounce, enthusiasm and affection. I remember her saying to Mum, in a huge rush of feeling, 'I love you, Ollie', wrapping my five-foot mother in a hug like a wrestler's so they both lost their balance and tumbled, laughing, to the floor. Once she came outside with me, when I went to chop wood for our fire, and told me, while she watched me at work, how she had chopped off her brother's big toe. He considered chopping wood to be man's work and, finding his sister doing it, he had put his bare foot on the block and told her to hand over the axe. She told him to remove his foot or lose his toe. He left it, and lost it.

Auntie Trixie had left Little Don with us for an unspecified time, and he was enrolled at Maungawhau School. She came to visit him at intervals which got longer as time passed, and finally stopped altogether. I heard it said that she was working on the trams as a conductor; then (in a whisper I was not supposed to hear) that she had had a baby. Little Don was to be ours until Big Don returned from the war.

HERE IS A MEMORY OF MY LAST DAY at Maungawhau School: there has been the usual atmosphere of excitement during the final afternoon in the classroom, and then Miss Someone has said her goodbye to us, we have given her a round of applause, and we are free. I walk down the steep back steps into the playground, between the shelter sheds (Boys' and Girls') and past the brick toilet block towards the steps into Ellerton Road. Under the firs or macrocarpas, the construction meant to protect us from bomb-blast, and the site of our 'mining' for those small white marble pebbles, is still there, but in a state somewhere between disrepair and ruin.

As I approach the exit I am thinking that I have been at the school many years, that I will never be a pupil there again, and that I ought to be feeling something significant, something I will remember 'for ever'. But there is nothing much more than the thought itself. I turn back to do a circuit of the school, intending to work up an appropriate, doleful sentiment, something that will cut a notch in the belt of the moment.

An informal game of cricket (not at all a common sight at that school) is happening and it captures my interest. The batsman is one of the 'big' Standard Six boys, Dave B., who is considered of anatomical interest to the rest of us because he is one of only two boys in the school to have reached puberty, and because he's one of the very few not circumcised.*

The bowling is weak and Dave is smacking it all around the field. He hits an almighty whack and the ball goes high. I watch it fly, wondering whether it will drop short. It disappears into the westerly sun, there is a pause, and then a bang on the head – no immediate pain, just a very brief moment of unconsciousness, and I am on the ground, a big lump coming up on my forehead and the soreness starting. When I get home I show the lump to Mum and the Grandmother and tell them how it happened. They both tell me I am a dreamer and should take more notice of what's going on around me. Mum dabs the lump with something that stings.

Only then I recognise that I have missed my grand moment and have no memory at all of my last passage through the gates of Maungawhau School.

* Circumcision was medically in fashion in New Zealand then, and for some considerable time afterwards.

II
THEIR SECRET WAYS

Words have their secret
ways of conjoining
of signing and
complaining.

Even under
a blue-eyed day
they can be the dark
living of the leaves.

NINE
LIVED BY HISTORY

Nineteen forty-five was an important year for me, and for the world. It was important for me because it was important for the world, and because in some way that I had been discovering as I grew older (once again, this was the culture of the family) the two, self and world, were interconnected. What happened in my life did not matter to the world, or mattered only in a sense so notional it was abstract, metaphysical; but what happened in the world, near and far, was part of my life. This was true of everyone everywhere, but not everyone everywhere knew it. To know it, to learn it, to make it part of your consciousness – that was politics in all seriousness. It was something which those who spoke of politics with contempt did not understand.

But there was also a limit to politics. Politics was a crude shorthand, necessary, essential for getting things done. There was another, more complex way of knowing the world. When my father propounded, with his usual clarity and logic, an opinion about what the government was doing and how it would affect our future – that was politics. When my mother played a Beethoven sonata, or a Chopin *étude*, that was an altogether different kind of knowledge, a different way of knowing the world, richer but more oblique.

And then there was poetry, with its strange way of steering a course between the two, keeping close to, yet keeping its distance from, both. As yet I knew next to nothing of that; but it was a poet, W. H. Auden, whose work, much later, would give me the phrase, 'We are lived by History'. 1945 was a year when, more even than usual, we felt ourselves 'lived by History'.

WHEN YOU WALKED FROM Brixton Road down the main drive of what was now Balmoral Intermediate School, you saw, if you were a child to observe such things, a creeper growing all over a tall wire fence on the left-hand side. It had white flowers, and if you observed closely you would see, here and there, a white butterfly with its head trapped in the centre of the flower. At first the butterfly would fight to get away. It would flap and strain. After a short fight it would tire, its wing beats would become slower, less frequent, there would be longer gaps, and soon it would give up the ghost. If you tried to help it get free you were likely to damage it, tear off its head or squeeze its thorax flat. But if you got to it in time, and squeezed the base of the flower, sometimes it would be released and fly away. Otherwise, it died there and, slowly, over days, its insides would seem to be sucked out. Was the flower feeding on insects? A carnivorous vegetable? It seemed unlikely, and it's something I have never checked on; but the plant was certainly engineered (by God, of course) to trap and kill butterflies. It was Nature's Bergen-Belsen, or Auschwitz, or Theresienstadt.

A day that came soon after first enrolment at Balmoral Intermediate is very clear to me. For the first few days, while we sat a series of tests, we had been randomly assigned to classroom and teacher. Now the whole school was assembled in the lower playground to be reassigned for the year. The headmaster, or principal, as he was called, Mr Pemberton, stood on some sort of platform and read out the names of every boy and girl in the school – first the Form Two classes, beginning with Mr Colquhoun's, then three further Form Twos, and four Form Ones – eight classes altogether, with about forty pupils in each. Mr Colquhoun was the deputy principal, and it was made clear that his was Form 2A, and that the others, ranged along the top floor of the main school building, one west and two east of ours, were Forms 2B, 2C and 2D. The same applied to the Form Ones on the lower level. But what excited me about this was not just that I was in the A form. The names were not alphabetical, and mine had come first. I concluded from this (and of course it is possible, though there is no way of knowing) that in those tests I had come top of the school.

That afternoon when I came home Mum was in bed, unwell, and being visited by Mrs Aitken, who sat in a chair by the big bed wearing a hat on her wig and being manifestly considerate and vaguely conspiratorial. There was an atmosphere of secrecy, as if I had interrupted confessions which would be continued only when I was out of the room. I came in full of excitement and explained that I was in the A form, and that it appeared that in the tests I had come top of the school. Mum, of course, knew this must be wrong. The boy who always came about the middle of the class in end-of-year exams, and who couldn't play even 'The Sailor's Hornpipe' without mistakes, was not going to be top of anything. If we had been alone she might have indulged it as one of Karlson's fantasies; but not in front of her friend, whose boy, Jack, never 'made things up'. She was embarrassed, and her face, her tone of voice, like coded signals ordered me to stop this nonsense. Now I, too, was embarrassed, and I left them to their secrets. *

Mr Colquhoun was a more interesting teacher than any I had had so far. Like all successful teachers, he was somewhat theatrical.

---

* I sent these pages on my year at Balmoral Intermediate to the current headmaster, enquiring whether my memories about academic performance could be verified. After a delay of some months there was a phone call to say that if records from so long ago existed it wasn't at present possible to find them.

I have the impression that he dressed well, with conscious attention to colour of shirt, pattern of tie, though always in the conventional tweed jacket and flannel trousers of the time. He seemed to single me out for attention. He smiled at me a lot, not a friendly, encouraging smile, but a mocking, challenging one.

He smiled that smile when he told you you were going to be strapped, and got you to hold out your hand. If the hand was not at exactly the right level, or not wide enough open with the fingers bent back, he would push it gently with the strap, up or down, or wider open, before inflicting the whack. He strapped me quite often, and never just one or two whacks but always two on each hand. To hold out for the second hit a hand that was red and stinging from the first took a lot of character. I find it hard to imagine how one would use one's authority as a teacher to inflict that kind of pain – routinely, or at all.

I had been strapped at Maungawhau School, where the boys were hit but not the girls – but only very seldom. In my year at Balmoral Intermediate it happened more; and yet it must always have been for minor infringements, because I cannot remember what any of them were. We were a bright class of pretty well-behaved kids, and Mr Colquhoun must have used the strap much more than even the punitive conventions of the time called for.

When I cast back and think of him, I have no memory of ever really disliking him, although I was scared of his habit. I remember that he interested me in almost everything he taught, that I was keen to please, that I accepted I would be strapped at intervals and that it would hurt; and that I sensed, without having a word for it, that there was a bit, perhaps quite a large bit, of the sadist in his character. There was no pretence that the strap was administered for my own good, or for the common good. Mr Colquhoun strapped for the pleasure it gave him.

His teaching might have been more interesting than I had experienced before, but that didn't mean I was not put through the usual torture of being required to keep an exercise book in which the talent I lacked for visual representation (only equalled by my talent at the well-tempered clavier) was revealed and put on record. Half the year had gone by, and my failings in the media of pencil, ink and paint were well understood, when we were given a poem to illustrate. I can't have thought much of the poem, because I remember nothing of it except that it was about a bird singing at evening. Norma was nearby when I was agonising over this task and she offered suggestions. The bird, she said, should be very near in the picture, so quite large (and she began to sketch it in faint pencil on the open page of my exercise book) and the scene, with trees and setting sun (more sketching) in a receding background. As she expanded her suggestions she began to apply paint, became interested, absorbed, and soon the illustration was done, with hardly a brush-stroke of my own. I was slightly anxious about it. She was two and a half years older, and had some artistic talent where I had none; but my homework was done and I was grateful.

Next day Mr Colquhoun got us to put our work open on the desks. He cruised around commenting, here with mild approval, there with amused distaste, and now and then leaving some sinner who had nothing to offer, and no supporting note from a parent, the promise of whacks to be administered later. When he came to mine he stopped. It was such a theatrical stop he might just as well have done several pirouettes and a leap. I had made him a gift.

'Girls and boys,' he said. And there followed a witty speech about how the muses had descended, the gods had chosen to wreathe the head of Incompetence with the bays of Talent. And then (the edge of malice, the threat, creeping in), 'All your own work, Karlson?'

I murmured that it was.

'No help. No other water-colourist at work here?'

I whispered something about my sister. I was required to speak up, to let the whole class hear.

'Ah, so we have a sister. A sister with talent it seems.'

I said she'd helped.

'Helped. I see. She did a little? She did a lot? *She did the lot?*'

And so it went on. There were not even the usual four whacks, two on each. I had given him such sport, there was no need.

I'm not sure why I didn't dislike him because, remembering, I disapprove of what I see in retrospect as his regime of self-entertainment and cruelty. I suppose it was another example of the child of those times (even, as I was then, the twelve-year-old child) accepting whatever presented itself as the norm – unless it was very clearly extreme and painful. Or perhaps it is just that, even when I was the butt, or the victim, what entertained him, although I was scared of it, entertained me as well. I had a part – a minor role – in his play.

I recognised very early in the year that he and Mr Pemberton disliked one another intensely. The principal, preceded by his very large belly, used to come into the classroom, not often, but without warning, interrupting Mr Colquhoun's lesson to set us a puzzle, sometimes verbal, sometimes 'scientific'.

'Girls and boys: what is an equine quadruped suffering from a cataract of the optic lens? The first person who can answer that can go home early.' I guessed the answer he wanted was 'a horse with a sty in its eye', even though I didn't think a sty and a cataract were quite the same. I was allowed to go home early, and Mr Colquhoun, seething but saying nothing, was left with the wreckage of his lesson.

Another of the principal's puzzles was a bit of bogus science about mushrooms. Nothing, he told us, could live without digesting food. (He appeared to digest a great deal himself.) But a mushroom could not digest anything. How did it live? I suggested it consumed food already digested by something else (I was thinking of the cow pats at Kaiwaka) and got out early for lunch.

Fashions go through schools – one moment spinning tops for the boys and skipping ropes for the girls will be 'in' and everyone will be doing one or the other; then it will be king o'seni for everyone, or hopscotch. There was a period when marbles became the fashion at Balmoral Intermediate. A value was put on the different kinds. 'Bottlies' were cheapest, almost worthless, 'steelies' were worth more, 'glassies' more again, and I've forgotten what the most valuable were called. If you won a lot, you could sell them back to the losers and make money. I was one of the better players – good enough to be making a few shillings a week. In fact (why be modest?) I accumulated five shillings and bought a trolley from a boy called Arnold who was teaching me the drums.

One day we had a visitor to the school and Mr Colquhoun was seen taking him around the grounds at lunchtime. After lunch he told us about this visitor, a Frenchman, who had watched some of us playing marbles. Mr Colquhoun had asked him whether French boys, before the war, had played marbles at school.

'Yes,' the Frenchman had said . . . but hesitating. (Telling the story, Mr Colquhoun imitated him.) And then he had added, 'The sissy ones did.'

As he told this story I felt Mr Colquhoun's eyes were on me. He was smiling that smile that mocked but also challenged. I had no understanding of what all this meant, or why I seemed to be its object. If I showed anything at all, it would not have been anger or resentment, only incomprehension.

AS THE YEAR WENT ON THE WAR became more exciting, more a cause for celebration mixed with fascination, horror and disgust. The death camps began to be overrun and revealed to the world, Auschwitz by the Russians, Bergen-Belsen by the British, and almost daily we saw new horrors – stick-figure survivors tottering on legs and holding out arms that looked like bare bones; corpses being scooped by bulldozers into enormous piles; soldiers and officials walking among the aggregate of rubble and body-parts with handkerchiefs over their noses; gas chambers in which millions had died, and ovens in which their poor remains had been incinerated; huge but neatly sorted piles of human hair, shoes, false teeth, spectacles. Together with all this came the stories of survivors, of the unbelievable cruelty that had been inflicted, of children torn from mothers, wives from husbands; of cattle trucks to transport the victims, whips and dogs to herd them; of inmates, sick with typhus, beaten to death because they could not stand up at roll-call; of doctors who had used inmates for medical 'experiments'; and of the monsters who had run the camps. Josef Kramer, Irma Grese – more than sixty years later the names randomly remain with me and float to the surface. It should have been an education in what the human species is capable of. Instead, it came like a confirmation of the propaganda of wartime. It seemed, at least to the child, to ratify all those war movies in which a German was a person who strutted about in boots and a brown shirt with a swastika armband, speaking, not German, but a peculiarly nasty kind of English, sprinkled with shouts of 'Sieg heil', 'Achtung' and 'Raus raus'. It was some years before I grew out of thinking there was something 'different' about Germans and recognised that evil in any degree can be done by any ethnic or national group, and in the name of any ideology or any religion or racial prejudice.

These revelations were truly a horror, searing to the developing consciousness. Nothing quite like it had been anticipated. It had been known that the Jews were being persecuted under Hitler's racial purity laws, and that Germany's expansion had meant especially bad times for Gypsies, occupants of lunatic asylums, Poles ('more animals than men') and other 'lesser breeds' east and south of the blue-eyed blonds; also that political rivals had been repressed in Germany, locked up, hanged, shot. My father had known these things, and had said, once or twice, that if we lost the war he, as a known leftist, would be one of those singled out. But the scale of what was now revealed, the whole machinery of the Nazis' 'Final Solution', was beyond anyone's anticipation. I doubt that even the Jewish refugees, who in the years of the war had so enriched New Zealand life intellectually and musically, had imagined the full horror of what they had escaped from.

So no one gave a thought to the present scale of the bombing of German cities, its indiscriminate cruelty, its random destruction of a great cultural inheritance. Even the fire-bombing of Dresden was only another bit of justice handed out, handed *back*, to the nation that had cheered as Hitler overran western Europe, invaded Russia, rained down death on London and the British cities, and, it was now revealed, had been inflicting this secret torment on, and extermination of, German citizens for the crime of failing to be Aryan.

It is in this historical context also that the use of the atomic bomb against Japan has to be seen. Did any of us really understand what a huge step up in the scale of human destructiveness that represented? I doubt it – and if we had, would we have cared? A war on an unprecedented scale was being fought. Bombs were falling and killing people every day. The sooner it was over and done with, by whatever means, the better. It might be true that there was an element of racism in this – Japanese were not Europeans; but if the Bomb had come in time, I'm sure it would have been used against Germany, and we would have been appalled (as with the Dresden fire-bombing) only later, in the long retrospect, when everyone looking back is wiser and more moral than those who were 'lived by History'.

I remember the news of the Hiroshima bomb for an odd and trivial reason – because it caused me a moment of embarrassment. We were at the table and Norma read from the *Auckland Star* the headline, 'ATOMIC BOMB DROPPED ON JAPAN', with a smaller headline that said 'City of Hiroshima Completely Destroyed'. Little Brother, who had never heard the word atomic (it was not in common use) corrected her: '*Automatic* bomb.' Big Sister held out the paper, and repeated with superior emphasis, '*Atomic.*'

Side by side, shoulders pressed together, we read the news item under the headlines. A single bomb, delivered by a single bomber, had destroyed a city. Normally (we took it for granted there were 'normal' ways of destroying a city) that would take many planes, waves and waves of them, over many days, each plane dropping many bombs. This was quite a bomb! I think that was how we reacted – marvelling at it, but with no comprehension of what it meant for the future, and that the Atomic Age had begun.

That was August 1945. In April (the month when Bergen-Belsen was liberated) Mussolini had been shot by partisans and his body hung up by the ankles, with his mistress and others, in a square in Milan. In the same month Hitler and his mistress, Eva Braun, were said to have shot themselves in a bunker under the ruins of Berlin, and a few days later the Germans had surrendered 'unconditionally'. In jubilant London the King and Queen and Princesses Elizabeth and Margaret Rose had appeared with Mr Churchill and Mr Atlee on the balcony of Buckingham Palace. And here at home we had celebrated VE Day (Victory in Europe Day), crowding into town on free trams, soldiers and girls dancing in the streets, kissing, singing, getting drunk and falling over. Now, a few days after the first atomic bomb, a second was dropped, this time on Nagasaki. The end, the very end, was in sight.

On an August morning I think less than a week after Nagasaki ('home of Madame Butterfly') had disappeared in a mushroom cloud, Mr Pemberton came into the classroom and stood, dramatic and silent, staring at us with a melting expression which I think was meant to represent (and perhaps did) his love for us, and for the human race. Mr Colquhoun stopped whatever it was he was saying and waited, repressing his impatience, not letting it become rage. How he would have loved to make Mr Pemberton hold out his fat hand; how carefully he would have adjusted it up or down, and pushed the fingers out straight, before delivering what would have been just the first of many, *many* whacks!

'Girls and boys,' Mr Pemberton said . . . And, after a pause, '*The war is over!*'

There was a rustle of excitement. Someone began to clap, and when that seemed acceptable, we all clapped. Then someone cheered. Soon we were all cheering.

'Boy,' Mr Pemberton said, pointing at me. 'Go and ring the school bell. Don't stop. Just keep it ringing.'

So I was the one who delivered the message to the suburb, or to those who didn't know it already. The bell was out in the grounds in its own small free-standing belfry, and you rang it by pulling on a wire rope. I pulled and pulled until my hands hurt, the bell rang and rang, and as instructed I kept it ringing. I was pleased and excited, because I was, on the whole, an obliging child, and 'pleased and excited' was what I was supposed to be. Victory had been promised for so long, to be followed by peace, when, it was understood, everything would be different, and much better, and we would have 'Dee-licious Tyne-brand herrings / Famous in days of yore'. But under the pleasure and excitement I felt a slight but quite distinct worry. It had been 'war' for such a large part of my life, anything before it was distant and indistinct. War had become the norm, and I wondered, with the anxious conservatism of the child, what peace would be *like*, different in what way, and would I like it – *really*?

WHEN UNCLE DON RETURNED FROM overseas he moved in with us. Little Don was sleeping in the second bed in Norma's room. Uncle Don slept on a canvas stretcher jammed into the small space of mine, now at the far end of the house. He was a silent chap who smoked and snored and counted his money from his new job in the cool-stores on the Auckland waterfront. On leaving for war he had taken me on his khaki knee and given me a pocket knife, and now he was back and never spoke of it. I wanted to hear the story, the stories; but the great adventure, which should have been full of terror, destruction, death and miraculous escapes, was a black hole, a smoke-filled silence. He had some notes of the currency printed by the Italians to be used by POWs inside the camps, and he gave me a few of those, one of which has survived:

Commando campo concentramento P.G.N 103 – P.M. 3200
L.it. 2   **Bueno per L.it Due**
           Valevole solo presso lo spaccio del campo
                Il Commandante del Campo

It was rubber-stamped, but those words, apart from 'di Bollo', had faded. I stared long and hard at it. Was it a 'concentration camp' of the kind the Germans had run? He told me only that it had been a very boring place – boredom was 'the worst kind of torture'. I felt that in the fighting before being captured, and even inside the boredom of being a POW (was there no tunnelling, no attempt to escape?), there should have been something memorable, a story or two worth telling; but if there were such, they were not for the ears of an enquiring nephew. Keith Sinclair, in his memoir *Halfway Round the Harbour* (page 104), records meeting newly released New Zealand POWs in England at the end of the war: 'They acted as convicts are said to, speaking in near-whispers out of the corners of their mouths.'

Uncle Don had reason to be thoughtful in any case, and perhaps depressed. His marriage, and the future of his and Auntie Trixie's child, had to be sorted out. It was arranged that she would visit and they would come to an agreement. This happened on a Saturday morning so we were all there, at home from school and from work. Little Don was not to see his mother – it might upset him. Uncle Don insisted on this, so Norma was instructed to take him away somewhere, not to tell him his mother was visiting, and keep him entertained until the hour had passed.

I was told Auntie Trixie wanted Uncle Don to 'take her back', and Mum hoped he would, but his face, grim and unyielding, didn't suggest that was what he had in mind. Dad remained neutral. He would support whatever they agreed to do.

Trixie arrived on her very good legs, her lovely black hair glinting in the sun, dressed in her best. There was no sign of her new baby. They went into the front room, the one with the grand piano. There was a murmur of voices, occasionally raised, dying away, then raised again, his throaty rumble full of anger and reproach. It went on for a very long time. I couldn't imagine what was being said, but I can now. He would have been asking who was the father of her new child, where he was now, and what other males there were in her life.

She would not have asked whether he had had 'other women' before being captured – she would have taken that for granted.

There was a long almost-silence when Mum and I (we were hanging about outside the door, ignoring Dad's hand signals waving us away) must both have imagined a reconciliation, the silence of a long embrace. But now came the unmistakable sound of weeping. Mum wept too. Dad looked grim.

Auntie Trixie left, and we never saw her again. I don't know that Little Don did either – certainly not, anyway, for a very long time.

The two Dons stayed on with us, not for long, but it must have been until the end of 1945, because I remember they were there when it had to be decided whether I would go to Auckland Grammar or Mt Albert Grammar. Our house was about equidistant between the two. These days people pay inflated prices for houses in the zone for Auckland Grammar, said to be academically New Zealand's top school; but then, as far as I was aware, there was no difference. Both Grammars had good sports teams. Both produced scholarship winners.

Neither of my parents had been to secondary school, Dad because his family could not afford to pay for it and needed him to go to work, Mum because, for the three or more years when she should have been there, she was living on Nauru Island being tutored, if at all, by her father. The choice was left to me, and I chose Mt Albert. My reason was simple: I was thinking of the problem of getting there by bike. The route to MAGS was downhill, the route to AGS distinctly up. It would be important to get there on time in the mornings; whereas coming home you could take as long as you liked.

There were forms to be filled in, and my parents had to choose a course for me. Would it include French and Latin, or just French? It seemed Dad had harboured a secret notion about me, and a consequent ambition on my behalf, that I might one day make a good lawyer. But for law you needed Latin, and Mum pointed out that Norma, at Auckland Girls' Grammar, was finding it difficult. That being so, she reasoned, it would certainly be beyond Karlson's powers – and Dad accepted that. Perhaps she was right. Or perhaps, on the other hand, she cost New Zealand a notable jurist. Who can say? For myself I regret the lack.* But it might also be true that if I knew more Latin than I do (which is still very little) I would not have felt free to make the ruthless raids I have made on Catullus, Horace, Ovid, putting their work to purposes of my own.

So I was enrolled for a sort of second-string academic course that included French but not Latin, chemistry but not physics. Academia for the handicapped. When the choices had been made and the forms returned, I took Little Don with me, 'doubled' him on my bike, to look at the school. It seemed to us both very grand indeed.

THERE ARE TWO EVENTS WHICH I CAN place with almost certainty at this same time, but which exist as memories seeming disconnected from all the rest.

The first begins with another of Mr Pemberton's grand entries, but this one specifically to call me to his office. There, he told me my mother was waiting for me in a taxi at the school gates and I should go to her at once. A taxi was something you read about in books, and saw people 'take' in movies – so far outside what for me was the normal order of things, it produced an inner panic that seared the moment on my memory. I couldn't imagine what it meant, except that it had to be something terrible. I made my way down the drive, past the feeble waving of dying butterfly wings, to the big black car ticking over in the street.

In a row in the back were the Grandmother and Norma on either side of Mum, who had been weeping – three generations of women, all in hats (Norma's the white panama with dark blue band of her Auckland Girls' Grammar uniform), a gravely serious trio united in

---

* If, by some process of palingenesis, I am assigned another life, I would like the gods who administer it to see I get an education which includes Latin, Spanish and French, with perhaps German as well, the living languages to be taught by ear only for a significant period before I am permitted to see any words on the page. And trained as a singer, please.

a grim resolve. I climbed in with them and a space was made for me. While the taxi made its way into town it was explained that Mum had 'had enough' (meaning of Dad). There was to be a divorce, and we were on our way to see a lawyer.

My parents' quarrels had been serious, even very serious, but there had never, to my knowledge, been talk of divorce. Once, long before, at the height of a conflict, Dad had packed a suitcase saying he was leaving. He had got as far as the gate, pursued and clung to by his two weeping infants, begging him not to go. There, understandably, his resolve had broken down, and he had returned.

In the lawyer's outer office Norma and I, sick with the awfulness of it all, waited while Mum went in and did and said whatever you do and say to a lawyer when you want a divorce and have brought your mother along for moral support.

And there the memory ends. I can record no retreat, no unconditional surrender, no armistice guaranteeing 'peace in our time' – nothing. The memory sits there, floats in isolation, but vivid and not to be doubted. It happened, but what followed at 63 Kensington Avenue was only more of the same.

The second of these vivid and somehow disconnected memories is Dad's attempted suicide. He had taken an overdose, but of what I never heard. Don was there, and Uncle Joe was called on our new phone. It was in the middle of the night. Joe, who I think was some kind of mechanic, had a little car – had had it for some years – and came straight over. I think I was told vomiting had been induced. What I do remember clearly is Dad slumped, grey and groggy between his two brothers, one arm over each of their shoulders as they dragged him, coaxed him, forced him to walk, up and down the hall from front door to bedroom and back again, up and down, on and on, while Mum and Norma, and I suppose the Grandmother too, wept and made cups of tea.

Again the memory is vivid; and the presence of Joe and Don together places it in time. But what was the cause of such despair? It might logically seem to follow from the other memory, the threatened divorce – and perhaps it does; but in my imagination the two are not cause and effect but parallel and failed attempts at escape.

What makes it especially puzzling for me is that it was never mentioned afterwards. It was as if it had not happened, so I never felt it was quite proper to ask about it; and now all the participants are dead. If Norma were alive, she would have something to tell me about it; but in her old age, when we talked often and quite freely about the past, and she laughed so much I used to be afraid she would fall out of her wheelchair,* it never occurred to me to ask what she remembered of the night Dad took an overdose, and whether she had any idea why he had done it.

Divorce and Death. It was as if the parents had tried and failed, one at each. Now there was nothing for it but to carry on. Did that represent another big D – Defeat? Or was it just reality setting in, acceptance of limit?

WITH TWO EXTRAS IN THE HOUSE Mum was now growing impatient – and perhaps embarrassed at the exposure it entailed. Little Don had been welcome; Big Don was another full-sized working male to cook and clean for. I had told her, not as a complaint, or to get him into trouble, but because it seemed such a marvellous, athletic feat, that Uncle Don, when he came home late from a party and didn't want to disturb them at the front of the house, was able to climb in through my bedroom window. The scraping of his big boots against the weatherboards made a lot of noise, so I would wake as he heaved himself up to, and tumbled over, the sill, breathing smoke and firewater. Mum told him he was disturbing my sleep and that she thought it was time for him to find a home of his own. So the two Dons, Big and Little, left, evicted, they probably thought, on a complaint from Karlson.

* Norma, mother of four, grandmother of eleven, died in 1999 aged 69 after many years of slow decline with multiple sclerosis.

TEN
TWO DUCKS ON A POND AND A LIFE INSCRIPTION

The bike I 'doubled' Little Don on to have a look at Mt Albert Grammar School was new. The old one, which had come, second-hand and already battered, from Uncle Joe, had done its time. Its wheels were buckled, the seat tended to slip suddenly upward with painful effect, the chain came off under pressure, one pedal was only half a pedal. I suppose someone, parent or the Grandmother, would have paid for a new one, but as it happened I paid for it myself, with help from a horse, a pacer called Benghazi.

Through his Labour Party connections Dad was often given tickets to the members' stand at Alexandra Park, the trotting raceway, and to Ellerslie for the gallops. I followed form in the newspapers, particularly the trotters, and went with my parents when they would take me. At one meeting I liked the chances of Benghazi, but Dad said at 120 yards behind he was handicapped out of the race. It was obvious everyone thought so, because the odds on him were exceptionally good. Big handicaps had spoiled his chances recently;

but seeing him paraded in the birdcage I thought he looked brilliant, big and strong and groomed as if someone had faith in him. The minimum bet was ten shillings, quite a significant sum in those days, and that was what I put on Benghazi, for a place. Dad thought I was wasting the only money I had. Mum, who had noticed my talent for picking winners, secretly followed my example.

Benghazi was a chestnut gelding, and I can still feel the excitement of the late run he made – so late, from so far behind, even a place seemed quite impossible: that red streaming mane going past horse after horse down the back stretch, his beautiful swinging motion seen from the front as he came around the last bend, his pace and power down the straight running him into third.

The bike I bought should have been named after the horse that paid for it, but it didn't seem to deserve a name. My problem in buying things was shyness. In familiar situations I was articulate and, though neither confident nor smooth, at least not socially incompetent. But I was always shy, and in shops it became so extreme I still remember, for example, the agony of buying a new tennis racket.

'I'll have that one please' (blushing).

'Would you like to try it, feel it for weight . . .' (and so on).

Too quickly: 'No thanks. *I've had one before*' – the blush burning at the recognition that this sounded, and was, not only untrue (it was a new make of Slazenger) but idiotic.

That's how I bought my bike. Boys in those days liked bikes that had some suggestion of dash, speed, style – some silver paint, some zigzag decorations, a trade name like *Speedster* or *Raleigh*, handle-bars, with white-taped grips, that curved down so you bent almost double when racing, but could sit tall and relaxed, one hand on the top part of the bars (or 'no hands') when tooling along at ease. The bike I bought, the one nearest the shop door and therefore quickest to pay for and be gone, was black and squat, with ordinary handle-bars, black rubber grips, a pump, a puncture repair kit hanging behind the seat, a small rack with spring-clip over the rear mudguard, two sensible brakes, and, worst of all, a black chain guard to prevent grease getting on legs or trousers. Mum thought it 'a good investment', as if it and I would grow old together. Don Cater asked, in a neutral, I think genuinely puzzled, voice, why I had bought *that* one. I said my parents had bought it for me, as if the choice had not been my own. Ian Lamont, another school friend, said (this was the unkindest cut) it looked like a woman's bike, and I saw that it did. All it needed to complete the look was the missing bar that let women get their skirts through, and a basket at the front.

It was a bike worthy of Philip Larkin and his cycle clips – or perhaps a clergyman in an English novel doing his rounds of a village parish. But I have to record I rode it every day to school for five years, and all over Auckland – to stay with Jack Aitken, to the beach at Waikowhai on the Manukau Harbour, up into the Waitakeres, even, later, with another friend, Barry Catton, all the way to Rotorua, 160 miles, and back again.

THE BOREDOM OF PRIMARY SCHOOL had decreased at Balmoral Intermediate. At Mt Albert Grammar it vanished altogether. Perhaps what made the difference was the continual changes of teacher – one or two periods with the English or French master, then, carrying your books in a bag over your shoulder, off to Social Studies or Chemistry, Music or Maths, General Science or PE. But the subjects interested me more – much more; and there was something about the bracing atmosphere of an all male school that felt (as I write this I surprise myself) liberating. There were scruples you didn't have to have; there was a boldness that was in you and was allowed to come out. You could be a boy there, full time, and try to become a man. And there was sport.

I was in III French, and our form master was Murray Print (later headmaster of Penrose High), known among the boys (every master had his nickname) sometimes as Pansy, but mainly as Pearly.

A master at the School House, where the school's out-of-town boarders lived, Pearly was young, eager-eyed, rather dashing, with straight hair parted in the middle, a complete tweed suit, almost pebble-dash in the assertiveness of its texture (tweed jackets with grey flannel trousers were more usual), and so many 'loud' ties it seemed he must wear a different one every day of the year. His voice and articulation were unusual, there was a clarity and deliberateness (perhaps a slight accent), which I can still seem to hear in my head but can't identify or describe. He was quite an enthusiastic user of the cane but not, by the standards of the time, excessive, and never brutal. He was what I think now would be called 'innovative' and didn't scruple to hand out Classic Comics so we could catch up on the stories of great books without having read them.[*] He also, now and then, 'took us to the pictures' at night, the whole form together to see the latest Hitchcock or Humphrey Bogart, which required long trousers and seemed very exciting.

He taught us French as well as English and had clearly never been within sight or sound of the French coast, or even of a French speaker. When the Grandmother heard I was learning French she produced some of the phrases she retained from her days in French Polynesia, and I corrected her pronunciation – a correction she accepted humbly, since I was the secondary school boy getting a real education. Much later I was embarrassed to recognise that her pronunciation had been right, and the one I'd learned from Mr Print was a sort of barbaric Franglais. He taught us that the feminine singular indefinite article, *une*, is pronounced een. Our teacher in the fifth form corrected this to oon. Neither is correct.

It was at this time that books became a serious part of my life, and poetry began to creep into it as a mysterious force. With Mr Print, even at third-form level, we 'did' some bits of Shakespeare,

---

[*] Recently I read that Murray Print as headmaster of Penrose High School (now One Tree Hill College) had bought works by major New Zealand painters, now a rare and valuable collection.

scenes from *A Midsummer Night's Dream*, and *The Merchant of Venice*, and I had my first scalp-prickling sensations of the life there could be in language. We read Sir Walter Scott's poetic narrative, *The Lady of the Lake*: and heroic poems – 'The Keeping of the Bridge', 'The Burial of Sir John Moore at Corunna', 'Drake's Drum' (we sang that), 'How they Brought the Good News from Ghent to Aix', 'The Charge of the Light Brigade', 'The War-song of Dinas Vawr' – even 'The Song of the Ungirt Runners'.

There was a man who came at intervals to take our English class, Mr McSkimming, whose job was to teach us specifically about poetry and 'dramatic art' – a sort of John Gielgud of the suburbs, with fine deep articulation and an admirable reverence for poetry and the theatre which he carried among us with the courage of a missionary among the heathen. We worked from an anthology that contained a very short poem the first two lines of which (I've forgotten the rest but it was in the same vein) went

Two ducks on a pond
A grass bank beyond . . .

Mr McSkimming told us he would rather be the author of that poem than have a thousand pounds. (In today's money, and in terms of the rhetoric, read a million.) I was starting to recognise that poetry was the door to a magic place, so I was able to honour this statement. But the beginnings of a poet meant the beginnings also of critical discrimination, and I remember trying to formulate in my head, as a joke but with serious intent, that I might just have to forego the thousand pounds, thanks, sooner than have my name attached to 'Two ducks on a pond'.

Mr McSkimming then asked us each to pick from the anthology a poem we especially admired. Don Cater was quick to nominate 'Two ducks on a pond' and at once sank in my estimation. Could he really have admired it, or exercised any thought at all about the alternative possibilities? It seemed unlikely. He was trying to please

– but even in that, surely, failing. Mr McSkimming had only said he would be proud to be the author *even* of such an insignificant poem; he would hardly have wanted it to be seen as one of the best in the book.

I am making a lot out of very little here, yet it remains with me, an exemplary moment: Mr McSkimming, the naïve, poetry-loving idealist, on the one hand and on the other Don Cater, the Everyman, with his uninformed and lazy goodwill towards whatever he was told, or thought he had been told, about a literary matter. It was like a microcosm of the world of literary taste, of best-seller lists, book awards and poetry prizes, about which, as yet, I knew nothing.

AT MT ALBERT GRAMMAR, YOU COULD say, sport *figured*. That it did was one of the things I loved about the place. Even before I got there I had been interested in high jumping, introduced to it first by Don Cater, whose brother John, already a MAGS boy, excelled at it. On grandfather Karlson's workbench I made myself a set of high-jump standards, used bamboo for a cross bar, and practised with Don on the front lawn. Once enrolled at the school I was captivated by the whole ambience of athletics, the 440-yard track laid out on the middle field, the final 220 yards marked in lanes for sprints, the two pits for jumping, the hurdles – there was a mystique about it, and about the boys who did it and won. Running, running easily and well as good middle-distance athletes do, is a pleasure in itself, like sex, something which feels natural, 'right', as if the body is telling you gratefully that this is what it was created to do and to enjoy. I had the legs for middle-distance running, and the style, but never the heart. * At the quarter and half mile I was an also-ran. Competent as a hurdler, good as a high jumper and, in my final year,

---

* At the age of 73 I discovered I have had all my life what is called patent foramen ovale, an imperfectly closed, and in my case 'prominent', hole between the right and left atria of the heart.

a discus thrower as well, I was in the senior athletic team in my last two years, not a star, but among some who were.

Of the real champions the best-known name is that of Les Mills, an all-rounder who went on to win New Zealand championships at shot and discus, compete in Commonwealth and Olympic Games, and start up the fitness centres that bear his name. He was even to be, for a few years in the 1990s, mayor of Auckland. The hurdler Linton Russell was another exceptionally fine athlete. Terry Lipscomb, a member of the senior athletic team in my final year, went on a year later to set a school hop, step and jump record that still stood half a century later. But an athlete who seemed to me even more remarkable than any of us was Graeme McDermott. He was a sprinter who had, by genetic inheritance, the kind of physique people these days spend years in Les Mills fitness centres hoping to create. He was not a beautiful runner to watch – there was too much tension in the arms and hunched shoulders – but he was impressive: fast, powerful and unbeatable. Truly, the ground shook when McDermott went by. He won the 100- and 220-yard sprints at MAGS at junior, then at intermediate, and finally at senior level, and, year by year, at the inter-secondary school sports.

Graeme was a nice, simple chap who appeared to do little serious training and claimed to eat seventeen Weet-Bix at breakfast, innumerable meaty sandwiches for lunch and two or three big steaks with sausages for 'tea'. He had a formidable mother who used to bring him extra food before a race, as if feeding a giant, or refuelling an aircraft engine. He had a strange but kindly sense of humour, and lacked the gravitas that normally went with the status of school champion.

In our fourth year (1949), in addition to the 100 and 220, McDermott was persuaded to enter the 440 yards – a distance he had never tried, and for which there was a special cup. He sprinted the first 220, cruised another hundred and staggered the rest, reaching the tape with wobbly knees but still well clear of Don Cater, who came in second. In his final year he stuck to his two sprints, 100 and 220, won them in record time, and then, at the inter-secondary school championships at Eden Park, ran 10 seconds and 22 seconds, 'even time', setting two New Zealand junior (i.e. under-nineteen) records.

It was always a puzzle to me that we didn't hear more of him as an athlete after we left school – though there was a story that he had 'suffered an injury, thrown his shoes into the back of the car, and given up'. If someone had taken him in hand he might have been another Peter Snell.* Janet Frame said to be a writer you needed, not just the talent, but the 'want', and perhaps the same is true of champion athletes. Now in his seventies and retired from a life in banking, survivor of a number of major operations, Graeme McDermott writes scolding letters to the *New Zealand Herald* on public matters such as the state of the railways, the decline of English, the New Zealand honours system (deploring the ending of knighthoods), the cost to the taxpayer when adventurers are lost in the bush or at sea, and the laxity of visiting rules in public hospitals.

AT MAUNGAWHAU SCHOOL AND AGAIN at Balmoral Intermediate I had played rugby. There was no other winter sport. Early on I had been asked whether I wanted to be in the forwards or the backs. I was quite fast and elusive at king o'seni, and, imagining the forwards would be the active ones, runners and scorers, while the backs were stolid defenders, I nominated myself for the forwards, only to find it was the other way about. Once designated a forward I seemed to get stuck there, even though I was a featherweight in the scrum. I played lock, and by Balmoral Intermediate had my own black headband with ear-protectors. I seemed to spend a great deal

---

* Triple Olympic champion (800 metres, Rome, 1960; 800 and 1500 metres, Tokyo, 1964), also a MAGS boy. I have been told that Arthur Lydiard, who coached both Snell and Murray Halberg, once said the three greatest natural athletes New Zealand had produced were Snell, Doug Harris and Graeme McDermott.

of the game labouring to get where the ball had just landed, only to find, when I reached the spot, that it had gone somewhere else. The rest was the heads-down bums-up stuff, inside scrums and what I think are now called rucks and mauls, a strange, intimate territory which the brotherhood who have been there speak of quietly among ourselves but are sworn to silence beyond.

My worst moment at rugby was being mistaken by a woman on the sideline for a boy called Gordon Stanaway, a brilliant back who had run in several tries in a game we from Balmoral played at Mt Roskill. Gordon and I were alike, and she heaped extravagant praise on me at the end of the game. It seemed simplest to behave as if I were Gordon; but as she went on and on, and asked me questions about myself, I had to admit I was really Karlson Stead. She was furious, as if I had deceived her deliberately, and began to look about for someone to 'tell'.

At Mt Albert Grammar in the first winter term I put myself down for soccer. I played on the right wing, and I still remember the exhilaration of racing down the far side of the lower field, discovering the pleasure of ball-control at speed, of going around and through the opposition, of accurate passing and centring. I played soccer from then on, moving to inside right and finally what was called centre forward (now it would be striker) – through junior and intermediate levels to the First Eleven in my final two years, and on from there to play for university.

THE FIRST SENTENCE OF OUR GENERAL science text-book in the third form read, 'The protozoan amoeba respires by simple diffusion through the cell walls.' Why do I remember that? Or, more to the point, what does the fact that I remember it signify? Only, I think, that I was a language person, not a scientist. It was a rather lovely and slightly arcane statement of fact, a poem in prose, a mantra. It was like the books of the Bible I memorised, not meaning to, but by hearing others repeat them. It was like the Labour Party's statement of intent about 'the socialisation of the means of production, distribution and exchange'. It was not that words did not mean; it was that they had a power, and mystery, beyond meaning.

Our chemistry master, J. L. D. Woolloxall, another future headmaster of an Auckland school, known among us as Jack, was the teacher who impressed me most. I always felt at ease with him. There was never the least kind of intimate interchange between us; but there was, or I felt there was, a mutual recognition and respect, the perfect impersonal relationship between teacher and pupil. What he taught came to me, clear and unambiguous, without obstacles. He was recently returned, as so many of the masters were, from war service overseas, and had the nervous habit, as he talked to a class, of pinching the back of one hand with the thumb and forefinger of the other, alternately east–west, then north–south, so the skin was always inflamed. I don't recall that he ever used the cane, nor that he had any difficulty without it, and without bluster or threat, in keeping a classroom under control and interested. He was sensitive, observant, and quick to react to what he noticed.

He was once checking forms, which needed our full names. I had put down only Karlson Stead, balking at acknowledging Christian, another name no one else I had met was lumbered with. He asked what the C stood for, and then at once recognised my embarrassment. What an opportunity for a Mr Colquhoun! Jack Woolloxall simply pushed a piece of paper across the desk and said, in a voice audible only to me, 'Just write it down.'

Because he was that kind of teacher, chemistry was one of my best subjects, and remained so through School Certificate and University Entrance, after which I asked to be allowed to drop it for my final (6A) year. By then I was writing poetry and short stories. I saw English and history as my subjects for university, and writing as 'what I wanted to do' (secretly, since it would have seemed worse than pretentious to say so). I needed the headmaster's permission to drop a subject, and Mr Caradus (nickname 'Granny'), himself the author of a chemistry text-book, forbade it on the grounds that my talent in chemistry should not be wasted. I dropped it in any case, in the sense that I attended classes as required, but took no notes and thought about other things. Jack Woolloxall was disappointed. He had wanted me for science; but if he had checked my maths results he would have known that was an improbable outcome.

We were taught maths in the third and fourth form by Mr Scott – Thomas Scott, known to the boys as Tammy. He had a small grey moustache, wore woven ties, grey flannel bags and a red-brown tweed hacking jacket. He was a talented amateur painter who had made a book commemorating the two hundred old boys killed in the war, one page to each, with name and rank, dates of birth and death, and a floral decoration around the lettering at the top of the page – each one different, unique to that dead warrior. A work of art and a labour of love, it was on daily display under glass in the school library, a page turned each day of the school year, and is still the school's major commemorative record of that war. Tammy told us, with great pride, and an intensity that caused me to remember it, that he had promoted the career of a young concert pianist, Colin Horsley, who was now becoming internationally famous.

Of the three branches of mathematics, there was, for me, no mystery about arithmetic – I knew the rules and could apply them, but (as with my scales on the piano) I was either slow and correct, or fast and inaccurate. SPEED KILLS was the working rule, and maths exams didn't allow you to do things at your own pace if your pace was as slow as mine. Algebra I did badly, struggled towards minimal competence, and never really understood. In geometry, however, I made a breakthrough.

As a game to interest us in our own progress, or to illustrate our lack of it, Tammy used to stand us around three walls of the classroom and work us through theorems. As you gave correct answers you moved to the left; wrong ones, or no answer, sent you the other way; so the class was soon arranged left to right around the walls from the most to the least talented. For a long time (this was in the fourth form) I hovered around the middle, always struggling to remember 'what came next'. And then, out of nowhere, came the recognition that these were not exercises in memory at all, but in logic. Each stage in any theorem followed as a logical consequence of what preceded it, and a stepping-stone to the next. I was immediately shunted in quick stages leftwards towards the top, where I remained – but only for geometry. It was not really a talent for mathematics, at which I would always be slow, but for logic.

In Tammy's class I sat at the front with a boy whom I will call, as I did in a previous account, M.* M was notable in the junior school for being an exceptionally gifted representational painter. He had a lot of hair, which he combed 'switchback', a clean-cut look, clear, friendly eyes and an affirmative temperament. We got on well together, without being close friends. We were not in the least rebellious or fractious, but there were a lot of jokes and suppressed laughter. We were right under Tammy's eye, but I failed to notice how much we were noticed.

One day, at the end of our maths class, Tammy asked me to stay behind. After everyone had gone he pointed to my name, C. K. Stead, scored on the top of the desk I shared with M. It was there, not prominent or extravagant, among many names and much other idle desk-top graffiti, so it must have taken a careful search to find it – but I could not deny that it was mine. He named a classroom upstairs, B8, and told me to be there at lunchtime. I supposed it meant a caning, but I hoped it might be something less unpleasant, because canings normally took place at once and in front of the class, and I had never seen Tammy use a cane.

The first swipe when it hit me was so hard I straightened up with the pain of it, but was told to bend over again – and again. Each swipe seemed worse than the last. There are some people for

---

* 'Poetry and Politics (and a beating)' in my collection of essays *Book Self*, Auckland University Press, 2008, pp. 103–10.

whom violence is not a release from anger, but a release into it, and it is impossible for me to convey the clear sense I had, even through the extraordinary pain, that the man I could just see behind me as I bent over, and whose fury I could feel, was losing, indeed had lost, control. I suppose he set out to administer what used to be called 'six of the best', though I had never seen or heard of any master going to the limit. In any case at five I could bear no more and took off, straight ahead between a line of desks, until I came to the wall and stopped, head forward against the cool panelling. I heard him go, and when he came back, I suppose twenty minutes later, I was still exactly where I had stopped. He held the door open and said, 'Get out.' I didn't feel cowed, and I'm sure didn't look it. What I felt, apart from pain, and the astonishment of pain, and what he must have felt as I passed him at the door, was something close to contempt.

I told no one but a few school friends about this beating. I don't know what my parents would have thought or done if they had seen the welts, the bruises, the broken skin where the end of the cane had flicked around and, even through the cloth of shorts, cut. There was nothing I would have wanted them to do. This was sadism, licensed by the times, and it had been carried out where neither boys nor other masters would see it happen.

For a long time afterwards I was keenly aware of Tammy watching me. It was as if I knew something about him he did not want known. I did – but only (I would have said) that repressed beneath the hacking jacket and grey bags, the neatness of the little white moustache and the arty concern for our war dead, there was a madman, a killer. I'm sure he would have seen in my face that I was still in a state of shock and hurt. But as the weeks passed I went back slowly to behaving normally in his class, because animal spirits revive, and to keep up the coldness would have been artificial. Perhaps he thought in the end I had accepted my punishment, 'taken it like a man'. I had not. I had (though I didn't know it) put it away for another day.

Many years later, in London in 1965, the painful memory surfaced and I found myself writing a poem about that beating,[*] in which I represented my name, carved on the desk with a pen-knife (a considerable exaggeration of my crime), as 'the bald style of a life inscription', and contrasted it with the death inscription of his commemorative floral paintings for the school's two hundred war dead. It was written as an anti-war poem, in the context of the anti-Vietnam War protests of the time, and it finished,

> I walked past him, and out.
> I looked at him, not 'daggers',
> But truly without feeling.
> He might have been a desk-top.
> My pride was exact.
> I would not go down
> In Tammy's book.
> He would go down in mine.

It was some years later again, also in the context of anti-Vietnam war protest, that I met M, not having seen him since school days. We talked about Tammy and he told me something which made a kind of sense, a story anyway (an unpleasant one), of what had happened. Tammy had encouraged M's painting and invited him to his home one weekend where they could paint together. After a pleasant afternoon Tammy said it was time for a shower. M didn't want a shower, and didn't understand why he should have one, but in the way boys in those days, told to do something by a schoolmaster, did, he got undressed and into the shower, where he was joined by Tammy. He didn't tell me exactly what happened – only that there was some kind of unwelcome physical contact and that he never went back.

[*] 'With a Pen-Knife', *Collected Poems, 1951–2006*, Auckland University Press, 2008, pp. 40–41.

Different readers may possibly make different sense of this story. I have reflected on it, and for myself the only sense I can make is that Tammy, secretly in love with M, had imagined our friendship, clearly visible to him every day in the front desk, was closer than it was in reality, and had found, in my name inscribed on the desktop, an excuse to turn sexual jealousy into righteous and violent rage.

The following year, 1948, the *Albertian* records, in a brief note which makes no mention at all of the memorial book, that 'after a long teaching period at Mt Albert' (he had joined the staff in 1926) 'Mr. T. Scott, B.A., left us to take up a position at Napier Boys' High School as Art Master'.

ELEVEN
THE NEW AFFLUENCE, AND POETRY

While I was at primary school the method used by everyone in the suburbs for washing clothes, linen and towels was 'the copper' – a large circular receptacle set in a surround of concrete on a concrete pad, with a small fireplace underneath and a small chimney behind. It was filled with water, loaded with sheets, towels and whatever else, soap flakes or powder were added, the fire was lit underneath, the contents stirred with a 'copper stick' and the water brought to the boil. A Reckitt's blue bag was added for whiteness. I don't know what it contained, but I remember a hoarding advertisement, seen from the tram, which showed a blue sea washing white over rocks and the slogan 'Out of the blue comes the whitest wash' – my first consciousness of a pun. The blue bag was also applied to bee stings to ease the pain.

Alongside the copper were ranged three concrete tubs with taps. When the wash was done it was hoicked, piping hot on the copper stick, into the first tub, already filled with cold water for the first rinse, and from there into the middle tub for the second. Between the second and third tub there was the wringer, two rubber rollers turned by a handle, and the washing was squeezed through so it went out to the line without excess water. Doing the washing was Dad's Saturday-morning job before he went down to his garden. Mine was to hang it out. Mum would be taking her Saturday pupils, and the Grandmother possibly cleaning the house with Norma's help.

In some cases the washhouse was out in the back yard; in others, as in ours, it was part of the house, but at the rear, the walls unlined. Ours had a space, beyond the three tubs, where a small smooth-sided barrel held wheat for the chooks. Two or three times a mouse got into it and found itself unable to scale the sheer sides to get out again. As in myth and fairy-tale, its dream of unending riches, a sea of golden wheat that would last forever, was fulfilled at the cost, it might be, of life itself. Each time this happened I caught the mouse by hand and released it outdoors, unwilling to bring the fairy-tale to its proper, cruel end.

Of New Zealand at the end of World War II Michael King writes, 'There was [. . .] the growth of a more overt form of materialism than had been apparent previously, centring on a desire for better homes and more consumer goods: washing-machines, refrigerators, family cars, fashionable clothing – the phenomena that came to be known as "keeping up with the Joneses".' It amuses me to think of us at 63 Kensington Avenue, positioned in the middle of the isthmus of Tamaki-makau-rau, only yards from the Maungawhau School polling station that moved consistently left or right with the mood of the nation, being lived in this case by social history. Our first phone (number 62 152) was followed, in such quick succession I am unsure in what order, by our first refrigerator, our first washing-machine, our first vacuum cleaner, our first car – this last a second-hand four-door Austin in pale green, with leather seats, chromium ashtrays, polished wood panels and dash. It was not as good as it was glossy, and was soon costing money in repairs, but it was very exciting.

Dad liked to drive long distances, and became more adventurous about holidays. He liked Rotorua especially, and we used to stay in a small flat there (a motel unit before there were such things) in a motor camp at Ngongotaha.

The new washing-machine was installed in the space previously occupied by the wheat barrel; the three tubs and the copper remained, and for a time the two kinds of washing overlapped. There was no spin-drying with those early machines, but a power-driven wringer.

So in a very few years of my infancy and childhood we went from pre-war Depression through wartime austerity to post-war affluence. Lacking car, telephone, washing-machine and the rest had not mattered before or during the war; in fact to have them would have marked us out as unusual. Now they became necessary indicators of social advancement. What was a state of quite reasonable comfort and adequacy in one period becomes, a decade or two later, poverty and deprivation needing the enhancement of the new. The actual quality of life has not changed, only the perception of what it ought to be and to include. That, alas, is the nature of progress in all societies in which no one is actually hungry or struggling to stay alive.

Dad's colleagues now were, many of them, lawyers and professional men. During the war he had been appointed, partly through Party connections, to the Auckland Land Sales Committee, set up by the Labour Government to control the price of property and prevent a boom, especially one that would make home ownership difficult or impossible for returning soldiers.* Memories of men returning from World War I to poverty, indifference and neglect were fresh and bitter, and the Labour Government, determined to do better, set the committees up partly as a protective mechanism. Along with what were called 'rehab loans' on very low interest, and

---

* The Servicemen's Settlement and Land Sales Act was passed in 1943, and J. W. A. Stead was appointed in June 1944 by Order in Council.

the already established 'family benefit', this meant the transition from warfare to suburban normality was financially easy, whatever shocks and deflations it might mean for the individual psyche.

There were three members of the Auckland committee (later renamed the Auckland Urban Assessment Court) – Mr Tuck, the lawyer, Mr Aimer, the architect, and Mr Stead, the accountant. It had the status of a magistrate's court. Evidence was presented, witnesses called and cross-examined. It did not sit all day every day so Dad was able to spend more time at home in his favourite brown armchair, smoking and reading his Left Book Club volumes as they came in, his British naval histories and the latest *New Statesman*. He had been glad to leave the Post Office, but Mum worried that his new position might not last because the scheme came under constant attack from the National Opposition, the newspapers and devotees of unfettered markets, who argued that it was an interference with free enterprise, and that payments 'under the table' were making it meaningless. Orthodoxy in the Stead household held that even if such illegal payments were being made, the existence of the Land Sales Courts was keeping the amounts minimal and preventing property inflation.

In the past Dad had talked about someone well-off as 'a thousand-a-year man', and it's possible he was now one of these himself, or close to it, at a time when the average annual wage might have been five hundred pounds. For years, like most workers, he had brought his fortnightly wage packet home (cash in a small brown envelope) and handed it over to Mum, who was clever and prudent with money, keeping for himself only enough to pay for his cigarettes, tram fare and incidentals. Now, for the first time, he had a cheque-book, which I suspect he used rather recklessly, sometimes when there was nothing in the account. A cheque-book, after all, was only a less convenient version of the credit card. You could get ahead of yourself, live up to your dreams.

A cheque account, a car, together with new status and respect – these were important. But what he craved still was that walk up the grey steps of the old Parliament Building, and all the possibilities and excitements that could be made to follow. His Party work continued throughout these years, and his connections were good. There is a photograph of him, with Mum and Norma, at a social occasion with Prime Minister Peter Fraser; and I still have the signed copy Fraser sent him of the report on the 1945 San Francisco United Nations Conference. 1946 brought a new election, and this time he put his name forward to stand for Labour in Roskill, the electorate previously held by A. S. Richards, who had moved over to the safer territory of Mt Albert. * Again he was unsuccessful; but if, this time, there was any trauma associated with the process and the failure, I knew nothing of it. Grammar, sport and reading were absorbing most of my consciousness, and I remember little of the election that year except that Roskill was lost, and that, though Labour remained the government, its majority was reduced to just four, exactly the number of the Maori seats, all of which Labour held. So for the next three years Minhinnick, the *Herald*'s unfriendly cartoonist, represented Peter Fraser in his homburg accompanied by a small round brown figure in a grass skirt with a taiaha and labelled 'Mandate'.

I HAD DEVELOPED BY THIS TIME WHAT I suppose could be called in retrospect my first 'intellectual' friendship. Barry Catton lived in Peary Road, and was at Maungawhau, and at Balmoral Intermediate (Mr Colquhoun's class), when I was there, but I got to know him really well only at Grammar. We were soon borrowing the same books from the school library, and I was struck by how quickly he read, often returning a book only the day after borrowing it. I tested him and found, if we read the same page together, he would be through it when I had still about a third to read; and when I questioned him he always knew the contents well, often better than I did, because I had been straining to read faster.

* Information supplied by David Verran at the Auckland Central City Library.

I soon recognised that while he read by sight, I read by ear. For me words were sounds, and patterns of sound, not visual short-cuts to meaning. The process was instantaneous; I was not mouthing the words. But the visual image, the word on the page, indicated sound, whether articulated or silently apprehended, not meaning. It was the sound which meant something, and brought with it, in addition to meaning, a sensuous content – flavours, colours, tones, music. I had no choice about this. Even when, much later as a research student, I learned to skim texts and documents for information, I did not unlearn my normal slow pace of reading fiction and poetry.

So Barry was always ahead of me, leading the way. We went through crazes for one kind of book, then for another. There was a period when we read only British school stories, with names like *The Ripswade Ring*. I liked them very much and regretted not being a boarder at the School House, where many of the conventions of the English public school persisted. Then there was a phase of Edward S. Ellis and James Fenimore Cooper, novels of the American frontier. I was gripped by what Balzac calls Cooper's 'poetry of terror', the 'ominous interest found in a tree trunk, a beaver's dam, a rock, a buffalo skin, a motionless canoe, a branch drooping over water'.[*] I tended to visualise everything in terms of what I knew already, so although I knew they were different, and did not see them as the same, nonetheless Kaiwaka and the bush were in my mind as shadowy substitutes for the North American reality. Later I would recognise that I was visualising people walking in the grounds of a great house in a novel by Henry James as if it were the grounds of Maungawhau School.

Murder mysteries (Agatha Christie, and our own Ngaio Marsh) took their turn; and there was a lot of P. G. Wodehouse and John Buchan. There was next to nothing of New Zealand. It was not great highbrow fare – though I did at this time discover in the school library a book by Bertrand Russell, *Marriage and Morals*,

---

[*] Honoré de Balzac, *Splendeurs et Misères des Courtisanes*, 1847.

which gave me a sense of how free the mind could be to reach its own conclusions. But we were third and fourth formers and we were reading – constantly.

There was also, with Barry, a lot of intellectual game-playing. We competed to be first to finish the *New Zealand Listener* crossword, and developed such an appetite for crosswords we bought whole books of them. Labour enthusiasts, we followed local politics. We experimented with mental telepathy, attempting to convey a shape, a colour or a number, by concentrated thought. We kept notes of successes and failures, and compared these against ordinary statistical probability. By this measure we convinced ourselves, while retaining a pinch of scepticism, that we were able to communicate images without words.

We also played chess, taught to us in the first instance by Barry's father, a watersider, Wilson Catton, who would lose his job in the lockout of '51. With another Mt Albert boy, Fred Foulds, who would one day be New Zealand champion, we joined a chess club in Dominion Road where we played against adult opponents. In my last year at Mt Albert I beat Barry to take the school chess championship, but only after Fred, who could beat us both, had left the school. Fred was also an amateur photographer and as a student took many photographs of me sucking on a pipe and attempting to look like a poet.

Barry was always early. In the mornings he came around to Kensington Avenue to call for me, and we rode together, crossing Dominion Road into Carmen Avenue, then, without stopping, half-dismounted and gliding crouched on one pedal, went straight under the wooden barriers built to force cyclists off their bikes, through an alleyway that took us into Volcanic Street, Pine Street, Oxton Road, and so on, by this back route to the school. I remember especially that dash through and under the barriers, just as I remember, later, our 4 a.m. races through the dark streets of Onehunga when we worked together at the freezing works.

There was, however, an area of my reading that was not shared with Barry nor anyone else. When I was in the fourth form Norma's pen-friend in Rugby sent her a copy of the *Complete Poems* of Rupert Brooke, famous as the epitome of beautiful young manhood killed in World War I. Norma was not much interested in poetry, so I appropriated the gift, and have it, still with her name in it. It was the first time I had owned a book of poems all by one poet. I read it many times. I looked at the frontispiece holograph of his most famous sonnet, 'The Soldier' –

> If I should die think only this of me,
> That there's some corner of a foreign field
> That is forever England. There shall be,
> In that rich earth, a richer dust concealed,
> A dust whom England bore, shaped, made aware,
> Gave once her flowers to love, her ways to roam . . .

It was (is still) pretty good of its kind. I would one day study poetic movements and critical fashions in the early twentieth century, and describe how the popular fashion for Brooke had been challenged and pushed out of serious critical consideration by Wilfred Owen and his like, whose poems refused heroics and represented war as it was in all its horror and brutality. But all that lay in the future. Here was the most famous of Brooke's poems, reproduced in his own handwriting, with even a phrase crossed out and another substituted. That was exciting in itself, humanising the process, yet also making it mysterious. What had caused him to alter the opening phrase of the sestet from 'Think, too . . .' to 'And think . . .'?

I looked at the photograph of Brooke, with his thoughtful finger running up his thoughtful cheek, his lavish hair, his huge arty cuffs and wide informal arty tie. Unlike Eric McCormick, who records a similar (and almost twenty years earlier) youthful attachment to this icon of male beauty, my interest was purely literary – or at least had no sexual overtones. I thought he looked handsome enough, though somewhat shiny-skinned under the studio photographer's lights; and the bland eyes, with their too close brows, didn't inspire full confidence. But the picture conveyed something of the romantic presence and importance of Poetry itself – Poetry and the Poet. I had already tried writing poems. Now I did it much more purposefully, writing Brooke-ish imitations, not about war, but about verandas at night, the moon on water, soft music, disillusion, the scent of flowers and dark female presences.

One thing the interest McCormick records had in common with my own was that our excitement had a distinctly provincial aspect. It was the response of colonials to the fact that this *important English* poet had travelled to our region, even to New Zealand itself, and that his poems from that period were full of images of the Pacific. For me it helped, too, that he was a Fabian, like my parents, and sided with the strikers of 1913. Brooke had tramped on the moors with Katherine Mansfield, and admired her writing; and Bernard Freyberg, on his way to Gallipoli where he would win a VC, had been among the party that carried the young poet's body to be buried on the island of Skyros.

These additional facts I acquired when I found, in the school library, a *Collected Poems* with a memoir about Brooke and his literary associates by Edward Marsh. Brooke, it was clear, had had an exciting life, with many young-women friends, and I tried, the naïve adolescent, to decide whether he had 'gone all the way' with them, or whether these were merely romantic encounters of a stuffy English middle-class sort. I hoped very much there had been real sex. Reading poems like the one called 'Lust', I decided there must have been:

> How should I know? The enormous wheels of will
> Drove me cold-eyed on tired and sleepless feet.
> Night was void arms and you a phantom still,
> And day your far light swaying down the street.
> As never fool for love, I starved for you;
> My mouth was dry and my eyes hot to see.

Your mouth so lying was most heaven in view,
And your remembered smell most agony.

Or this one, written in Waikiki and dated October 1913:

Somewhile before the dawn I rose, and stept
Softly along the dim way to your room,
And found you sleeping in the quiet gloom,
And holiness about you as you slept.
I knelt there; till your waking fingers crept
About my head, and held it. I had rest
Unhoped this side of Heaven, beneath your breast.
I knelt a long time, still; nor even wept.

It was great wrong you did me . . .

That Brooke had died of septicaemia after being bitten by a
mosquito was hardly heroic. A sniper's bullet in No Man's Land,
a hand-to-hand bayonet engagement, a shell blast blowing him 'to
bits' (like Mansfield's Leslie) or 'his head off' (like my great-uncle
Owen) – any of these would have been better. But death by mosquito bite was still Death. Heroism wasn't essential, and sometimes
there was a false ring to it. I decided I cared more about what he did
with those young women than how he felt about going to war.

The reading of Brooke at this time was combined with a redis-
covery of Robert Louis Stevenson, whose novels had provided
entertainment while I was still at primary school. Now I read about
him as a traveller in France; about his courageous journey across
the Atlantic and across America to rescue the woman he loved from
poverty and heartbreak; about his adventures in the South Pacific
and his writing of *Treasure Island* to entertain his stepson, Lloyd
Osbourne. I read his letters from Vailima in Samoa, and about his
death and burial there. All this, and the fiction of Joseph Conrad,
mixed in my imagination with those images that filled the house at
63 Kensington Avenue – tropical islands, sailing boats, beautiful

brown-skinned Polynesians and browner-skinned Melanesians, my mother as a child tied by a rope to the mast and 'washed into the scuppers' in high seas; and finally my grandfather buried in Noumea under a stone none of us had seen, or would see, but which we knew (or thought we knew) was inscribed with lines by Stevenson.

The romance of it all helped, but it was not, really, the point. I don't think it's too much to say that in this period my life found, in poetry, and in the mysterious richness and power of language, its focus, purpose, direction.

I THINK IT WAS IN 1947 THAT 'Dickie' Bedgegood, head of physical education in the school and the only master with a doctorate (it was in education, from London University), decided he would do a health report on every boy in the school. He was a rather dry character, and the story that went about was that he caned backhand or forehand depending on the severity of the punishment called for by the crime. Presumably the forehand was stronger, but I never saw him use a cane on anyone, and the story might have been enough in itself to ensure good classroom discipline.

Dr Bedgegood's health examination consisted in thrusting his hand down the front of each boy's shorts, cupping the testicles, and instructing the subject to cough. If the cough caused the testicles to move up, it meant there was no hernia. If they failed to rise, I don't know what followed – reference to a proper medical authority perhaps. That the testicles were duly descended was recorded with a small 'pb' on the health report.

There must have been close on one thousand boys at the school, and it's hard to imagine a schoolmaster now inflicting on himself the chore, or (if that is what it was) allowing himself the pleasure, of 'feeling up' every one of them in the name of a health check. But I doubt anyone suffered from the experience. Many bad things happened in those days, and many others passed harmlessly, for want of undue diligence.

TWELVE
LES, HERBIE AND HEDGIE, BARRY, JEAN AND VIDA

T he boy I knew in fourth-form French as Les Parker came to MAGS after spending his third-form year at Seddon Tech. His full name was Grenfell Bertram Louis Parker,[*] known to his family as Gren. Disliking all his names, he had, in making the transfer from Tech, selected Louis and shortened it to Les (as I had shortened Karlson to Karl).

Les was short, dark and possibly handsome, anyway with a lot of very curly black hair and chunky white legs. He seemed to attach himself to me, I think because, noticing that he knew no one and was ignored, I was the first to behave as though he was in the room and engage him in conversation. Thereafter, during that first week of the fourth-form year, he was at my side as we went from one classroom to the next, and as we rode home towards Balmoral. Inadvertently, I had acquired a new friend.

---

[*] I always seem to remember triple forenames. Don Cater's was Victor Donald Bradley.

Les had boxed at Tech and had his own gloves and hand-bandages, his own soft-leather bootie-looking shoes. He trained at the gym, punching a bag, rope-skipping, going for runs interrupted by repeated darting, feinting and jabbing. He entered, that year, the school's annual boxing competitions, which were presided over by Mr Boulton (known to the boys as Hedgie), and persuaded me to join him. I was fourteen, and weighed in at under 9 stone 7.

All I knew about boxing was what I had learned years before from John Surridge's father – the straight left and the right cross. Still, I was doing very well in my fight against a 4A boy, Darryl Harry, clearly winning on points, until I began to tire. How could three minutes, the time of each round, last so long? I was exhausted, and still there was no sound of the bell. Had we been forgotten? Out of puff, I dropped my arms and looked around, Darryl hit me with the haymaker he was noted for, and Hedgie stopped the fight.

I wasn't 'laid out', but I must have had a few moments of unconsciousness because I have no memory of getting out of the ring – only of being outside it, recovering on the floor – and then an extraordinary exhilaration, a Zen moment, enlightenment, *satori*! Perhaps a brain specialist would be able to explain it. It seemed, however, a rough and risky route to the *dharma*, and not one I intended to take again, so my record as a boxer remains: fights, 1; wins, 0; losses, 1 (t.k.o. in round one).

But Les was the boxer – or so he said – with his fancy soft bootie-shoes, and I awaited his fight with interest and only a very slight headache. The first surprise was his manner of fighting. It was unorthodox to the point of absurdity, and consisted of bounding around the ring like a kangaroo, so that although it was difficult for his opponent to hit him, it was equally difficult for Les to land any significant blows. This went on inconclusively, with grumbles from Hedgie about 'mixing it', and 'getting on with it', until late in the third round when Les's opponent pinned him in a corner where effective bounding was impossible, and knocked him out – cold. Les was carried out of the ring and didn't come to – or not properly. Hedgie, still mounted in the elevated desk from which he judged the fights, showed some slight signs of concern. Another master, Mr Horrocks (our soccer coach), was worried and decided Les should be taken home. Did anyone know where he lived? Yes, someone said, Stead knew, so Stead was to go with them in the car.

By now Les was beginning to protest that he was all right, didn't want to be taken home; but he was still groggy, and Mr Horrocks insisted.

Les's mother, when we arrived, was immediately angry – first because I referred to him as Les (his name, she said, was Gren), and then because he had been allowed to fight. He had had a head injury, a concussion, and had been forbidden to box again until further notice, or possibly ever. Mrs Parker was slightly intimidated by Mr Horrocks, and so directed her wrath at me.

After that Les's head injury was mentioned from time to time when he and I were together. He had, or pretended to have, 'blackouts'. These usually occurred when we were riding our bikes. He used to come and watch me play soccer for the school (his own winter game was rugby league), and as we were ambling home on our bikes, he would suddenly stand on the pedals and sprint – straight at a wall, a ditch, a tree, a parked car. At the last minute, when a crash seemed certain, he would pull away and stop, put his hands up to his forehead, shaking his head slowly as if confused, asking what had happened, insisting that he'd had 'another blackout' and had no recollection of what he'd done.

Were these little melodramas simply an act, or were they real? If real, why was he always able to veer away at the last minute? But, on the other hand, perhaps there was just enough consciousness for self-protection. I could never decide, and still can't, and wonder whether or not they represent behaviour an expert in brain injury would recognise and be able to explain.

IN WHAT I WROTE SOME PAGES BACK about high jumping I was evasive. 'Good at' – yes, and no. In some ways my self as high jumper illustrates how the inner life has its own dimensions, its own brilliant light and gloomy shadows, areas of pain and pleasure which no view from the outside could possibly suggest or reveal. High jumping was a passion, and my Zen – literally, because I had read, very early in my days at Mt Albert, an article about Zen and archery, and had taken on something of the Zen idea, something that would remain with me, coming and going in different forms throughout my life.

I competed at the high jump. At MAGS you competed at everything. You got used to coming second, or nowhere, or, now and then, if you were lucky (or if you were Graeme McDermott) first. This is frowned upon now by many enlightened teachers: too tough on sensitive souls and delicate egos. But in those days *compete* was what you did, and what most boys loved to do. So I competed; but as important, more important, than the competition with others was the competition with myself – and in field events, where you are not racing for the tape, but attempting to jump higher or throw further than you have done before, that is much more what you feel.

A modern reader has to understand first, however, that comparisons of actual heights jumped, then and now, are irrelevant – almost (but not quite) like remarking it cost an adult a shilling to get into the pictures (ninepence on 'Guest Night') then, and costs twelve or fifteen dollars now. There has been inflation. There has been the Fosbury Flop, the now standard high jump, in which the athlete goes over the bar more or less on his/her back. If anyone had done the Fosbury Flop then, had thought of it, had tried it and, without the piles of foam rubber a jumper falls into now, had cleared the bar and fallen straight down into the sandpit on the back of the neck, the injuries could have been fatal. No foam, no Flop; and there was none – only sand – to fall into. For jumping styles there were the scissors, the eastern cut-off, the western roll and the straddle.

The school record in 1949 was 5 foot 6.[*] I equalled it once, but not officially, in competition.

I graduated from the scissors to the western roll. On the floor of my bedroom I used to lie in the position of going over the bar – on my left side (I jumped off the left foot), left shoulder turned forward, left knee slightly bent, right leg lying over the left, right arm reaching forward in the direction of the jump. That was how I went over and I had to imagine it so body and mind learned it together, accepted the imprint and could repeat it endlessly.

Then there was the practice, which became, in time, the jump in competition. You knew how many paces you would do in the run-up – in my case five, accelerating. You stood looking at the bar and imagining going over. You did not decide when to begin your run-up. You imagined it, there was a moment of blankness, and you found yourself already into your run. I think it was important that there was very little *will* about it; no sense of conscious effort, of trying very hard, of deciding *now!* – just a glide into an action that would, nonetheless, get the co-ordinated best out of your body.

What is embarrassing looking back on this interior drama is the recognition that this almost mystical approach to high jumping, which was itself (I still affirm) a valid and rich experience, also trapped me into superstitious behaviour. What I needed was a bit of science. What I needed was a coach.

When you won or came second in your school competition, and won the right to wear the Cambridge blue and gold colours, vest and shorts, you next aspired to come somewhere in the inter-secondary school competitions. In my third year I won the MAGS intermediate (i.e. under-sixteen) high jump and represented the school at the 'Inter-secs'. In the morning competition, when the bar reached 5 foot 2, the field was reduced to five for the final. I was the only one

---

[*] My late historian friend (Sir) Keith Sinclair's claim, in his memoir *Halfway Round the Harbour* (Penguin, 1993), p. 43, to have jumped 5 foot 8 inches at MAGS in the late 1930s can't be right. The record in 1940 was 5 foot 5, broken by Des Rainey in 1948 with a jump of 5 foot 6, and raised to 5 foot 6¼ by A. D. Grover in 1958.

to clear it at first attempt. There seemed every reason to suppose I would get at least a place, and probably win in the afternoon.

I didn't know anything about 'warming up', about how muscles don't perform when cold. I thought I should 'conserve energy'. In the afternoon it rained intermittently and I lay on the wet grass in my track-suit pants waiting for my event. When it came, the bar was set for the first jump at 4 foot 11. I failed at it three times and was out. I was baffled, deeply disappointed. Why had I not been able to reproduce my form of the morning? I had no idea.

Next year, a sixth former, I entered for the school championship. I don't know what happened beforehand but I was evidently warm for it, without intending to be, because I won. All I remember is the final jump, I don't know at what height, only that everyone else had missed it three times and I had missed it twice. I needed to get over to win. It had been raining and the ground was wet. I stood imagining myself going over, waiting, then finding myself, as always, already two paces into my run-up. As my left foot drove down hard for the leap I felt it slide slightly in the wet, and in the slow-motion way an athlete apprehends, and retains in memory, the details of a performance, I thought, 'I'm going to fail this jump', while at the same time I felt myself clearing the bar, faintly brushing it, making no effort (for fear of dislodging it) to arrange how I would fall, how I would land, just collapsing into the pit knowing I had won.

So in my fourth year at MAGS I had made the senior athletic team. Next year, my fifth, I was expected as school champion to win again. One afternoon, after intense training for the hurdles, I saw the high-jump bar already set up somewhere around five foot. Without stopping, only deviating from my trot back towards the changing rooms, I jumped the bar in the unfashionable eastern cut-off style, a sort of moderated front-on scissors, with a lot of extreme lean to keep the centre of gravity where it ought to be. It was such an effortless and joyful leap, I went back, set the bar higher, and then higher again, and finally at 5 foot 6, the school record, and each time using that style, cleared it at a first try.

It didn't occur to me to ask why I was jumping so well. Having no coach to discuss it with I thought I must be better at this style than at the western roll, and that I would use it in the championship. When the day came I felt I had a secret weapon. Once again I lay very still in my track-suit, conserving energy, marvelling at the sight of my main competitor, I. B. Turley, foolishly (as I thought) wasting it by warming up.

So it was a repetition of what had happened two years before. I came third to Turley and a boy called Hooper. As I missed for a second time, Herbie Towers, still remembered in Auckland as a notable athletics administrator, checking off our jumps on his clipboard, asked in a half-suppressed bark, 'Where's your western roll, Stead?' It was the only 'coaching' remark I ever got at the school. Turley (a good friend during that last year at MAGS) won, and went on to do well at the inter-secondary school competition.

That is almost, but not quite, the end of the story. Some of us had gone to a weekend coaching school at Auckland Teachers' College where an expert had shown that discus throwing didn't depend only on strength and weight. What the arms and shoulders did could be less important than what the hips and thighs did; and to begin with you should train with that lower part of the body, letting the arm bearing the discus follow loosely behind. I learned a technique, practised it for a few days and came second to Les Mills, who broke the school record in the MAGS open event. I had failed as a high jumper but earned my place again in the senior athletics team.

That final failure at the high jump is hardly significant, but I always remember it with an inward, anguished groan. Why the disappointment should so vividly remain is something I don't understand; yet it is real. What made it worse, then and still, is that, for the first time, Dad had come along to watch me perform. He had suggested before that he might do this, and this time I had not discouraged him, thinking, I suppose, that he would see me confirmed as school high-jump champion, and perhaps this time a record-breaker.

That was 1950, my last year at MAGS and the end of my athletics career. Six years later, when I was a new lecturer in an Australian university, Frank Sargeson collected, from a second-hand shop in Takapuna, twelve shillings for the sale of my spiked running shoes. He offered to send me the money but I insisted he keep it and buy himself a book – a variant, perhaps, on turning swords into ploughshares.

In the mid-1960s, returning somewhat reluctantly to New Zealand after my second period in London, pacing the decks, I found myself jotting down in green ink on the inside flap of a copy of Samuel Butler's *Erewhon* (the nearest thing to hand) the outline of a poem apparently about high jumping, which I called (remembering Tennyson) 'Crossing the Bar' – only 'apparently' about high jumping, because really it was about the relation of art to life. High jumping was a manifestation of life, representing nothing but itself, serving nothing but itself, existential, *Zen*: 'only the whole man jumps his own height'. Poetry (i.e. art), on the other hand, served something beyond itself – served life. So it was only 'second best' – and I contracted my life to it.

> Poets at the last are deft.
> I contract to that end
> My second-best art.
> It will serve to praise the first.
> The first served only itself.

At the launch of my *Collected Poems* in Auckland in November 2008, I quoted those lines, written 45 years before.

1948, MY FIFTH-FORM/SCHOOL CERTIFICATE year, was also the year of the polio epidemic, when New Zealand learned to call 'infantile paralysis' poliomyelitis. For most, perhaps all, of the first term, schools throughout the country were closed and we worked at home by correspondence. I retain this as a general fact, and one particular memory confirms that indeed assignments came from school to home and went back again to be marked. Doing a geography essay for Hedgie Boulton I wrote that some part of Germany was known for 'brewing bear'. Instead of correcting 'bear' to 'beer', Hedgie corrected 'brewing' to 'Bruin' and added a question mark. It was the sort of beakish joke that appealed to me.

Of all the MAGS masters who were returned soldiers from the recent war, Major Boulton was by far the keenest to talk about it. As a teacher he seemed bored and was consequently boring. He used to sit behind his desk droning on in a gravel voice about some remote part of the world, its climatic character, its crops and industries, gesturing now and then, without getting up, towards a map at his back. He could be coaxed out of these monologues by a question, even one patently diversionary, about the desert campaign, 'Monty' and Rommel, Freyberg and Kippenberger. Reminiscence and anecdote would replace geography. Hedgie became animated, got up from his chair, came closer, settled with one leg over a front desk. The battles at Tobruk and Sidi Rezegh figured often. Then there had been the night break-out at Minqar Qaim, when New Zealand forces escaped from Rommel's closing trap, though with heavy losses. Hedgie had been in the blinding arena where life and death put their heads together, and nothing afterwards was ever going to match the excitement. Did I wish I had been there? Yes, I think a part of me did. But I also enjoyed it when a cruel sixth-form cartoonist, whose work was often pinned on a notice board in the upper floor art studio, did a spoof book jacket, featuring Hedgie leading a bayonet charge against 'Jerry', and the title *How I won Two World Wars* by Hedgie Boulton.

Hedgie had gingerish spiky hair, cut short and standing to attention. He commanded the school's military training, which took place in the final period every Wednesday afternoon, and meant on that day we had to come to school wearing the abrasive khaki uniform supplied by the New Zealand Army. There was an atmosphere about this militarised period I disliked and resisted. It was not just the time-wasting inefficiency and consequent boredom, but the increasing politicisation that came with the Cold War. Churchill had spoken of an 'Iron Curtain' coming down across Europe. Berlin, now an international city within the Soviet eastern zone of occupied Germany, was a source of tension. In June of that year the Russians blockaded roads through their zone, and only an airlift by the Western Allies, continuing into 1949 when the Russians relented, kept West Berlin alive and viable.

So one was being asked to accept that in a very short space of time our evil enemy Germany had become our close ally ('Ich bin ein Berliner', John F. Kennedy would soon be saying) and that our erstwhile heroic ally, the Soviet Union, was now the foe. This turnaround required a flexibility, or superficiality (choose your own emphasis) I lacked. I strongly resented military training in which the enemy was now preordained as 'Red'.

In class, Hedgie began to tell us, with relish and with envy, that we should prepare ourselves for the next war. Our grandfathers had fought in the First World War, our fathers in the Second, and not too far away in the future would come 'our turn'. Since it was unavoidable that both sides would soon have nuclear weapons, this seemed a kind of insanity, or at least a failure of imagination. It was also insidious. Even in someone like myself who thought there could be no new war like the one just fought, and that it was useless training us as if there could be, there was, nonetheless, a corner of my boyish consciousness that lit up with excitement at stories of how Charles Upham had won his two VCs, and at the thought of 'going overseas to fight'.

WHATEVER ASSIGNMENTS CAME AND went by mail, that first term of 1948 felt more like an extension of the summer vacation. The cousins got together. The public baths were closed, but there were expeditions, picnics, swimming at beaches. Barry Catton and I, with a neighbour of Barry's called Sid, a Seddon Tech boy, went out to Piha by bus, carrying rucksacks of supplies and a tent. We had each five pounds and the plan was to see how long we could make it last. Sid left after a few days but Barry and I stayed on, eking out what we bought from the store with fish, mussels (plentiful in those days) off the rocks, and occasional 'borrowings' from local orchards and vegetable gardens. Barry (met again recently after half a century) claims he had his school assignments sent to the motor camp by his mother, and returned them to the school marked 'not known at this address'. I don't remember what I did with mine. We learned to give due respect to the west coast's often dangerous surf, its unpredictable and shifting undertows, holes and rips. We swam, tramped in the bush, grew very fit and brown, and drifted to sleep in the dark of the tent smelling the scents of kerosene, canvas and crushed pennyroyal, hearing moreporks calling between the breaking of the waves.

I remember walking north along the beach in the evening, Lion Rock looming behind, low green hills rolling away to the right, to the left the blue and white sea rolling in, and ahead perhaps a flat mile of iron sand glinting blue-black, with now and then a human figure, or two human figures, brightly lit by the downward sun but their forms hazy in spray skimmed and blown shoreward by the constant westerly. We had eaten a huge meal of mussels, and boiled potatoes flavoured with sprigs of mint, and it was one of those youthful moments that register and remain, because the sense that there are obstacles and difficulties vanishes. Everything was possible.

Back in town again Cousin Ngaire was now in the National Junior Orchestra, preparing for a concert which was to include Dvořák's ninth symphony ('From the New World'). In the second movement there is a beautiful solo based on a Negro spiritual, normally played by the cor anglais. This had been re-scored for the oboe, and Ngaire practised at our house, accompanied by Mum on the piano. My dog Skipper was always deeply moved. He would listen until he could bear it no longer; then, casting sad eyes heavenward, his big spaniel ears drooping on either side, he would break into a long, melancholy howl. Or perhaps I misread him; he was not sad at all but just 'singing along'.

I played a lot of tennis, and table tennis, especially with Jean Lamont, a year older and a year ahead of me at Auckland Girls' Grammar. The Lamonts, a few streets away from Kensington Avenue, and close to the Whitworth Tennis Club, were friends from Maungawhau School. Her brother Ian, my contemporary, had been enrolled as a boarder at the MAGS School House because their father had died while they were still at primary school, and their grandfather, who took responsibility for the family, thought Ian needed the discipline the House would provide. I played soccer with Ian; but it was Jean who became my close friend during that year, and for some time afterwards.

She was very intelligent, a reader, a good talker, great company, a writer of clever, somewhat rebellious school essays (one in the AGGS school magazine was called 'Sport is a fetish'). We began to have the sort of needlessly prolonged telephone conversations teenagers have, or used to have (now they chat by thumb), where, when everything has been said, still neither wants to be the first to end it. We went together to watch the early rounds of the New Zealand tennis championships at Stanley Street Courts, where we bought ourselves salmon and cucumber sandwiches and cups of strong brown English tea. When we competed, as we did constantly – at tennis, or table tennis, or who would get higher marks in English, or anything else – the loser had to buy the winner one or more milk shakes.

I liked her very much, her cleverness, her athleticism, her sense of humour. I was entirely at ease with her, but it never occurred to me to think of her as a 'girlfriend', I suppose because I had never had one, and because she was a year older, which seemed significant at that age. We spent many hours alone together in the Whitworth Tennis Club, a sort of concrete bunker, playing game after game of table tennis. Sometimes between games she would half sit on the edge of the table, her arms behind her making props, her pelvis thrust forward, and there would be a deep brown-eyed silence in which it seemed something was required of me; but I didn't know whether I was imagining this, and if I was not, what it might be.

One afternoon, when Jean and I had played seventeen games (not an invented, 'for example' number, but a precise memory), Norma, who did not belong to the club, appeared there red-faced and out of breath to tell me Mum wanted me at home. When I got home I was not wanted at all – yet Mum had sent Norma to fetch me. I was puzzled, which is why I remember it. Now it seems to me clear: a mother's imagination was running, apprehensively, a long way ahead of the story.

LABOUR HAD ESTABLISHED A 'child allowance' of ten shillings per week for each child up to the age of fifteen, and beyond while the child continued at home and was in full-time education. At a time when the average wage was probably five pounds per week, this was a generous supplement, and from quite early in my time at MAGS, and beyond when I was a student, Mum gave it to me as pocket money. Since everything at home was supplied free, it was easy for me to save for special things. I bought a book about photography, including developing and printing, and then the necessary chemicals and photographic paper. Mum let me borrow (in reality gave me, since she never asked for it back) the family camera, a Kodak, which opened with a bellows or concertina action that pulled the lens outward from the film. I turned my bedroom into a darkroom simply by buying a red globe for my desk lamp. Cameras were bigger in those days, and films were as wide as ordinary 'snaps', so you could do what were called 'contact prints' without need of an enlarger.

On a Rotorua holiday I took photographs of trout in the pools at Rainbow Springs, of the marvellous clear surging waters of

Hamurana, of a waterfall at the Buried Village (where Dad thought he had had a heart attack on the steep climb back from the foot of the falls),* of Mokoia Island at evening across the lake, of the Ngongotaha Stream and of the best trout I caught there. In Auckland I tried some 'art' photography, including setting my camera on its back in the centre of the Auckland museum foyer and photographing light coming through the glass panels far overhead.

They were black and white photographs; and because I had no enlarger, and no way of screening light from the print-paper beyond the image, the edges of all my pictures were black, as if commemorating a death or recording a grief. It was all very crude, unmistakably amateurish, but absorbing.

Once when I was in the middle of developing a film I was called out to meet some visitors, Dad's cousin Gwen (vividly remembered from my childhood visits to Kaiwaka), and her husband, a returned soldier and farmer whose name was Jock Upton. I said the necessary politenesses and then explained what I was doing and that I had to get back to it. Jock expressed an interest in the process and came with me to watch. He was a big, shy chap, and we sat in the strange reddish twilight of the darkroom, I with my hands in the white developing dish that looked pink under the lamp, watching the images emerge as the developing fluid performed its magic – and then switching them (I wonder as I write whether I am remembering the process correctly) into the dish of 'hypo' where they were 'fixed'.

Jock said nothing for a very long time, but because I was occupied and he was interested, it was not an embarrassing silence. And then, out of this silence, he told me I had beautiful hands.

What does a fifteen-year-old boy say to a farmer who tells him he has 'beautiful hands'? This one could think of nothing, and thought only that blushing would not be detectable under a red light.

---

* A Maori village buried by the eruption of Mt Tarawera in 1886. About 150 Maori and half a dozen Pakeha were killed. Dad's maternal grandfather, Police Constable Abrams of Rotorua, riding to help out at the disaster, fell off his horse when it shied, breaking his wrist, and never reached the scene.

Jock thanked me, and returned to the sitting room. I thought he was strange – a nice man, but quiet, melancholy, needing a black edge like my photographs; and I remembered that thought when, less than a year later, news came that he had taken a gun out into the bush and shot himself, leaving a note saying 'God bless you all', that everything was wrong and, to Gwen, 'It is not your fault, darling.'

AT THE END OF 1948 I GOT MYSELF A vacation job – the first of many. I was taken on at 'Dominion Road South', as the Mt Roskill Post Office was called, to do various menial tasks during the Christmas rush. There was one day a week when a lot of extra money came into the office, for pension payments due next day, and I was soon working out a scheme for getting in on that particular night and robbing the safe. I don't remember the details, and I don't suppose it would have worked, but its point for me was fiction. Being in that office gave me details, facts, circumstances, characters – everything fiction needs – and I was soon writing a story in which such a robbery was successfully carried out. I don't remember much else about it (all early work, I'm pleased to say, was destroyed in a succession of burn-ups during my student years) except that the thief, a sort of ur-self, rowed out and hid the loot in one of two disused barges, at that time to be seen moored off Northcote, and carried on his life until the fuss had died down. When he came at last to reclaim his treasure, however, something had gone wrong, or went wrong (the money destroyed by the weather? taken by a friend/enemy who had been needed as an accomplice?), and I don't think that question had been resolved when school started again and the whole thing was abandoned.

One of my tasks was to phone telegrams, handed in over the counter, through to operators in the CPO in downtown Auckland. Doing that job, I got to know, by voice, a girl called Vida. We talked almost every day. I told her where I played tennis, and she told me later she had come on her bike one weekend to have a look at me, had seen me coming out of the club room with Les Parker, a visual test of acceptability which I must have passed because she now invited me to come with her to the Midget Car Speedway at Western Springs.

We met outside the gates, I having received various ways of identifying her. I no longer remember her face, though I was about to spend quite a few hours up very close to it. She had a blanket over her arm and a cushion under it, and led me high up into the pines, though there were, as I pointed out, plenty of seats closer to the racetrack. I told her that Roly Crowther, one of the top midget car racers of the time, who would be racing that night, lived in our street and had his workshop nearby in Queens Avenue, and that I knew his sister who was 'crippled' (the word used then) and in a wheelchair; but Vida seemed unimpressed by these attempts at conversational connection and pushed on up among the trees.

This was the first, the most innocent (I was shy, uncertain of what was required, and slow to get started), of what for the next five or six years would be a succession of encounters that could be described as 'sexual', but of which I could say afterwards, like Bill Clinton with Monica Lewinsky, 'I did not have sexual relations with that woman.' I didn't then know Yeats's line, 'the young in one another's arms', but I was always in the arms of a girl, always wanting sex, which was always denied; though whether the denials were intended to be understood as absolute, whether no always and invariably meant no, as feminists would later insist, was never quite clear. It was not only fear of pregnancy that determined the behaviour of young women, but a fear, in that strangely puritanical time, of being classed as wanton, sluttish, 'bad girls'. Maybe a little show, not of force but of forcefulness, shifting responsibility for 'what happened next' to the male, would have been welcome. But, though loaded with surplus testosterone, I had so little of the rapist in me, I needed something close to a formal invitation to be sure I wasn't unwelcome. No did mean no, and the condoms I armed

myself with, bought at a huge cost, not in money but embarrassment, went unused.

But all of that lay in the future. Not even the junior bar was
going to be crossed this time. For the moment all that was required
of me, as night came down and the unmuffled engines roared
around the floodlit track, was kissing, very exciting to begin with,
but finally tedious, as if you were required to kiss your mother or
your sister goodnight, on and on into infinity.

I don't think Vida and I met again, but I tried to write a poem
about our encounter. Our fifth-form English master, Mr Cornwell,
had recently introduced us to the work of Alexander Pope. I was
beginning to understand how the various poetic forms and metres
worked, and decided I would write in heroic couplets. This might
have worked if my intention had been satiric, but it was not. I
wanted to edit out the wordless tedium of the kissing and make
something romantic of the night, the roar and whine of engines, the
diesel-scented smoke floating up through arc-lights and dissipating
among the pines, and a girl's face, her eyes, her lips . . .

I would have done better to stick with Rupert Brooke for model,
or to have taken a step forward into Keats, just now beginning to
take a firm hold on my imagination.

TO CONCLUDE THIS CHAPTER I WILL TAKE a very short step back in
time. Term has ended; we are at the end of the 1948 school year. I
am at home with Mum and the Grandmother, soon to start my job
at the Post Office. Norma, who failed School Certificate in 1946,
and went to business college in 1947 to learn shorthand and typing,
is at work at the Lands and Deeds Office in Auckland, where she
has acquired the nickname Rusty because of her habit of bursting
into gales of laughter which she can't suppress but cause her to
blush with embarrassment. We are at the lunch table when Dad
comes in, unexpected. He looks at me, smiling, and holds out his
hand – his left, as it always has to be, turned on its side – reaches

out to me through the silence his entry has caused. Puzzled, I shake it. He says, 'Congratulations, son.'

I have passed School Certificate. He has been so anxious about it he has got a friend in the office of the *Auckland Star*, where the results are about to be printed, to check for him.

I remember the moment with great affection, of course; but also as a measure of how little had been expected of me.

THIRTEEN
GOODBYE LABOUR
AND GOODBYE JEAN

But perhaps I exaggerate. Yes, it's true Mum never could reconcile the hope engendered by the three-year-old, who could sing infallibly in tune, with the keyboard-incompetent who came later. But there is a danger of making too much of it, in the interests of colour, and at her expense. She was not stupid. And maybe she was not altogether wrong. There was, not always, but quite often, something laborious about my personality, a sort of Prometheus in gumboots, flightless, anxious, explanatory. Third finger! *Third* finger! How often did she have to tell me? Perhaps she was right to be surprised at my successes. I was surprised myself, and was consequently given to making them known, not intending to boast (though that is how it must have seemed), but as if something out of the normal order of things had occurred: an earthquake, a meteor, a tsunami, an A-pass in English!

I think my mother had an inner life which none of us in the family recognised or imagined, and she looked out of its high window, like Tennyson's Lady of Shalott, not directly, but by means of a mirror, hoping for the fatal Lancelot who never came. He might have come in any form at all – a brilliant concert-pianist son would have done as well as any. My faulty fingering put an end to that hope; and my continuance at the keyboard, day after day, even if it was by her own edict, was just another distraction from her secret task, which was to keep her eye fixed on that mirror-image of the river and the fields, hoping for the one who would come singing among the barley-sheaves, the sunlight flaming on his greaves.

Meanwhile she had to put up with pedestrian jokey Jim, the one-arm gardener who was 'not a handyman', the politician who could not get himself a seat in Parliament – Jim and his smoulder-ing disappointments, his smoking and snoring and endless reading, and, worst of all, his loud angers and what she called his 'violence'. Was he violent? Sometimes, when I or Norma as infants had been very 'bad', the ultimate penalty was promised. Dad was to be told, and when he came home from work we would be punished. This happened very seldom indeed; and though there was a lot of huffing and puffing, and carting one or other of us off to the bedroom where the hitting could occur, I never remember anything except a belt waved about, and squeals of anticipation from the criminal. If any blows were landed there was no pain. He was supposed to punish us but couldn't bring himself to do it. I have sometimes thought, when hearing that So-and-so was a good teacher, or a good parent, because no child was ever hit in anger, only for correction, that I could respond that no child in our house was ever hit *except* in anger, and then not very hard. Of course all hitting is wrong, and should be unnecessary; but the latter seems more natural.

But was he violent with her? She said it so often I believed it; and because of the special (and very real) bond there was between mother and son, I always took her side against him. But on care-ful reflection I have come to the conclusion that it must have been almost entirely bluster on his part and hysteria on hers. I never saw bruises or black eyes, blood or abrasions; there were certainly no injuries requiring medical attention. If this was 'domestic violence' it was at a level which, I imagine, would cause an experienced cop in South Auckland to bite his pencil and wonder what to write in his notebook.

Dad did once, or so she claimed at the time, try to smother her with a pillow – not so effectively that we didn't hear her cries for help and rush in to save her. And there was a time when she ran across the road to the Willetts family to tell them of his cruelty, and he went after her and dragged her home again. Back indoors, however, he was so grey-faced, breathless and depleted by the effort, I thought we would have to call an ambulance for him not her, and nothing followed. I'm sure he was driven to fury by her agile tongue; that he threatened her; that he went close to the border – maybe got in the odd cuff or rough shove. His behaviour was bad, I don't doubt; but I don't believe that significant violence occurred. And I think her determination to drag the children in on her side, to involve us as allies, to weep and play the victim before us, especially when we were very small, was deplorable. Later, she must have recognised, from two sets of steely adolescent eyes attending to her version of events, that she was being judged, and sometimes disbelieved.

So in retrospect I absolve him of the charge of assault. What there was between them, however – the verbal assaults, the bad blood, the shouting, sulks and tantrums – was destructive. Usually, like the nor'-easterly storms that blow into Auckland from the tropics, each one lasted three to four days, poisoning the household. I think our parents were high-powered and under-used, bored with their lives, addicted to one another and to their battles; and we, their children, learned to live with, but never to be less than deeply unhappy about, their endless alternations of love and war. When I was small, and half-believed in prayer (or anyway practised it), the only thing I ever prayed for was that they would not fight. As I grew older, and recognised that prayer was a phone line with no one at the other end, I escaped into sport, school, friends, the landscape and animals. Norma, I later came to think, was more seriously marked by the parental warfare, her long-term health affected, her insecurity deeper and longer lasting. How my younger sister, Frances, coped only she could say, since by that time I was off the premises; but she is a sturdy personality, deputy principal of a school, mother and grandmother, a success in life, and if there are scars, they don't show.

Despite the rows, I never doubted that my parents continued to be lovers; one somehow knew that it must be so, without dwelling on the question or knowing how one knew. So it was not a total surprised when Norma told me in 1949, my sixth-form year, that Mum, too embarrassed to tell me herself, was pregnant. My immediate thought was that it would relieve me of some of the attention I was finding irksome, the enquiries about what I did, who I was with, how I passed my time away from home. Her maternal anxieties would be engaged elsewhere.

AFTER DAD DIED AND WHEN MUM WAS old and ailing (or seemed so, though only in her late sixties) she once asked me to drive her to Ponsonby, to what in her childhood was Disraeli Street and is now Dickens Street. We parked outside the house she had lived in for some years from the age of eight. During the patriotic fervour of World War I she had sometimes been chased home from school by children who decided, because her name was Karlson, that she must be German; but she looked on it only with nostalgia. At the back there had been an orphanage, and as an eight-year-old she used to look over the fence at the orphans and feel for them, not just abstract pity but real compassion. Her own parents had returned after leaving her for three years with the Quelch family, then living in Parnell, while my grandfather went on one of his assignments to the islands. Medical advice had been that little Olive was not a strong child and might succumb to tropical ailments. It had been a trauma for all three. The Grandmother always remembered, and wept recounting it, the morning they were to leave, going to take a last look, unseen, over the fence of Parnell School, knowing that the little five-year-old she could see in the playground would be eight when she returned. And Mum remembered how she kept a photograph of her parents always beside her bed, and how the memory of them, and the faith that they would return to her, faded and became less and less real as time passed. Looking at the Dickens Street house she told me she would like to die there. She had wanted to see it again, knowing the sense of peace and security that modest wooden cottage would bring her. She could look at it and contemplate death without fear – almost with a sense of luxury.

The relationship between parents and an only child is often intense, because the parental emotion (and the Grandmother was a very loving woman) is not dissipated by numbers; and I suppose the feeling between this mother and this daughter, even though the daughter was intellectually so dominant, had been made even more intense by that painful hiatus of three years. Then, in adult life, circumstances had dictated that the Grandmother live on with us, or we with her – and that, surely, must have made the wars between Jim and Olive worse. Now Mum was pregnant and there was going to be a third child. The Grandmother, who had been an extra parent and live-in baby-sitter when Norma and I were infants, was beginning to fail in health and in her mind. She would be, not a reliever of the burden, but an addition to it. Mum, I can see now, though I did not know it then, was about to go into a kind of twilight zone, where her ailing mother and her new baby would strain her to the limit, while Dad struggled on with the recognition that his dream of political success was never going to be fulfilled.

From all of this, with the healthy blindness and brutality of adolescence, I escaped into sport, social life, school and (soon it would be) university.

BUT ALSO INTO LITERATURE, AND BY TWO quite separate doors. One was the school, where in English we graduated in the sixth form to studying the English Romantics, and most notably for me, Wordsworth and Keats. The other door was contemporary poetry and book reviews and occasional essays, as found locally in the *New Zealand Listener*, and internationally in my father's weekly *New Statesman*.

In studying Wordsworth we were directed to the scenic quality. That was there, and I responded to it. But there was something else, something elusive:

> Once again I see
> These hedge-rows, hardly hedge-rows, little lines
> Of sportive wood run wild . . .

It was not just the adjective 'sportive' and the image of hedge-rows running wild like children threatening to grow up to be woods; and not just the lovely alliterative patterning; even more, it was that hesitation and slight self-correction. There was an intimacy, informality, immediacy that must have been new at the time the poem was written and were still fresh. Voice, personality, presence, tone: I perceived such things and felt them almost physically in reading; but I had as yet no language for them in the classroom or in exams. They were strong, but so much my own I couldn't credit them with any merit outside the space of my own head.

'Tintern Abbey', a poem about bearing up in the city, supported by recollections of self and nature, spoke directly to the boy who had so often escaped from present boredom or misery into thoughts about Kaiwaka, the landscape, the bush. There was a strength of feeling in Wordsworth I responded to as if it had been my own voice, as if he had been speaking, not to me, but for me:

> I cannot paint
> What then I was. The sounding cataract
> Haunted me like a passion: the tall rock,
> The mountain, and the deep and gloomy wood,

Their colours and their forms, were then to me
An appetite; a feeling and a love
That had no need of a remoter charm
By thought supplied . . .

Even more exciting was Keats's 'Ode to a Nightingale'. Again there was the scenic quality, especially in the fifth stanza, where, with beauty and economy, the poet tells us what he *can't* see in the darkness –

> The grass, the thicket, and the fruit-tree wild,
>   White hawthorn and the pastoral eglantine,
>   Fast-fading violets covered up in leaves,
>   And mid-May's eldest child
>   The coming musk-rose, full of dewy wine:
>   The murmurous haunt of flies on summer eves.

The texture there was even richer than Wordsworth's, playing so much upon the ear that it 'made *sense*' even before making sense. You could slide right past 'meaning', not because it wasn't there, but because it was less potent than the verbal music, which was where the primary aesthetic experience lay. Meaning was almost an excuse for the music, rather than its purpose.

But then, in the next stanza, Keats took (and took me, aged sixteen, with him) a step further, somewhere beyond 'scene' into the mysterious power of language itself:

> Darkling I listen, and for many a time
>   I have been half in love with easeful Death,
> Call'd him soft names in many a musèd rhyme,
>   To take into the air my quiet breath;
> Now more than ever seems it rich to die,
>   To cease upon the midnight with no pain
>   While thou art pouring forth thy soul abroad

In such an ecstasy!
Still wouldst thou sing, and I have ears in vain –
To thy high requiem become a sod.

The whole stanza, which was about hearing and not hearing, as the previous one was about seeing and not seeing, seemed to build towards the final mysterious line, where the vowel sounds of 'thy high requiem' suggested something spiritual, eternal, otherworldly, but were brought right down to the poor, clipped, dark reality of that last word, 'sod'.

The school gave me no language for these responses. How could it? That would come later. But it gave me my introduction to the poets, and for that I was, and remain, hugely grateful. I could have said to my teachers (though I wouldn't then have had the confidence, let alone the arrogance), 'Thank you for introducing me to Mr Wordsworth, and Master Keats. You can leave me alone with them now.'

Quite a different kind of excitement, but complementary, was the discovery of the living world of literature, the fact that it was being written and published now, reviewed and read, argued over. Dad read the front of the *New Statesman*, I read the back. Of course Dad read some of the book reviews as well, and I kept up with world politics and watched the Cold War getting colder; but that was how our chief interests divided – a Jack-Sprat-and-his-wife arrangement. The issues came weekly by sea-mail so were not up to date, but that hardly mattered in a world which moved at a slower, more deliberate pace. I read new poems by contemporary British authors as well as reviews of their work. The *New Statesman* could be generous with space for poetry; and I think I read there, for example, most of Louis MacNeice's *Ten Burnt Offerings*, a sequence of long poems, as they came out over a period of many months. Dad and I would both have been surprised to know that I would one day write for the paper, and that he would read me there, both in poetry and prose.

But equally, and in some respects more, important was the discovery that the phenomenon of literature went on locally. Oliver Duff, ignoring instructions to keep the *New Zealand Listener* completely focused on broadcasting matters, had resolved not to follow public taste but to mould it, and the paper had become a point of focus for the nation's writers and intellectuals – something which Monte Holcroft, when he took over the editorship towards the end of the 1940s, continued. There I read my first poems by James K. Baxter, Louis Johnson, Ruth Gilbert, Basil Dowling, Keith Sinclair, W. H. Oliver; short stories by O. E. Middleton, John Reece Cole, W. H. Gilbert, Dennis McEldowney; and many reviews of books, the visual arts and music.

In this same year, 1949, I had discovered in the school library a copy of John Mulgan's novel *Man Alone*. Mulgan, I would later learn, had lived not far from Kensington Avenue and, before I was born, must have gone past our house every day on his way to Maungawhau School. He had graduated from Auckland University College, gone on to Oxford, graduated there with first-class honours, joined the British Army at the outbreak of the war and then transferred to NZ Div in the desert. He was a heroic figure, and myths had grown up around him, some of which I would later challenge.* He had survived the war and then mysteriously taken his own life in Cairo.

Man Alone was a dourly told story with strong political overtones, exciting partly because it was (at last) a serious novel about the country I knew at first hand; but also because Mulgan had read his Hemingway, his Joyce, the Modernists of fiction who in their various ways had broken the mould of middle-class formality and the conventions of language that went with it. Almost every New Zealand work I read from that time on for the best part of a decade had for me this double attraction – that it was dealing with a known

---

* See, for example, 'John Mulgan: A Question of Identity' in my *Kin of Place: Essays on 20 New Zealand Writers*, Auckland University Press, 2002.

world, and that it was using language in ways that broke with older, more formal, essentially British and middle-class conventions.

Among these writers was Frank Sargeson, whose work I was first introduced to by Mr Cornwell, another returned soldier, who told me, in a moment of informal chat, how he had once crouched in the shelter of an olive tree in Greece or Crete while low-flying German planes went over, and had watched the leaves flickering in sunlight as the bullets went through. He had shown me a Sargeson story I now know to be one of his best and best-known, 'An Affair of the Heart', in which the narrator tells of a mother devoted to her worthless son whom she waits for every night until the last bus has gone, though she hasn't seen him in years.

Mr Cornwell asked me what I thought of it. I said nothing about the content (though in fact I had been moved by it) but remarked instead on the mechanics of the writing, that there were no inverted commas for spoken dialogue.

We agreed it was very colloquial, very modern.

Shortly afterwards, in Whitcombe & Tombs in Queen Street, I saw a novel by Sargeson, *I Saw in My Dream*, published in London by John Lehmann. I stared at the photograph of the author on the flap, and read the note that said he was born in Hamilton and, after a visit to England and Europe, had spent the past eighteen years living in Auckland. So it was possible to be a writer, published in 'the world', and living in New Zealand. That seemed surprising, and wonderful. I imagined he must be rich. The novel cost ten shillings and sixpence, which I didn't have; but even without my buying it, it had given me a message.

English at Mt Albert Grammar under the famous J. G. ('Butch') Brown was very literary. Recently I saw again copies of the school calendar and reading guides for the years I was there, which say 'All School Certificate Candidates should have read most of the following novels by their third school year.' I remember that injunction very well, and how guilty I felt that there were many books on the list I hadn't yet read. But I had read a lot of them, a good representative sampling. Under headings School Stories, Historical Novels, Detective Novels, Romantic Novels, Humour, Travel, Didactic Novels and Suggestions for Play Reading, it included Dickens, Sir Walter Scott, Jane Austen, George Eliot, Wilkie Collins, Conan Doyle, R. L. Stevenson, Rider Haggard, John Buchan, H. G. Wells, Swift, Defoe, Charlotte Brontë, Mark Twain, G. B. Shaw and Oliver Goldsmith, a list that might make most modern teenagers, and their teachers with them, quail – or, more likely, laugh out loud. But what a grounding; what a language-loam for the developing mind; and what a reservoir of stories! This, along with Shakespeare and the major British poets, was an education for the literary talent which no course in 'creative writing' could ever match. And now I had in addition that expanding horizon of contemporary and local writing to draw upon and to imitate.

Nor was School Certificate easy. I had the impression that only about half of us got through. The rest either left school at that point, as Norma did, or, like Don Cater and Graeme McDermott, repeated their fifth-form year. Others among my friends, Barry Catton and Ian Turley, for example, passed School Certificate, but then failed the University Entrance exam.[*] So those who made it into 6A (in later years called the seventh form) were the élite survivors of quite a demanding obstacle course.

WITH SCHOOL CERTIFICATE SUCCESSFULLY behind us, Barry and I began 1949 with a heroic trip to Dickinson's Motor Camp at Ngongotaha on the shores of Lake Rotorua, where I had been on holiday with my family – 'heroic', because we rode there, 160 miles (250 kilometres), with packs on our backs and camping equipment (pup-tent, ground sheets, poles and pegs) strapped to

---

[*] Barry's serious myopia, which he concealed successfully for years, was diagnosed only in 1950. He went on to graduate MA, taught during his OE years in UK schools, and spent most of his working life as a lecturer at Waikato Teachers' College.

our bikes. The plan was to do the first 80 miles (125 kilometres) and camp the night, but, finding ourselves ahead of schedule at Hamilton, we pushed on to Cambridge. Barry has a photograph taken while we were resting by the Waikato River. I am holding an eel, which he claims I caught with one hand, leaning down into the water from the bank, though I have no memory of this. After Cambridge we cycled past the Karapiro hydro station and saw the new dam being filled. We both remember the pain and dehydration of climbing the Mamakus before the final cruise down into Ngongotaha.

Once settled we had bikes for sight-seeing, and ranged far and wide. We cooked for ourselves in the camp kitchen. On the last night we met two girls, Catholic cousins. I was quite seriously smitten with mine, and what we did together in the moonlight under willows by the lake, and only too late realised there had been no exchange of addresses or phone numbers. I wanted very much to see her again, but then, some months later, recognising her coming towards me in Queen Street, I was struck dumb. She hesitated and then, put off by my silence, walked on.

We made the return journey only the day before school was to begin, so set out to ride the whole distance. In Barry's recollection we get to Pokeno, in mine to Papakura; in both we load our bikes on the guard's van of a train and ride the final 30 or 40 miles in second-class luxury.

IN THESE YEARS DAD AND I DISAGREED about politics, not in loyalty but in emphasis. Like Peter Fraser, Dad seemed burdened by the increasing bitterness of the exchanges between America and Russia. As the Cold War got colder, he tended to side with the Americans, whereas I retained the loyalty of my childhood to the great Soviet ally. Even as it became apparent that the USSR was just another corrupt power bloc imposing its will on the weak abroad and opponents at home, still the more I read the greater my distaste for

America became, because that was *our* side, and we were allied to, and implicated in, what it did.

Dad was still the Labour man, still the Fabian; but I think he was becoming in some ways more conservative, more cautious; and it was at this time that he dabbled briefly in something called Moral Rearmament, which had begun in Oxford in the late 1930s and proposed that the betterment of the world had to begin in observance of the highest standards of morality in private and public life. Why my father should have been detained for longer than a few seconds by this thumping proposition is beyond me; but it was said to be a world movement, and perhaps he saw it as offering, by extension, a 'Third Way', a sort of middle-of-the-road, neither-socialist-nor-capitalist, neither-one-thing-nor-the-other hope for the future. A series of plays on Moral Rearmament themes were put on somewhere in the region of Karangahape Road – possibly in what later became the Mercury Theatre – and Dad took us to see them, father-mother-son-daughter, the morally rearmed, or morally observant, nuclear family. We struggled through each of these laboriously acted-out play-propositions as they ground towards exemplary conclusions, until Mum was heard to murmur, as we emerged from the last, that she had been bored stiff and couldn't face another. No one argued, not even Dad, and Moral Rearmament went back into the toy-box.

1949 brought an election. Peter Fraser had wanted to legislate for compulsory military training for eighteen-year-olds (meaning eighteen-year-old men, not women) but his own caucus opposed him, and he compromised by putting the question to the electorate as a referendum. I wanted Labour to win the election and the CMT proposal to be lost. The electorate meanly welcomed Fraser's proposal, and voted him out of office.

Barry's parents held a party on the night of the election. I had just turned seventeen. Labour had been in power since I was three – as long as I could remember. It was like ringing the bell at Balmoral Intermediate and wondering nervously what peace would be like

– but much worse. We were to have Sidney George Holland as our new Prime Minister. Barry and I had been to his biggest meeting in the Auckland Town Hall and heckled him. He was (as we saw him) an insignificant little man who as Prime Minister would be an international embarrassment. His foreign policy had consisted of a promise to 'help dear old Britain' and to close New Zealand's legation in Moscow. His declaration on being sworn into office – 'There will be no more socialism in New Zealand – today, the peg has gone into the wall' – was meant to signal the end of all those good things Labour had done; and it could be argued that it did. They would never be quite wholeheartedly or unequivocally restored. I began to recognise that the problem with raising the poor out of poverty was that it made the affluent a majority, many of whom, motivated by self-interest, ceased to care about the class they had come from and now saw it as a costly and powerless minority, to be controlled rather than fostered. Perhaps that's what Moral Rearmament meant to Dad – teaching people to vote disinterestedly (in the proper sense of the word) for what is good for the group, not what is good for oneself.

So the party at Peary Road, which was meant to be a celebration, turned into a wake. I tried cider and discovered what it felt like to be drunk. I went into the kitchen and there was a stocky man standing on one leg, leaning well forward but with head raised, holding one arm to the front, the other to the rear. 'I'm the man who stands on one leg,' he said, repeatedly. His wife explained to me that he had been an athlete, a sprinter who ran in the Olympic Games for New Zealand, and that he had posed for the nude statue over the gates of the Auckland Domain.* The bronze figure (an unusually good one in a city where most public statuary is badly executed) was placed so that it gave a better view of his testicles than anything else. I had often as a child glanced up at them nervously and looked away. Adults never mentioned or looked at the statue, and behaved as if it wasn't there.

* His name was Allan Elliott and he ran at the Los Angeles Games in 1932.

MY FRIENDSHIP WITH JEAN LAMONT continued – and then it
stopped. She was a year ahead of me, so in our School Certificate
milk-shake competition we had to compare my end of 1948 results
with hers of the year before. I had beaten her in chemistry (76 per
cent) but she had beaten me in English (my mark was 73). I suppose
a milk shake passed each way. Our phone calls continued, and our
games of tennis and table tennis. I was now playing tennis for the
school as well as at the club. I was also (I learn from school records)
singing bass in the secondary school's music festival, which explains
my ability still to find tune and words, though no longer voice, for
the hymn from Milton's 'On the Morning of Christ's Nativity':

> Ring out, ye crystal spheres!
> Once bless our human ears
>   (If ye have powers to touch our senses so);
> And let your silver chime
> Move in melodious time;
>   And let the bass of heaven's deep organ blow;
> And with your ninefold harmony
> Make up full consort to th'angelic symphony.
>
> Yea Truth and Justice then
> Will down return to men,
>   Orb'd in a rainbow; and like glories wearing . . .

– Milton at his most Miltonic and fruity, but somehow the
composer had made the words singable.

So life went on. Then one day (this was 1949, before the election)
Les Parker told me it was all over for me with Jean. She was now
his girlfriend. He had met her somewhere, taken her somewhere,
something had happened, declarations had been made . . .

'Girlfriend?' Until that moment I had never thought of Jean as
my girlfriend. But of course she was! Why had I never kissed her?
What an oversight! All at once, having felt nothing of the kind, I felt
possessive; I experienced sexual jealousy.

I phoned expecting her to confirm that Les was mistaken, deluded. She confirmed that he was right. It was over between us. Over before it had begun! I was crushed. It was very strange to find myself retrospectively 'in love'. I felt anger, jealousy, even pleaded my case.

Les was triumphant. In one of our classes we sat together and he took to singing under his breath, from a current popular musical, a song that went

> Don't you know, little fool,
> You never can win.
> Use your mentality,
> Wake up to reality.

It was the word 'mentality' that irritated me more than his tuneless-ness and tastelessness. If you wanted to say 'use your brains' you should say it; not employ a non-word, not even for (or especially not for) the sake of a rhyme! How could he bear to sing those words? The literary-critical self distracted me from my role as sad forsaken lover. Very seriously I asked myself how Jean Lamont, a young woman of intelligence and literary refinement, could attach herself to this tasteless kangaroo boxer, this head-banger with his real or fake 'blackouts'.

But they, Les and Jean, were serious – 'in it for the long haul', he would have said. I am ransacking memory here, but I think he qualified as a pharmacist first, and then, possibly after they married, as a doctor. The last time I remember seeing them was in Albert Park at the end of 1951, my first university year. I told them (oh God, yes, of course I did! – what else?) that I had A-passes in first-year English and history. Not that it wasn't true. But why did they need to be told? How could I have made myself so vulnerable? They thought it very amusing.

FOURTEEN
A MARRIAGE, A DEATH, A BIRTH, AND THE HALL OF DISTINCTION

In 1949 Norma, aged nineteen, met John Datson at one of the dances held weekly at the Crystal Palace on Mt Eden Road. He was ten years her senior, returned from the war, and began to take her out. In summer I often slept in a pup-tent on the front lawn (hidden from the road by a high, stone, ivy-covered wall) and, hearing them talking at the gate, I sometimes went in pyjamas and joined in, they on the street side of the gate, I inside it. John probably found it deeply frustrating, but he was a patient, tolerant man with serious intent, and showed no sign. Soon he was coming to dinner, visiting often, and they were engaged. John was full of stories from his war experiences, first in the Middle East, then the Italian campaign. He had joined the New Zealand Scottish regiment, and his work had been in Army Intelligence, which in his case seemed to be keeping track of stolen equipment (including vehicles, often trucks, 'borrowed' by our own men wanting a brief holiday) and keeping some kind of lid on the black market. He didn't seem ever to have been involved in close combat; but there had always been dangers, especially from the skies.

His stories were full of humour, and peppered with the weak puns he had a taste and a talent for, which I enjoyed and Dad pretended to deplore. John's closest friend right through the war was Graham Perkins, who would be best man at their wedding (I was 'groomsman', Barry Catton and Don Cater were 'ushers'); and a few years later, when I bought Kendrick Smithyman's first book of poems, *The Blind Mountain* ('Oh, so you bought the other one,' said Ken, wry about sales), I found there was a sonnet addressed to Graham. Graham, Ken and John had been schoolboys together at Seddon Tech.

I always attended silently to John's stories, enjoyed them, and tried to imagine beyond the beginning, middle and end he gave them. I noticed there was one recurring part of the overall narrative that might start anywhere, as if arriving unbidden, and never came to a conclusion. John had been stationed for some considerable time at Senigallia on the Adriatic coast just north of Ancona, and was billeted there with a local family who had a daughter, Gina. It was clear (though John didn't say so directly) that he and Gina had liked one another very much; and also that Gina's family had been very fond of him. As defeated people, uncertain what to expect from the occupation forces, I'm sure they would have found him wonderfully easy-going and generous.

It seemed to me I saw two possible untold (withheld) stories here. In the first there had been a real affair with Gina and a tragic parting. He couldn't forget her and she couldn't forgive him. He had moved on with his advancing army, and never gone back. He had thought of doing what he was charged with preventing others from doing, 'borrowing' a truck, going back to her. Perhaps that is what he had promised to do. But . . . And so on: a Hemingway war novel, with elements of Scott Fitzgerald.

In the second story, the old stone house, the twisting cluttered streets of the little town, the views of the Adriatic, the fisherman's painted boats, the smells and sounds of the sea, the moon on the water – it was all charged with a love that went unspoken between them. He loved her, and slowly was able to believe that she loved him. But he knew he would soon move on with his army; that he could not make a life for himself in Italy. And could he ask her to give up this beautiful place for New Zealand? Perhaps even the thought of his rather conventional mother, and how she would deal with an 'Eyetie' daughter-in-law came into it . . . This was a Henry James novel, redolent of place and unspoken passion, in which nothing happened while below the surface everything was toil and torment.

I am no doubt elaborating beyond what I would have been capable of then; but I saw these two possibilities, and saw them as fiction – novels. Given John's temperament, I thought the second more likely than the first, though either would make a good story. On reflection it seems disloyal of Little Brother to have been inventing a whole other life for Big Sister's betrothed, who was clearly in love with her; but writers, even novice writers, are not to be trusted. Very recently I met Kathy, third child of Norma and John, and asked whether she had ever heard anything of John's Italian friend, Gina. She said she had known nothing until after his death, when a bundle of Gina's letters was found. They were all in Italian and Kathy had no idea what they contained. To me this seemed a wonderful confirmation, not just of memory, but of adolescent intuition.

For their wedding present I raided my vacation earnings and bought them a rather fine tea-trolley, or tea-wagon, in darkly varnished wood. These absurd domestic vehicles had an upper and lower deck and were loaded with tea-pot, hot water, milk, sugar, cakes and scones, and wheeled into the sitting room when visitors came for morning or afternoon tea. They were very fashionable at the time. I was pleased with my gift, and so were they.

I bought my first real suit to fit the role of 'groomsman'.

AFTER MY JOB AT DOMINION ROAD South Post Office I found myself
vacation jobs regularly. The next was at Foodstuffs Ltd warehouse
(suppliers to Four Square Grocers). Of that job I have a general recollection of long dull hours filling trolleys with orders from individual
shops, and twice daily sweeps of the floor on which I was instructed
first to scatter damp tealeaves from the smoko-room, a very effective
method of collecting the dust. Apart from that there is only one
particular memory. I was coming down the steps at the end of the
day, talking to a dim young fellow-worker about a book he had seen
me reading in the lunch hour about soil erosion. It was called *Down
to the Sea in Slips*, and I was laboriously explaining that this was a
pun, because you would normally say . . . And so on.

My dim fellow-worker suddenly brightened, because he had
thought of a joke. 'Down to the sea in *shits*,' he said. At this moment
I saw that Dad was at the bottom of the steps, waiting to pick me
up. I could see that he had heard my laboured explanation, and the
response, and that he was either embarrassed for me or, more likely,
worried, thinking I was becoming such an intellectual I didn't know
how to bring my conversation down to the level of the smoko- and
shower-rooms. He was wrong of course; but it is the job of a parent
to worry needlessly.

After Foodstuffs Ltd came, in the next vacation, a job at one
of the wool stores in lower Parnell, wielding a hook and wheeling heavy bales about for the sorters and classers. Fellow-workers
were interesting, especially the union radicals, idealists often, with
Midlands, Geordie or Scots accents. I worked a sixty-hour week,
and made twice the basic wage; but the pain and boredom of those
long hours were not to be forgotten, especially later when I sat in
a well-appointed university office, with books and pictures around
the walls, preparing lectures, or conducting tutorials, waiting for
my next sabbatical leave and feeling inclined to complain about
my lot. University teaching is much harder work than those who
look in from the outside imagine; but it is a life of leisure, diversity
and constant entertainment compared to the daily wage-slavery

('wage-slaves' was another weapon in the Grandmother's rhetorical armoury) of the ordinary unskilled worker.

The hardest work I did while still a schoolboy was at a job Barry Catton and I took in the fellmongery at Hellaby's Freezing Works, where the pelts of slaughtered sheep were scoured of wool, washed in vats of brine (or possibly acid) and 'fleshed' in roller machines to remove any remaining fat from the skin. Barry called for me soon after 3 a.m. and we rode at speed, 10 miles (16 kilometres) through the dark streets to start at 4. That first shift until a big breakfast at 7.30 was hard, but I think each got harder, until knock-off time at 5 p.m. We worked slightly shorter days on Saturdays and Sundays, and earned very big wages, setting us up for the remainder of the year. The work itself was heavy, loading pelts from the vats into big trolleys and wheeling these to the workers on the fleshing machines, mainly Tongans and Samoans, among them a musical group (electric steel guitars and singing) who were heard often on the radio and, though none was 'Hawaiian', went by the name of 'Billy Wolfgramm and his Hawaiians'.

There was an old fellmongery retainer who entertained himself with endless jokes that involved 'catching you out'. He would ask, 'What's the biggest drawback in Africa?' When you said you didn't know, he said, in a tone of triumph because he had 'caught you out', 'The *elephant's foreskin*.' Another was to ask very casually whether you were 'going over on Saturday?' When you said 'Over where?' the gleeful reply was, '*Over your balls with a scrubbing brush.*'

Such games didn't amuse the Islanders, who preferred to sing, and let me sing with them. But they had their serious side. When, in response to a question from Billy Wolfgramm, I admitted that I hadn't yet 'gone all the way' with a girl, he explained to me, very precisely, and in the tone of a tribal elder instructing a younger protégé, the useful physiological and psychological effects of playing with a girl's 'titties'.

In the smoko-room at meal breaks an illegal crown-and-anchor game was run by a Maori whose patter ('Place your bets, gentlemen.

Any more for the more?') was worthy of the croupiers I would hear many years later on the tables at Monte Carlo.

Elsewhere in the works, sheep were driven up a ramp to the knifemen (no preliminary stunning in those days), and whisked away on the chain, a hook through one rear leg, their scarlet throats hanging open. Penned bobby calves, crying pitifully, were hammered to death by a single slaughterman who waded among them like a lunatic gardener in a bed of red roses. One grew used to these horrors, or learned how to screen them out; but not without reflecting on the Nazi death camps.

The ride home, most of it uphill in the heat of evening, seemed sometimes beyond endurance. Then there was energy only for a meal and bed. But at the end of those hard weeks Barry and I awarded ourselves another holiday in Rotorua. This time we left bikes at home, got a lift down with Barry's Uncle Bill, and stayed in a small cabin in the same motor camp. Lacking bikes we were less mobile; and, exhausted from our stint as fellmongers, we spent much time doing very little, mooching along the railway line to play a pinball machine in the takeaways shop, or throwing sheath-knives at a target we pinned to a eucalypt on the edge of the camping ground. The noise we made at this game annoyed a camper who one morning signalled his displeasure by pinning to our tree a cartoon of ourselves tied there while a camper – himself – prepared to throw a tomahawk at us. The style was unmistakable. We had seen it five days a week for most of our lives. The displeased camper was Gordon Minhinnick of the *New Zealand Herald*.

Coming back to Auckland we hitched a lift with a friendly truck driver from the Ngongotaha sawmill.

THE 6A (I.E. SEVENTH-FORM) YEAR WAS one of quiet confidence and many pleasures. Life was still full of embarrassments (that would not change); but one was permitted, even encouraged, to take a certain pride in having got through the examination obstacle race.

We were the school's academic élite, and sat in the gallery of the hall during school assembly, removed from the prefect surveillance that went on in the body of the hall and distant from the eyes of the masters on stage in their academic gowns. It would have been better if one had been a prefect as well, and I crouched behind the parapet as the first list was read out, and then, a week or so later, the second, and was deeply disappointed not to be among them. There was a strong representation from Hedgie's defence force, which I had resisted in my lower sixth-form year; but some who were not significantly military had been chosen, and I wondered why I had missed out. I would like to be able to report that I didn't care; to ask, in a lordly (Yeatsian) fashion, 'Why would a poet want to be a prefect?' That would have been admirable. Alas, I did care, and demonstrated to myself at those moments that I was not a brave non-conformist, just a failed conformist.

We had a different, easier relationship with the masters now. Mr Coldham ('Georgie'), head of French and famous for conducting the school's massed singing, asked would I mind phoning him on Wednesday evenings when the BBC comedy programme *ITMA* ('It's that man again') was broadcast, because he was forgetful and didn't want to miss it. So there was a weekly call: 'It's Stead, sir, phoning to remind you . . .' 'Ah yes, thank you, Stead. So glad you did.'

Mr Brown ('Butch') used to put on his special threatening snarl-and-bark, the one that frightened the life out of third and fourth formers and junior house boys, but it was now a snarl in inverted commas, not to be taken seriously. He had his ceremonial joke cane, wound about with barbed wire, mounted on the wall behind his desk, but for us there was to be no caning.

Mr Calder ('Jasper' or 'Jazz') taught us history in the style of H. A. L. Fisher and J. R. Green (and Thucydides, I suppose – it goes back a long way!) – history as a big story, containing many smaller stories: the human comedy, as full of tragic fragments as a fruit-cake is of fruit. Jazz relished the fruit, especially the dark bits, and told us some things (the way Edward II was murdered, for example) which preyed on my mind and made me wish he hadn't. Years later I would encounter a snobbery (as I saw it) among academic historians, contemptuous of colleagues who still practised history as narrative rather than as interpretation. My response was always the same. Remembering Jazz Calder, I would say, 'A narrative *is* an interpretation.' High intelligence and critical detachment were also necessary, and an eye for the significant detail that would, so to speak, speak *for* you, and for itself.

We had a number of study periods every week, left alone in room A3 to make our own way with a subject. A lot of talking went on and not a lot of study, and I rediscovered there, from time to time, my old talent as Tusitala to Standard Two, retelling a novel, a movie, an historical or biographical incident. I remember recounting the whole of a movie, *The Golden Salamander*, with a sense that everyone was choosing to listen (anyone could turn away at any moment, or say 'Turn it off, Stead – I'm working') only because I was getting the telling right. I had puzzled over why some of Wordsworth's simple-to-the-point-of-simpleton poems had worked at the time they were written, and went on working now, and had decided it was nothing to do with 'poetry' (the eloquence that was so strong in his reflective poems), and everything to do with narrative. He was simply telling stories very intelligently and, quite by the way, putting them into rhyme. It was something that required, moment by moment, a clear and conscious separation in the story-teller's mind of what he knew (the facts, and where they led), and what the listener knew thus far. It was a special talent. Wordsworth had it; so did Jazz Calder; and so did I!

MAGS had a weekly Friday-night dancing class for senior boys, conducted in the hall along with girls from Auckland Girls' Grammar, supervised by Pearly Print and one of the AGGS mistresses. Partly what I liked was finding a girl who lived somewhere close by, who could be 'walked home' in the dark – the kissing and touching, the skirmishing on and around the foreshores of sex. I seemed always to be at ease with girls, sure of myself in a way I was not, or not always, in all male company – possibly because I had grown up with a sister and no brothers; or (putting it another way) with three generations of loving women, and a father who did his best but found me somewhat mysterious and unpredictable and so was not quite at ease with me. But apart from the girls, I loved the ballroom dancing for its own sake, for the satisfaction and sheer physical pleasure of doing it well. It was music again, music and the body brought into accord, as if the limbs and muscles had ears of their own, and heard and responded directly to the music.

I was soon going to public dances with Ian Lamont, Jean's younger brother, my exact contemporary, who had spent three years as a House Boy (boarder) at MAGS, and was now an apprentice motor mechanic. Aged seventeen, Ian and I were both desperate to 'go the whole way' with a girl – any girl really: better if she was 'really nice looking', but not essential. It was even a competition for who was to be first – one Ian was to win. But there were real obstacles. First the girls themselves, who seemed physically inclined but socially programmed to refuse; then the lack of opportunity – the fact that almost everyone, in those days, at that age, lived at home with parents, so you might be making good progress somewhere in (or, in summer, outside) the house, only to be interrupted by a light going on, an enquiring voice, an anxious mother or protective and threatening father.

Ian and I found ourselves in some strange places and at some surprising parties. I have a photograph from that time of myself with a young woman on my knee, beside a young man of my age with a young woman on his knee. I have written the names of my three companions on the back of the photograph, and the date, but I have no memory at all of two of them, nor of the occasion. I'm quite sure I never saw them again. In the photograph we are all carefully dressed (suits and ties, party dresses), posed and self-conscious. I do remember being in a bedroom with that young woman, I assume at or after the same party. No doubt I was applying the Billy Wolfgramm manual of seduction. Having said the usual no, but an enthusiastic kisser and toucher, she changed her mind and said yes. The light was off, we were still wearing most of our clothes, and I wondered about the logistics of getting them off – in what order? Shoes first, obviously. And in the dark I had to find the condom, which was in my jacket hanging on the back of the door. By the time I had it, and had my shoes off, she had changed her mind. I was sorry, but relieved. Masturbation was not as good as 'going the whole way' was going to be – I was sure of that; but it was a lot simpler.

Ian was quite tough, and brave. I admired him. Once he got into an argument with a dangerously large lad on the dance floor. It was agreed they would 'sort it out' later. I went as Ian's second, and the large lad had his own. I and the other second waited, silent on the main road, holding the combatants' jackets and ties (we all wore ties to those dances), while they disappeared into the dark of a side-street. After quite a time Ian emerged from the shadows, very cool, his white shirt stained with blood. The other second rushed off to find his friend. I asked Ian was the blood his. He said it was not, and we walked on home. I wanted to ask about the fight, but clearly he had won, and I could see he preferred this rather grand silence. No one carried knives in those days, so I assumed the large lad's nose had been bloodied.

Very occasionally Ian was allowed to bring out his grandfather's Rover, a wonderful car which I think he was charged to keep in running order while the grandfather was away overseas. But soon he had his own motorbike, a powerful Norton, and took me for fast spins along Dominion Road extension and out to Waikowhai. He worked with a motor mechanic who used to describe in vivid detail, which Ian passed on to me, the ways he had sex with his wife, including standing up in front of a mirror; and later how he had gone about fucking his son's girlfriend.

We went to a lot of movies together, and arriving home we used to wrestle in the dark on the front lawn. Wrestling was another physical pleasure. It involved pain as well, though one could always give in and concede the bout; and neither had any anger, or any wish to do more than win. But even the pain was a kind of pleasure. Our wrestling happened without talk, without preliminaries of any kind, and seemed such a natural, primitive, almost programmed thing to do, I see it now, at this great distance in time, as one would see two young male animals in a nature documentary, practising their fighting skills, learning, by doing it, what in time they would have to do in all seriousness, even to the death. It was something I always remembered, years later, when I lectured on *Coriolanus*, and came on the lines in which Aufidius speaks of dreaming of their contests:

> Let me twine
> Mine arms about that body, where against
> My grainèd ash an hundred times hath broke
> And scarred the moon with splinters . . . .
> Thou hast beat me out
> Twelve several times, and I have nightly since
> Dreamt of encounters 'twixt thyself and me:
> We have been down together in my sleep,
> Unbuckling helms, fisting each other's throat,
> And waked half-dead with nothing.

I was much closer to Ian than I knew. When he was killed a year later I felt such grief I remember lying face-down on our front lawn in the dark, holding on to the grass with both hands, with a strange, dizzying sensation that I was going to fly off into space. I had seen him, the evening of his death, down at the Balmoral shops, cruising on his bike, looking for me. I waved out but at just that moment he decided to turn, leaning wide, curving around and back through traffic, and roared away. He hadn't seen me and it was my last sight of him. Somewhere between Balmoral and Landscape Road he turned left up one of the side streets, accelerated, ran at high speed into the back of a truck parked in shadow between lights and was killed instantly. Someone in his family rang next morning to tell my parents to break the news to me.

I was by that time into my first year of university. I was given a lift to the funeral at Waikumete and was shocked that Ian's relatives chatted and joked as if nothing had happened. These were distant relatives and my reaction was absurd, part of my own inability to understand how the world deals with such events, and to know how I should deal with it myself. I was not, as T. S. Eliot would have said, or not yet, *un homme qui sait se conduire*, and didn't know (Eliot again) how 'to prepare a face to meet the faces that you meet'. In fact I went about for some days with a long face, as if it was necessary to *show* what you felt, like hanging a sign around your neck: GRIEVING. I began to write an elegy for Ian, a sequence of poems, which I sent, handwritten, to Charles Brasch, my first offering to *Landfall*. Brasch declined it, though saying he liked its 'freshness', and it was soon burned in one of my periodic literary incinerations. But the last of the sequence remained in my head, and became the earliest preserved poem in my *Collected* volume:

> Earth, you are frozen now,
> The dead-cold centre of a doom-darkened winter.
> Yet from this spiny row
> Of waxen, wasted willow-sticks must grow
> New life in spring.
> The sun will be warmer then
> And velvet leaves will spin
> A net of new-born comforts round old signs.
> Persistent sapling shoots in lines
> Of contradicting green
> Will not admit
> That dead-brown death has ever been.

My second, or strictly (remembering the one-hour life of little Irene) my third, sister was born at the beginning of 1950: Frances

Caroline. I was often the baby-minder. I learned, during that year and the next, to change nappies, give bottles, walk her up and down the hallway in my arms putting her to sleep, or sit in the dark on the floor beside her cot, one hand through the rails until I felt her release her grip on my finger and I could crawl to the door and out. I photographed her among flowers. I felt, over that time, bonded to her, as if I was as much part-parent as brother.

At school, in Butch Brown's 6A English classes, there was a lot that was random and almost pointless; and then moments that were flashes of illumination. Butch had many dog-eared sets of notes on important Eng Lit topics, and would sometimes dictate from these – the very worst kind of teaching. Then, before the notes had been completed, he would grow bored and change quite randomly to something else. He was not really a great English teacher, but a serious one, and a great personality; and perhaps those moments of illumination were the best one could hope for, because they were memorable, and stayed in our heads.

One such for me was the day he came into the classroom and looked around at us all with such an accusing, melodramatic eye, we all fell silent. He let the silence go on for a time, and then, in his snarling but curiously effective voice, he quoted,

> This short straight sword
>   I got in Rome
>   when Gaul's new lord
>   came tramping home.
>
> It did that grim
>   old rake to a T –
>   if it did him,
>   well, it does me.
>
> Leave the thing of pearls
>   with silken tassels

to priests and girls
and currish vassals:

Here's no fine cluster
on hilt; this drab
blade lacks lustre –
but it can stab.

It was a poem so suited to Butch, and to Butch's delivery, and so
good – economical, stark, direct – it seemed an electric moment.
None of us knew who had written it, and we were treated to Butch's
now in-inverted-commas snarl. We were 'an ignorant pack of slobs'.
This was a poem by a *New Zealand* poet, R. A. K. Mason, and we
should know it, and know his work. I made it my task to see that I
did, not to please Butch (I could have predicted that he would never
mention Mason again, and forget he had told us about him), but for
myself. It was probably by that route I came to Allen Curnow's *A
Book of New Zealand Verse*, and so to Curnow's own work, and to
the opinion (unusual at the time, but one I didn't waver from, and
waited confidently for the New Zealand literary world to catch up)
that Curnow was our major poet.

The other most memorable of these Butch-moments for me
occurred in the school library. We were all reading silently when he
interrupted and told us to listen. What he read was my first introduction to T. S. Eliot, in particular to *The Waste Land*, then hardly
more than twenty years old.

The river's tent is broken: the last fingers of leaf
Clutch and sink into the wet bank. The wind
Crosses the brown land, unheard. The nymphs are departed.
Sweet Thames run softly, till I end my song.
The river bears no empty bottles, sandwich papers,
Silk handkerchiefs, cardboard boxes, cigarette ends
Or other testimony of summer nights. The nymphs are departed,

And their friends, the loitering heirs of city directors,
Departed, have left no addresses.
By the waters of Leman I sat down and wept . . .
Sweet Thames run softly till I end my song,
Sweet Thames run softly, for I speak not loud or long.

My scalp prickled. I had never heard the conventional notion of poetic beauty so flouted, to such poetic effect. Butch had set me off on a pursuit that would only end (if it ever ended) years later when I had published two books in which Eliot, and the piece of literary history he occupied, and in part created, were right at the centre.

A third significant literary moment of that year had nothing to do with Butch or MAGS but came from a notion of my unpredictable father's, that he and I should go together to see Marlowe's *Doctor Faustus*, performed in the Town Hall concert chamber by Auckland University College students and produced by Professor Sydney Musgrove. Musgrove (though at this time I had never heard of him) was head of the English Department in which I would soon be a student, and would, later again, be employed. What put the idea into Dad's head I can't imagine. Had he read a review? Was some residue of his childhood Catholicism engaged by the thought of a story written by an atheist that ends in what seems unequivocal damnation? Or was it the appeal of a story about a person 'born of parents of base stock' who hopes to learn by magic how to gain 'A world of profit and delight / Of power, of honour'?

My vivid memory of it means it must have been well produced and well performed. Musgrove was as much actor as academic, and I would later notice how his lectures, delivered from tattered old notes, yellow and curling at the edges, would spring to life when he needed to deliver a dramatic passage from Shakespeare, crucifying himself against the blackboard, casting despairing eyes to the heavens, howling Lear-like into the storm. He would have coached his student actors well.

A schoolchild of recognised academic bent in Britain would, no doubt, by the age of seventeen, have seen any number of good productions of plays by Shakespeare and his contemporaries. We had read Shakespeare at school and acted out scenes; but this was my first full play production, and I was deeply impressed. The drama was simple and powerful, and I'm sure I was not bothered about whether there were God, Heaven, a devil and damnation *really*. For the purposes of the drama there were all those things, and to suspend one's disbelief with such encouragement was easy. That Faustus barters his soul in particular for the favours of a beautiful woman, and that he speaks his pleasures in such richly textured lines –

> O, thou art fairer than the evening air
> Clad in the beauty of a thousand stars . . .

> More lovely than the monarch of the sky
> In wanton Arethusa's azur'd arms

– all that was wonderful lead-up to the damnation itself, to the hero's courageous agony, his dismissing of his well-wishers from danger against the striking of the clock that marked the end of his life (the lines lengthening, mimicking the protraction of each last second) –

> See, see, where Christ's blood streams in the firmament!
> One drop would save my soul, half a drop: ah my Christ!

In a young and receptive mind it is surprising how a single and quite small door can open on a vast space. I had stepped into the field of Elizabethan and Jacobean drama and poetry, and once in, wherever else I went, I would take it with me.

I was writing poems and occasional stories at this time, and just once offered a poem for publication in the school magazine, the *Albertian*. I received no response from Butch, who was editing, and waited in hope. It didn't appear. So the man who would later include me in two of his *Verse for You* anthologies was the first editor to turn me down. I look at the *Albertian* for 1950. It is full of rhyme and schoolboy banality, as you would expect. My poem is long gone, a victim of the burn-ups; but I remember its opening two lines:

> No light there was, no sound nor sense,
> No moving shadows broke the night.

Perfect tetrameters. The first line might be improved (though it could be argued either way) by reversing its poetic inversion ('There was no light . . . '). I'm quite happy, even now, to reclaim the second.

IN JUNE 2008 I WAS INDUCTED INTO Mt Albert Grammar School's 'Hall of Distinction', along with two deceased Albertians (no longer 'Old Boys', because the school now admits girls). One was J. A. W. Bennett, a great scholar, fellow of Merton College, Oxford, and then professor of Medieval and Renaissance English at Cambridge – also the author, however, while still a solemn schoolboy, of the school's execrable hymn. ('Dusk on the walls and the twilight lingering / Darken yet lighten our half-dimmèd gaze, / While on the panels still bright with his fingering / God writes this legend in golden rays.') The other deceased inductee was the man who was New Zealand's first, and for many years almost our only, significant publisher, A. W. Reed.

I hadn't been in that hall for close on sixty years. It was there I had been t.k.o.'d by Darryl Harry; there I had crouched behind the parapet of the balcony, disappointed not to hear my name among the new prefects; there I'd received a number of certificates at prize-giving, and a small cup as school chess champion. Now I was unsure whether I was an unusually fit 75-year-old, or not long for this world. Possibly both were true. Over the previous summer I had reached a score of 100 (my challenge to myself, and a new personal record) swims out to the yellow buoy at Kohimarama. On the other hand, on the afternoon before the induction I'd had two stents implanted in a coronary artery, and spent the intervening night in hospital with heart and other monitors making sure everything was working as it should.

I still felt slightly tottery from the procedure, but I had made it and was on my feet. In response to the customary encomia I made a short thank you speech meant to encourage those who were, as I had been, apparently undistinguished. I said I had not been a star at the school, had not captained a team, had not won a scholarship or been made a prefect. I had left my face on a few sporting photographs but not my name in gold leaf on the walls. None of the masters of my time, I was sure, would have predicted a 'Hall of Distinction' career for me. I told a story about an Auckland lawyer who used to put his arm around me at parties, after I became known as an academic and a writer, and announce to the room, 'This is Professor Stead, whom I beat for the Lissie Rathbone Scholarship in 1950.'

I said my reply to this was always the same: 'It's important not to peak too soon.'

III
FROM FAR DARK WORLDS

Close in our white blades knife a harmless breeze,
Children brawl, the Gulf winks and beckons,
While down the fleeces of our sky blue signals ride
From far dark worlds where it is always raining.

FIFTEEN
151 DAYS AND A GENERIC FOR HEMLOCK

I enrolled as a first-year student at Auckland University College (as it then was – a college of the University of New Zealand) at the beginning of March 1951. At some time during that first day a fellow-'fresher' introduced himself as Rob Dyer, saying he had approached me because I 'looked like a poet'. When I found a way of admitting that I wrote poems, or that I tried to, he told me that he did, too – that was why he had approached me. Perhaps he had responded to an uncannily accurate inner prompting. Or perhaps he had approached three or six others before me, saying to each that he or she 'looked like a poet', and I was his first success.

Rob was very young, and came to university on a national scholarship, with a reputation for brilliance in languages. He had been placed seventh in New Zealand on the scholarship list in all subjects, and seemed destined (and I'm sure that is how he saw himself) for academic greatness. In that he was perhaps another case of 'peaking too soon'.

He had soon organised a group of mainly first-year students who wrote poems, and we met in what was called the Men's House Committee room to read our work to one another. We were mostly, but not entirely, chaps. The numbers varied that year and in the two years that followed, but there were more than a dozen of us, some distinctly talented, some less so. Some poems from that time and that group stay with me; one in particular I can still quote:

> You recalled the bay
> The still, out-stretched evening sky,
> The firm rippled sand
> And the gull's cry.
>
> And heroic battles we fought
> A burnt boyhood ago
> With delicate toi toi lances
> Like shaken snow.
>
> Now you are changed and older
> But I caught you a moment there,
> Naked, shouting with laughter,
> Wind in your hair.

That was Jack Tresidder, who became a journalist and now lives in France, author of a dictionary of symbolism and of several travel books. Few of us were so felicitous. Geoff Fuller had great potential, and was the first, I think (unless I was, with a poem in the *Jindyworobak Anthology* in Australia) to have an editor outside the university accept his work. 'Nothing belongs / To the woodwinds', Geoff wrote,

> when
> The melancholy note is slaughtered by the following gong
> (Yet the care is great in the player's stroke).

The Night cries, 'Follow me; and I will teach
You all you need to know . . .

The Night cried in vain, however. Geoff qualified in law, moved to Hamilton, and fell silent. Ted Sturmer, a Byronic figure, who looked like an angel and wrote like poor Poll ('Let me scale the scoriac slopes of Sumna / And stub my toe on the Matterhorn') went on to practise law in London where he discovered an ancient statute that made possible the merging of major banks (National and Westminster becoming NatWest was his first), and later would fly back and forth between London and the Americas, disentangling the web of deceit that was the Banco Ambrosiano. He now lives between a nice house in southern France and an apartment overlooking the Thames. Brian Horton, scion of the family that owned the *New Zealand Herald*, had a poem that began 'The clock decides twelve', and ran down into dim sonorities, where 'a falling star defies / Thirteen primordial equations'. He was to go on to Oxford and a distinguished career, first as Berlin correspondent for Reuters, then its managing editor in London; later foreign editor, then managing editor, of the *Times*, followed by early retirement in Spain. Paul Temm became a judge, Sue Renshaw a journalist, Bernard Clark (the one who beat me for the Lissie Rathbone Scholarship) a lawyer,[*] Douglas McArthur an academic, Phil Rau an army officer, Jeremy Commons an international expert on Italian opera, Peter Goddard a schoolmaster and schools inspector, Jenny Cooke a wife and clergyperson, later prison chaplain. We all had pretty good careers; but only Jack Lasenby and I survived as writers of poetry and fiction. Jack wrote poems about the bush, retired into it for his deer- (or was it opossum-?) culler years with the popular writer Barry Crump, and then emerged as a successful writer for children.

---

[*] Bernard died in February 2009 while this book was in preparation and Brian Horton (whose sister was married to Bernard for some years in the 1950s and '60s) in August the same year.

Rob Dyer was, in style, possibly the best of us, because he could be more measured in a language and tone that owed everything to the classical Roman poets.

On the lone long foreshore of his birthland
A man stands dusty, grimed from a journey
Through an imagination of ruins
And a pride of mindful words.
And he watches the sun evolve from the sea
Where only the ships of the bold set outward.
His heart has travelled too far to be bold
And begins to wear out at the knees.

My own poems showed technical competence, but tended to the lugubrious. I didn't stand out in that crowd, but I did have 'the want'. In an unpublished memoir written many years later Rob described me as 'much the best writer' (this was wisdom after the event), but 'shy to the point of nausea' about reading my poems to the group.

Rob and I were probably the most serious in our aspirations. We talked poetry a lot, and for him there was no embarrassment. For me, much more the typical Kiwi lad of those times, poetry was not something you admitted to in general company; and I remember asking him to keep his voice down when he shouted above the rattle of a tram, 'I thought that poem you wrote yesterday . . .' This inhibition was in part ridiculous, and in part a useful monitor of what I was writing. When I felt uncertainty about a poem, I would try to put it out of my head entirely and then let it back in during a soccer match, when the action was down at the far end of the field from where I (playing centre forward) was positioned. If, in those rugged circumstances, the poem didn't seem ridiculous, 'soppy', 'poetic' in the bad sense, then I could go back to it, and maybe even offer it somewhere. This was a time when I was learning, from T. S. Eliot and the Modernists, that 'dryness', 'hardness', the urban reality rather than romantic nature and the broken heart, were what poetry in our twentieth century called for.

During World War II Rob's father, Colonel Humphrey Dyer, though a Pakeha, had been for a time commanding officer of the Maori Battalion, and had been in the thick of extraordinary battles. I had not known Rob very long before he told me how, in the battle for Crete, his father had shot a mortally wounded Maori soldier who didn't want to be left by his retreating mates, and asked them to kill him. After the war the Maori family put a curse, a makutu, on Humphrey Dyer. The curse, it was said, was not because of the shooting, but because Dyer had shot the soldier in the head, and the head, to Maori, is tapu. Rob believed, then and for many years afterwards, that the curse extended to him as well, and that his problems in life, academic, domestic, and (while it lasted, through several marriages) a failure to have sons, were due to this curse.

Four decades after this first meeting with Rob, I was to embark on a novel about a World War II New Zealand soldier I called Donovan O'Dwyer, who was, I suppose I could say, one third Humphrey Dyer (the Crete experience), one third Dan Davin (the Oxford experience) and one third invention. What I found, however, in doing my preliminary research, was that there were two versions of the shooting of the wounded Maori: there was what I called 'the sanitised version', which (understandably) was the one Rob as a child had heard from his father, and which he continued to believe; and there was the true version, which Humphrey Dyer had written in a notebook and deposited in the national archives, evidently wanting the darker truth to go on record. In the version Rob had heard, the dying soldier begged his comrades to shoot him; in the secret notebook record, he was being dragged along by two of his mates, who refused to put him down and abandon him, and as the enemy was closing on them fast, and it seemed certain they would all die if they continued at this pace, Dyer shot him in the back of the head. These two versions formed an important crux in my novel *Talking about O'Dwyer* (Harvill, 1999), which has since appeared also in German, Spanish and Croatian translations.*

Rob was to cruise through his years at AUC, graduating with high honours, and make it to Oxford on a scholarship where, however, in some way not entirely clear, he came to grief, partly through conflict with his New Zealand-born tutor, G. F. Cawkwell, who, he said, tried to turn him into an English gentleman. Since Rob not only believed in his own English aristocratic lineage, but was also something of a New Zealand nationalist who took pride in his family's settler roots, this was bound to lead to trouble. In some accounts he was said to have thrown a meringue at Cawkwell at high table; in others it was a brick through the tutor's window. These stories, which had currency for a while, may of course be untrue; or, on the other hand, it may have been, at that time, in that place, quite a fashionable kind of behaviour. (Karl Miller, writing of this period, records that in a racecourse tent his Cambridge friend Rory threw a potato at the attorney-general, Sir Reginald Manningham-Buller.) Whatever happened, Rob never completed his Oxford degree. He came home, taught briefly back at his old Auckland school, King's College, then at Canberra University College, and was to spend most of the rest of his working life as a classics teacher in a rather posh American high school – good service, no doubt, and a worthy life, but not quite what he expected of himself in 1951.

On that first day, and for as long as I knew him as a fellow-student, Rob was intellectually both interesting and eccentric, rather patrician and well schooled in manner, yet socially awkward, too, especially with women. Certainly he was to confound expectations as much in this regard as in scholarship, marrying four times, the first wife a great-niece of the composer Rimsky-Korsakov, the latest a granddaughter of novelist and Nobel Prize-winner François

---

* In the German and Croatian translations the title is *Makutu*; in Spanish it is *Recordando a O'Dwyer*. I have since had reason to wonder whether both versions are true: i.e. that Dyer shot more than one of his soldiers.

Mauriac. Now retired, Rob lives in Paris with this distinguished and beautiful scholar-wife, chair of a committee charged with editing Proust's manuscripts. Since she is also mother of their three sons, Rob must at last feel that the curse has been lifted.

NOT MANY DAYS AFTER ENROLMENT I caught my first sight of Allen Curnow, walking up through Albert Park, and recognised him from photographs. The memory is still sharp, because already I had placed him first among the New Zealand poets. He was to be my tutor in second year, lecturer and mentor in my MA year; but in 1951 he was just one of a number of lecturers teaching in the Stage I literature course I was enrolled for. At the invitation of Professor Musgrove, who had been impressed by the long critical introduction to his *A Book of New Zealand Verse*, Curnow had just come from years as a journalist on the Christchurch *Press* to a lectureship in Auckland, and was now faced with the task of preparing everything from scratch. At a time when most of his colleagues still wore gowns and delivered formal, written lectures, Curnow's notes were hasty annotations in the margins of books and scribbles on scraps of paper. The pressure showed, and for a time he appeared seriously stressed, his normally copious hair falling out in handfuls, the random patches of bare scalp dusted with something prescribed as a cure.

Curnow's lectures at that time were often compared unfavourably with Dr John Reid's. Reid was a publicly well-known ball of energy, reviewer of films and books, Catholic proselytiser (tending at times to bigotry), who would soon publish good solid academic studies of Coventry Patmore, Francis Thompson, Thomas Hood, and one called *Bucks and Bruisers* about Pierce Egan and Regency England. Reid's lectures on Dickens might begin by announcing that there were 'seven levels of meaning' in the novel under discussion, and proceed to list them one by one, with illustrations. Students, especially younger ones, found this reassuring, and

Curnow, by contrast, unpredictable and disconcerting. What I soon recognised was that, with Curnow, you had to listen carefully, and wait. Sooner or later he would come up with a gem, an aperçu, one, often, which took even him by surprise, so that you saw the moment of recognition arrive, the light go on. It was like watching someone digging for treasure – and then finding it! That was your reward for an hour's attention, and it was always worth the wait. Reid was diligent, dependable, intelligent, organised; but there was never, or not for me, the shock of true intellectual discovery that there was with Curnow.

At close quarters Curnow was less a conversationalist than a monologuist; and once started, he was hard either to escape or to interrupt. In my second year, 1952, he was my tutor, and these sessions, which were really meant to be a conversation about a set text between a lecturer and a group of eight or ten students, were always, with him, solo disquisitions. Once into his stride, Allen didn't welcome interruptions. They confused him, put him off his developing thought. In general I was happy with this. I was still burdened with adolescent self-consciousness. Even to walk into the library, knowing that those up in the gallery could be looking down and watching (of course they weren't, and I knew that) made my shoulders freeze and my limbs move awkwardly. I preferred in class not to have to speak; but now and then the need that something additional, or other, be said, became more compelling even than shyness.

This happened once in a tutorial about a poem by Shelley, 'Epipsychidion'. I had read the poem, about which my feelings were distinctly mixed, and then a booklet about Shelley in which Stephen Spender suggested it ends in a 'collapse' – referring to the lines

Woe is me!
The wingèd words on which my soul would pierce
Into the height of Love's rare Universe,
Are chains of lead around its flight of fire –
I pant, I sink, I tremble, I expire!

Curnow was soon deep into his exposition of the poem, and it was clear that the only dialogue was going to be between tutor and text. As was his way with all poems he chose, either to lecture on or to anthologise, he was its advocate, its defender, its protector; and this was particularly so, now, of the lines in which Shelley writes with horror of conventional marriage, saying he never was 'one of that great sect' who choose a single partner for life, and as a consequence,

> With one chained friend, perhaps a jealous foe,
> The weariest and the longest journey go. *

For the young Stead, by now seriously engaged by the poems of John Donne, Shelley was temperamentally alien, stylistically slack, intellectually limp-wristed, and inclined dreadfully to *run on*. I wanted to hear at least a word of doubt or reservation. None came, and the hour was passing. I, of course, had no way of knowing how much this poem, this message, spoke to Curnow at this moment in his life – not stylistically but morally.

Tutorials occurred in the lecturer's office where smoking was permitted, and the chink in the otherwise impenetrable armour of Allen's monologue was his pipe. He had to stop, sometimes even in mid-sentence, to re-light it, and I used this gap to stick in my oar. Rather crudely (but one had to be quick) I said, 'Stephen Spender thinks the poem collapses.'

Curnow blinked his pained-lizard blink, where the lower lids seemed strangely to be the ones that closed, upward. 'What?'

I repeated Stephen Spender's opinion, adding, with ironic emphasis, that last line, 'I pant, I sink, I tremble, I expire!'

There was a significant silence, during which he clung to the pipe but didn't draw. 'Oh why,' he said at last, 'doesn't Granny Spender *get on with her own knitting?*'

---

* Hence E. M. Forster's title for his second novel, *The Longest Journey*, and its point.

Long afterwards, around a dinner table, I recounted that moment. It produced shock and disapproval. A tutor should not 'put down' a student who is trying to offer constructive comment. I can see, looked at in abstract, that if I had not been the student, if it had been someone other . . . But I *was* the student, and I had not felt 'put down'. Honour was satisfied. I had registered the one negative the hour would hear about Shelley and his 'Epipsychidion'; and I had elicited such a memorable and witty response (Stephen Spender was a bit of a 'granny'), I would retain it a lifetime later.

Entirely different, and almost a prototype of what tutorials were supposed to be, was the one I attended in history, conducted by Bob (R. McD.) Chapman, later to be the university's first professor of political studies and mentor of two Labour Prime Ministers, first David Lange, then Helen Clark. Chapman had a round, baby face, plump, pompous jowls, and the manner and voice of a Grand Old Man. He wanted to be counted among the poets, but only ever published a handful of very clumsy poems; he aspired to academic leadership, yet was never to publish a significant book, nor even to finish his doctoral thesis. But if the word 'intellectual' means anything (and something that is not simply disparaging or dismissive) that is what Chapman was. He was remorselessly, and rather abstractly, a 'thinker' – one who wrestled with ideas valiantly and not always with complete success. If he had arrived on the scene half a century later, he might have made a top-rate literary theoretician, where the confident opacity of his thought, and his inability ever to make perfect sense, would have been seen as virtues.

The Chapman tutorial I was assigned to, in which Bernard Clark (my Lissie Rathbone nemesis) and Barbara McKay (who claimed she had beaten us both, and only failed to collect the scholarship because her school had forgotten to enter her name) were also members, produced the most stimulating classroom interactions I would experience at least until I was an MA student in 1955. Chapman recognised our intelligence and engaged with us. No doubt there were others in that class, but I remember it as if there had been only three students and our tutor.

Another notable history lecturer of those first two years was Bob Tizard, who lectured to us on the causes of the First World War. Bob, later to be MP, Cabinet Minister and finally Deputy Prime Minister under Norman Kirk, was intelligent, hard-working, sure of himself, combative, and faintly boring, like one of those tuis that sing over and over just six notes, the first five unchanging, the sixth a harsh territorial squawk. The poetry in the family, the dash, the fizz, the panache, belonged to his wife, Cath. The Tizards gave great parties to which bright students were occasionally invited, and at the end of one such I was kissed a lengthy and unforgettable goodbye by the hostess. Cath was at that time mother of four, just getting started on late academic studies in zoology. Later, when her marriage to Bob was breaking up, or running down, they moved to a townhouse in Freemans Bay where their daughter Judith's friend Helen Clark boarded for a year or two. Judith was to be Minister for Auckland in Helen's Government. Cath became mayor of Auckland, and then Dame Cath, our first (and uniquely eloquent) woman governor-general.

WITH IAN DEAD AND BARRY AT TEACHERS' college, my social life was now lived entirely within the university – with my fellow-students in English, history and French, my teachers, my fellow-poets; and I had met Diane Henderson. Diane* was the daughter (only child) of Hubert Henderson, who had come to Auckland in 1950 to be district superintendent of education, and of French-born painter Louise (later Dame Louise) Henderson. Hubert, a New Zealand graduate, had gone as a soldier to World War I, after which he had stayed on for a time in Europe and graduated from both Cambridge

---

* Pronounced as in French, the i as in tea-tree, the a as in manuka, elided so the stress falls on the second syllable.

and London universities. During that period he had met Louise, a Parisian, who followed him to New Zealand where they were married in 1925. After the birth of Diane in 1933 Louise's parents came to Christchurch, so Diane, brought up in a house with three native French speakers, was bilingual; and in fact French was probably her first language.

It would be hard to exaggerate what an expansion of my consciousness the Henderson household was. They were intellectuals with a distinctly European flavour. The floors were polished wood with fine rugs. The walls were plain (no patterned wallpaper), hung with paintings, many of them Louise's, but one or two by her Auckland mentor John Weeks, and by members of the Thornhill Group with whom she exhibited her work in Auckland. There were white bookshelves, and many books, French as well as English.

The Henderson house was a meeting point for a cross-section of Auckland's intellectual community. A lot has been written about the Lowry house on the lower slopes of One Tree Hill; and as a senior student I went to exciting parties there and met exciting people. Louise and Hubert were less raffish, more refined, more *haut-bourgeois*, less dependent on alcohol-as-lubricant (though they drank good wine). I met poet A. R. D. (Rex) Fairburn there, painter John Weeks, critic and scholar Eric McCormick, Auckland Art Gallery director Eric Westbrook, architect Vernon Brown, liberal-left lawyer Frank Haigh and his wife, Honey, who was said to be Fairburn's mistress.

Hubert was a small man with a neat military moustache, a pipe, a big voice, and a large generous enthusiastic personality. He was a natural teacher, guide and mentor. When I showed signs of thinking myself rather fashionably left of Labour (which he supported), he asked had I read the *Communist Manifesto*, and when I said I hadn't, he gave me a copy. This was quite neutrally done, neither as advocate, nor on the other hand as critic. But it suggested, without saying so, that if I was going to argue in favour of something I should at least know what I was talking about.

Louise exerted a rather old-fashioned pre-feminist feminine power, often oblique, always intelligent and articulate, and with the added charm of a marked French accent. She was formidable, sexy, not altogether scrupulous, charming when necessary or advantageous, unpredictable – a strong personality, clear in her judgements, determined in the pursuit of her art. In that, she had the complete support of Hubert, her most devoted admirer, framer of her pictures, negotiator with galleries and buyers. She was also, it should be said, a painter of exceptional talent. I have lived a lifetime with some of her work, and the respect endures.

Diane was the product of all this, nature and nurture. There was possibly more of her father's temperament in her than of her mother's; but the manner, the manners, the acquired or conditioned temperament, were all Louise. Diane was slim, graceful, beautiful, charming, and I was in love with her. Of all the set books for Stage I English that year (and I remember most of them, and the pleasure and excitement they offered, as if I had read them only last week) possibly the one that seemed to speak to me most nearly and directly was F. Scott Fitzgerald's *The Great Gatsby*. Summer nights . . . Gatsby's parties, where 'men and girls came and went like moths among the whisperings' . . . Daisy with her charming stammer, 'p-paralysed with happiness' . . . The eyes of Doctor T. J. Eckleburg, blue inside their yellow frames above the valley of ashes . . . Golfing, grey-eyed, 'incurably dishonest' Jordan Baker, and sinisterly physical Tom with his bulging thighs . . . But above all, Gatsby looking longingly from West Egg across the moonlit water to the green light on the dock that marked Daisy's mansion . . . That was how the world seemed to me – glittering, so full of promise it might explode.

Was it how I saw myself in relation to Diane, I yearning, she so close yet ultimately unattainable? Perhaps yes, in some part of my brain; but I didn't doubt that she was in love too, as Daisy was with Gatsby. Diane would say, 'When we're married, will you let me choose your clothes?' – and when I answered 'Yes, of course' (not minding at all the implied dissatisfaction with what I was wearing now – I didn't like it much either) it was an affirmation, not just of the choosing of the clothes, but of our future together. Only (I would have said) something large and unavoidable, like fate, could prevent it. Or perhaps something small – like chance?

On 17 October that year, my nineteenth birthday and her eighteenth (that we shared a birthday seemed hugely significant) she gave me a copy of the beautifully made and printed, limited and numbered edition of Alistair Campbell's first book of poems, *Mine Eyes Dazzle*. Before coming to Auckland she had been at Wellington Girls' College with Fleur Adcock, now Campbell's young and beautiful poet wife. Alistair was beautiful; the poems were beautiful; everything was beautiful. Delicacy abounded:

> And now you rise
> And kiss me with such grace, I know
>   A goddess has usurped
> Your place, or a willow casual
>   As the wind, leans
> With its cool beauty through the room.
>
>   A small bird sings
> And breaks the frail morning. My dear one,
>   Turning from me
> You bend a shadowy brow and sigh
>   For one bird singing,
> One bird in the miraculous sky,
>   Singing, singing.

That was Campbell at his most delicate. I am not mocking, but I was mocked, especially by my poet friends, Peter Goddard and Phil Rau, who thought my passion for Diane, and the mournful poems that came from it, faintly, or more than faintly, absurd. One day that spring she left three kowhai flowers on my desk in the library, with a note that read, *J'ai chanté au bon Dieu et il a fait tombé trois cloches d'or dans ma main. Les voilà. Je te les donne. Aussi la larme au fond de l'herbe. Je l'ai pleurée dans un rêve. Travaille bien, mon amour. Diane.* [*] Phil had read it before I returned to my desk. He was merciless. He hugged himself, he pranced, he mocked. I was impervious, enchanted.

But there was a problem. I was in and out of the Henderson household; she was never within a mile of mine. I never invited her, nor told her anything about my family apart from the fact that I'd had a Swedish grandfather – because that seemed 'interesting'. Was I ashamed of my family? Perhaps – and if I was, that is itself shameful. I was certainly embarrassed at, and shied away from, the idea of taking her there. It was not just the differences in style, in sophistication, in taste; it was also the fact that my family seemed to have gone into an eclipse. With the change of government and the scrapping of the Land Sales Courts, Dad had lost his good job. Reluctant to go back to the drudgery of the Post Office, and with hopes for a seat in Parliament dwindling as Labour lost popularity, he had taken a job as accountant for the North Shore Bus Company and, when he was not at work, sat at home smoking, reading, casting the dark shadow of defeat over everything. Mum, with a new baby, was struggling at the same time to look after the Grandmother, who could hardly walk any more, needed to be dressed, and was slipping, probably into incontinence, certainly into dementia. To a young man for whom everything, even the commonplace, even consciousness itself, was in some degree an embarrassment, the thought of bringing the delicate, the ethereal, the ultimate Diane, into that precarious environment, presented itself like a wall. It would have to happen, wouldn't it? Yes, I supposed so, but for the moment it was consigned to the future.

---

[*] 'I sang to the good God and he made three golden bells fall in my hand. Here they are. I give them to you. Also the teardrop deep in the flower. I wept it in a dream. Work well, my love. Diane.'

Meanwhile other young men were attracted to Diane but were not encouraged and didn't persist. She went out once with Brian Horton in his large car. Brian had an eerie charm but was rather aloof, and it seemed, from her reports then, and his many years later, they didn't like one another much and the experiment wasn't repeated. Rob Dyer, having first dismissed her as a flirt, fell comprehensively in love with her, declared himself, and when declined, or rebuffed, or let down gently, decided 'life without Diane could not be endured',[*] and attempted (or so he told me soon afterwards) a classicist's suicide, brewing up hemlock and drinking it. In the memoir written many years later, however, he revealed that, lacking real hemlock, he had in fact brewed rhubarb leaves. 'It may have been fear alone, or the chemical properties of the leaves. My heart raced and pounded in my chest. I lay down on my bed and passed into oblivion.' He woke eighteen hours later, 'refreshed and whole, and went out to do some gardening'.

Diane had another suitor, whose name and face elude me – said to be rich (these faintly irritating distractions were often well-heeled) and to own a yacht. He invited her to his house, but said something that gave offence, something hurtful, and then refused to acknowledge fault or to apologise. She wept, and ran outside into the overgrown summer garden, while he sat at the piano playing Ravel's *Boléro*. This scene, as she recounted it, struck me so vividly I wrote a poem about it, which appeared quite some time later in the *New Zealand Poetry Yearbook*.

> outside the thin rain falls
>   on steaming leaves
> the curved and buttressed walls
>   dry under eaves

---

[*] This and the sentences that follow are quoted from the 1992 memoir referred to a few pages back.

down urn-flanked steps she runs
    among the trees
mist and the fragrance stun
    her velleities

and still the notes repeat
    from the hot room
ravel's *boléro* beats
    on the afternoon

mad she whispers mad
    her satin stained
shoes crushing fruit gone bad
    in the summer rain

delicate fingers play
    across her mind
the steps are ivory keys
    not left behind

and still his casual grace
    inflicting pain
tears and her ruined face
    and the drifting rain.

Diane went through phases of youthful self-re-creation. She was briefly a poet, and published a poem in French in the student magazine *Kiwi*. She turned singer for only a matter of days, and was heard about the house – a good voice, but not a lot of tune. But under these experiments, which might have been no more than the only child trying to discover something truly remarkable about herself to offer, and match, truly remarkable parents, there was, I was sure, pure gold – a loving heart, a firm personality, a charm that was all her own, and (incidentally) beauty of face and form.

1951 WAS THE YEAR OF THE WATERFRONT STRIKE, or Lockout, that lasted 151 days. The watersiders asked for a modest pay rise, and when it was denied, they refused to work overtime. The ship owners retaliated: overtime-refusers lost their jobs. So it was a lockout or a strike, depending on which side you favoured. But there was a division of forces within the trade union movement itself. The watersiders belonged to the radical Trade Union Congress (TUC), and were not supported in their action by the more conservative Federation of Labour (FOL). I supported – passionately – the watersiders. Walter Nash, Labour's leader of the Opposition (Peter Fraser had died the previous year), declared that he was 'neither for nor against' them, a political mistake which gave his enemies then and for some time to come a weapon: he was, they said, vacillating, indecisive, facing-both-ways, and so on. I suspect that was Dad's position too.

What radicalised the whole debate was that Sid Holland's National Government invoked the emergency regulations that had been enacted after the Queen Street riots (the ones I attended briefly in the womb) nineteen years before. This was what put passion into the argument, and made it a matter of principle. It was, after all, a fairly routine industrial dispute; but in a Cold War atmosphere in which the Korean War and the fear of international communism could be constantly played upon, the Holland Government treated it as a matter of national security.

Under the emergency regulations striking unions were deregis-tered and their assets seized. The army was brought in to work the ships. It was illegal to assist the striking workers or their families, even with food or clothing, or to argue their case in print or in public. Civil rights, rights of free speech, were effectively suspended. Governing without reference to Parliament, Sid Holland made free use of the radio on which any other reference to the crisis was denied.

The student body was riven. *Craccum*, the student newspaper, under the editorship of a portly and pompous youth, Gerald Utting, turned pro-government and anti-union. There were angry meetings. Resolutions were passed. I distributed pamphlets in the night on behalf of the workers, risking prosecution. The dispute lasted from 15 February to 15 July, by which time the militant unions were broken. The government, sensing it had the public on its side, then called a snap election, which it won with an increased majority, 54 seats to 26.

It was for me a bitter lesson, that New Zealanders were not deeply concerned about democratic rights, were shallow in their political perceptions, and easily manoeuvred, especially by fear, into voting against their own best interests. As Bill Pearson was to reflect in his 1952 essay 'Fretful Sleepers', 'New Zealanders may well wake up one day to find a military dictator riding them and wonder how he got there'. It was part of what lay behind my writing, some years later, a political fantasy, *Smith's Dream*, in which, in a time of crisis, the country acquiesces to a right-wing takeover and suspension of democratic rights.

IN OUR ROLE OF ASPIRING STUDENT POETS, Rob and I met James K. Baxter visiting Auckland – he in his grand role as *enfant terrible* of NZ Lit, the stern and drunken moralist who in an already famous address to the Writers' Conference in 1950, had told his fellows that the poet must be 'a cell of good living in a corrupt society'. Like Curnow, Baxter was a monologuist, but rather worse in that he didn't stop talking even when he had run out of things to say; and not either when he needed to relieve his bladder in the night on the tennis court outside the student union. There was a frightful Presbyterian monotone, and monochrome, to his talk, castigating New Zealand and our collective moral turpitude until a part of me wanted to affirm something really despicable and truly lightweight, or simply break into song and dance. But that urge was well suppressed. Baxter was, after all, a force, both on the page and in person. I admired his poems, and was no doubt trying, from time to time, to write Baxter-like pieces; so I gave him due respect. Rob took a rather loftier, faintly disparaging tone with him, and afterwards, in conversation and in letters, always referred to him as 'Jimmie'.

True to form in Auckland, Baxter went out to the West Auckland wineries with printer and publisher Bob Lowry, and the same evening, at the start of a poetry reading, was seen to pass down the aisle of the university hall pressed hard between Rex Fairburn and Allen Curnow – a puzzling entry, until one saw from behind that each of the older men had him firmly by an elbow, and that the galoshes he was wearing were hardly touching the floor. Legless for the moment: but he had time to recover. His two carriers went first, and then R. A. K. Mason, who (to put Garrick's aphorism about Oliver Goldsmith in its proper order) 'wrote like an angel and [read] like poor Poll'. When Baxter's turn came, he lurched forward into the light from the lectern, still wearing what I came to call his Presbyterian raincoat, and after a silence we all thought was going to last for ever, delivered his poems, unfaltering and all from memory, in that unforgettably resonant voice. Not, however, without giving new offence to the more sensitive among the audience by delivering a ballad which (from memory – I don't think I have ever seen it in print) contained the line 'some for a woman's fanny cry' while the 'I' of the poem insisted that he preferred 'to piss my money against a wall.' Such improprieties were to become commonplace in the 1960s; in the grim and proper '50s they produced just the kind of shock their author intended.

It was during that visit Baxter gave me a copy of *The True Confession of George Barker*, a poem sequence which, he said, T. S. Eliot had turned down for Faber; so it had appeared in a little cheap pink-covered edition. I say 'gave me', but perhaps it was a loan I forgot to return. In any case the little book was clearly important to him, and a strong influence on his poems at that time, mixing as it did cynicism about love, confessions of lust, and appeals to God for assistance:

I confess, my God, that in
   The hotbed of the monkey sin
I saw you through a guilt of hair
   Standing lonely as a mourner
Silent in the bedroom corner
   Knowing you need not be there:
I saw the generic man had torn
   A face away from your despair.

Like Barker, Baxter was always seeing God (and soon it would be the Virgin) through 'a guilt of hair'; and some of his lines seemed less original in the light of that little pink book. But that is how poets learn to be themselves; and if I could learn from Jim, why should he not learn from George? Bad poets borrow, T. S. Eliot was teaching us; good poets steal.

Baxter had given me the name of a pub in Wellington where the poets met, and I intended to return the Barker book when I passed through later that year on my way to play soccer at a winter tournament. Also, I hoped there might be a chance to tell Alistair Campbell that Fleur's school friend Diane had given me his *Mine Eyes Dazzle*, and how much she and I both admired it.

I found the pub, and Campbell was at the bar – yes, beautiful probably, though I don't think I noticed – just recognised him from his photograph in *Landfall*, and approached with due deference, asking was he indeed . . .

He confirmed that he was, and waited. What to say next? Forgetting my script about Diane and Fleur, I asked where would I find Jim Baxter, and when he said, with understandable huff, or miff, that he didn't know, I left, deeply embarrassed and cursing my social ineptitude. Many years later Campbell recorded a memory of the young C. K. Stead coming to pay him homage in that pub, wearing a long varsity scarf and carrying a hockey stick. There might have been a scarf; there was no hockey stick – and the homage was never paid, but it was intended, so his intuition was sound.

SIXTEEN
PAINS OF LOVE
AND WAR

I was not beautiful, but I talked well and was said to have good legs. There were three young women, friends of Diane, one of whom, P, took a special interest in me, and insisted (I was told many years later) they, the three, go to the student review in which I appeared as a Roman conspirator wearing a toga. I have a photograph of myself among the conspirators, wearing flattering make-up, though the legs are not in the frame. Barry Rodewald is there, dux of MAGS in our final year (he peaked too soon); T. J. McNamara, for decades, and still, the *New Zealand Herald*'s art critic (many peeks, no peak); Peter Salmon (who clearly got it just right) now his Honour Justice Salmon, recently charged with reporting to the government on 'the future of Auckland' – and others. I wonder whether all this promise showed in our singing. Those were the days when, whatever might be said for or against my legs, I did have a voice. I look at the photograph and remember a chorus sung to a melody from *Il Trovatore*:

What's become of Cassius?
What a silly ass he is.
He's a vegetarian –
His diet's unvaryin'.

P, I was told, also persuaded someone to take her by car, or possibly to take the three friends together, to 63 Kensington Avenue to view the address in secret during the summer vacation, because 'no one had ever been there' and my other life was considered something of a mystery. The story, as told to me, was that I was seen painting the roof. I have no recollection of painting the roof, but I suppose it might be true.

P, it seems, believed that I was in love with her – she had seen ample signs of it, and knew I was too shy to declare myself.

In the French class we both attended I had done a translation of a poem, 'Étoile d'Amour' by Alfred de Musset, not just a literal translation, but one carefully crafted into metre and rhyme. I thought it rather good, and gave her a copy. The last stanza read,

We're taught acceptance that your light must fade
Love's Star, étoile d'amour,
But pray you turn a moment at the door
And smile upon the folly you have made.

P believed this was my declaration. She arranged to meet me one night after lectures, and explained, as we walked to where she caught her bus, that my message had been understood, my love was welcomed and returned.

Poetry is dangerous stuff. I tried to explain that the poem was Alfred de Musset's message, not mine; that I was in love with Diane and there was no room for anyone else. Unfortunately, I felt the blow should be softened, and hugged her; and when it was clear she wanted to be kissed as well, I obliged – no more than a comfort kiss, but it made everything worse. She wept, walked on, letting her bus go by, holding me by the hand, drawing me with her up past Grafton Bridge, where great-grandfather Robert Flatt to the left, and great-great-grandfather Martin McDermott to the right, offered no advice to the distant fruit of their loins.

We had got to the top of Symonds Street and turned into Khyber Pass Road before I decided there was no use persisting. I had explained myself. She would have to accept it. I left her weeping and headed back towards the university, feeling as if I had left a blood-stained corpse on the pavement. Then pity gripped me, and I turned back to try again to help her understand. At the corner we hurried into one another. The tears were gone. That was what astonished me – the speed and completeness of the transformation. She was furious, her face set like iron. It is something that stays with me, an image, I suppose, of the will – the other face of love.

I said I just wanted to be sure she was all right. She said, coldly, that she was, and we parted.

IN THE MAY OR AUGUST VACATION OF 1951 Barry Catton and I got work as yardmen at AFFCO's Southdown Freezing Works. We were put on a small gang out of doors building a fence around the manager's house. It was terrain typical of much of Auckland, a thin but very fertile topsoil over (in geological terms) quite recent scoria from a lava flow. So to make the fence-posts we had to go through the topsoil and into the scoria. Holes were 'drilled' in the rock, charges laid and exploded, and the posts cemented into the resulting cavity. I put 'drilled' in inverted commas because what happened in fact was that one member of the team lay on the ground and held a steel spike about a foot in length, and another, the foreman, swung an enormous iron hammer and drove it into the rock where the explosive was to be set. Barry and I were the youngest, and the only non-union men, so it was our job, turn and turn about, to hold the spike. Looking back it seems (like so many things one agreed to do at that age) a kind of madness. It would have taken only the slightest deviation of that hammer, left or right, and a wrist or arm (or head) would have been smashed beyond repair. We should have refused, but that would have been seen as, and would have felt, shameful and cowardly.

That was the last time Barry and I worked together; and very nearly the last time I saw him for the space of what has turned out to be a lifetime. I was due now for compulsory military training (CMT); he was excused on the grounds of myopia.

In fact Rob Dyer had devised a scheme meant to save himself, me, and anyone wanting to join us, from military service. He had checked and been told officially that the only accepted ground for conscientious objection was religion; so this son of a war hero had, with my help, devised a new religion, Dionysianism, in which a primary tenet would be pacifism, and had written to the Department of Internal Affairs attempting to register it, and ourselves as the Society of Dionysiasts. Many weeks went by and we had long since given up any hope of official recognition when a letter came telling us what we had to do next. Unfortunately Rob's original letter had been handwritten, and we were addressed as the Society of Drompiasts, whereupon the joke lapsed. I think Rob's military service was deferred more than once, and in the end he got away to Oxford without being called in.

So at the end of that academic year there were for me only a few weeks of well-paid work at the wool stores. At the end of December I was called to report at Papakura Camp for an initial four weeks' basic training, after which I was assigned to the Signals corps and sent to Trentham for a further six. We were paid, but very little (in a letter I mention eleven shillings per day), and most was spent in the canteen, or on Friday night leave, and on fines. My first charge came within days of arriving, when my hat badge was deemed insufficiently dazzling at morning parade. This offence was not dealt with summarily, however. I had to appear before a court presided over by an officer. Not permitted either hat or webbing, escorted by the Regular army corporal who was in charge of our platoon hut,

I was marched by a warrant officer before the CO of our company. 'Prisoner and escort, quick *HARSH!* Prisoner and escort, *HALT!* Right *HURN!*' The charge was read: '328175 Recruit Stead, you are charged with conduct to the prejudice of good order and military discipline in that you did appear on the Papakura Parade Ground with a dirty hat-badge, how do you plead?'

When I went to plead a case for the offending badge, and naturally unbent a little from the position of standing to attention, I was bellowed at from behind by the WO, who, like all of his kind, made a virtue of voice-volume: 'Stand to ten-*SHUN!*' It is very difficult to argue a case while standing rigidly upright, arms at sides.

The army was full of absurdities of this kind, rules, orders, discipline, regimentation, morning parades and inspections, marching and saluting, with few rewards and many punishments – fines, 'confined to barracks', extra parade ground duty, cleaning toilets and peeling potatoes, the latter known as 'vegetable fatigue'. It would not have mattered so much if the whole system had not been full of solemnity, self-congratulation, reverence about itself. The little corporal, my escort in the hat-badge drama, was so in love with the army, he found it hard to believe that those of us who had already passed some units towards a university degree, and could therefore have enrolled for Regular force officer training, did not do so at once. He told me his CO had told him *his* only chance of a commission was if there was 'a scrap' in which he did something heroic and won a medal (a VC for example); so he hoped for war and the chance to prove himself. Hedgie Boulton (whose report on my years as a school cadet, still preserved in army archives, says I was 'not willing to work at the job') would have understood. I did not.

I think it was Britishness that made it especially absurd – the class divisions, officers who were gentlemen and non-commissioned ranks who were not; and all the potential that followed – for deference on one side, swank on the other. We were forever standing about waiting to know what we were to do next, while officers either knew and couldn't say because they needed, first, an order from above; or pretended to know when they didn't. Only a British tradition could produce so much muddle and confusion out of so much shouting. More orderly people (here speaks, probably, the wishful Swede) manage themselves better with less fuss and noise.

I know the piety is that in the desert, and in the campaigns that followed, the New Zealand troops, because they were less wracked by class-war and class-privilege, were more independent, self-reliant and efficient, better soldiers – and perhaps they were. The charming story goes that when Monty complained to General Freyberg that the New Zealand soldiers didn't salute much, Freyberg replied, 'Just give them a wave and they'll wave back' – and it's probably true. But we were still in the grip of empire; and only a year or two later when the new young Queen was crowned there was a renewal of loyal enthusiasm, amounting sometimes in New Zealand to fervour, as if the wave didn't diminish on its journey outward from the centre, but reached greater heights the further it travelled.

And finally, and perhaps most significantly, there was the Cold War emphasis military training now took on. Following World War II there had been the J Force – New Zealand's contribution to the occupation of Japan; and now we had troops fighting in Korea, helping the Americans 'save us from communism'. The fact that during our exercises the enemy was always designated as Red was one of many things that made me a reluctant, indeed resistant and sometimes recalcitrant, soldier. It was not that, for me, much of the old leftist idealism about the Soviet Union ('all that corn and ballet in the evening', as Peter Sellars put it) survived; more that my focus was on our primary ally, America. I was disturbed by its policies abroad and by its McCarthyite repressions at home. In particular the execution of the Rosenbergs, Julius and Ethel, Jewish parents of two small boys, seemed to characterise the shadow that was falling over 'the land of the free and the home of the brave'. I didn't know whether the Rosenbergs were guilty of passing secrets to the Russians, and didn't care too much, because the idea of the

United States alone possessing nuclear weapons seemed hardly less frightening than the two superpowers both possessing them; and in any case it was a state of affairs impossible to preserve for long. So the death sentences seemed needlessly brutal; and the offer to commute Ethel's sentence if she would confess, and betray her husband, thus confirming the justness of his execution, seemed cruel. It made a heroine of her for refusing, and victims of them both – he with his small moustache and rimless spectacles, both dressed in their dark, proper suits, and their foolish '50s hats, leaving behind only uncertainties, and two infants orphaned by the state.

There were things about barracks life I enjoyed; and I was surprised to notice there was no one I really disliked. But I was never going to give my Signals corps CO, Major Pope (an amiable army sentimentalist), an easy time.

The transfer to Trentham was a welcome change of scene, and made our training more (but not very) interesting. I was now a signalman and went with my fellows on expeditions in trucks and jeeps into remote countryside north of Wellington, bearing old zc1 transmitter/receiver sets, as up-to-date as the .303 rifles that were also standard issue. But I now had new friends, in particular John Edwards and Dick Jessup. Dick was (or said he was) a communist who would later climb high on the business ladder in the world of insurance. John was a science student, tramper and mountain climber, who would go to Cambridge on a scholarship, become a world expert on the African assassin bug, and spend much of his academic career as professor of zoology at the University of Washington (Seattle).

Of the three of us, John's resistance, or protest, was the most effective. He had less ego, or more confidence, and was not unwilling to pretend to incompetence. On the parade ground at Papakura he pretended to be unable to march in step, and put on a show of huge corrective hops and bounds as he mimed the actions of a simpleton trying to 'get it'. He drove instructors mad, because the incompetence was so well acted, the lack of co-ordination so apparently genuine. (This was the man who would, years later, be one of the team that made the first successful winter ascent of Mt McKinley in Alaska.)

There would be those, including poor dear Major Pope, to ask what was the point? Our behaviour was 'immature', irksome to those inclined to take the whole enterprise seriously. We – Dick, John and I – would have answered that we were victims of the war-nostalgia of our elders. The regimentation seemed pointless. It subdued the subduable and made enemies of the intelligent and independent. I found recently a copy of ROUTINE ORDERS for 1 Div. Sig. Regt at Linton Camp for 29 November 1953. Under the strange heading 'Extracts from Sqn Casualty Returns' it records 'Promotions', 'Cpl V. D. B. Cater to Sgt'; and 'Punishments', Sigmn C. K. Stead fined two pounds for 'disobeying a lawful command'. Ah Kensington Avenue, how I had failed you, and how proud you must have been of Sergeant Cater!

On the other hand, we were living mostly out of doors, in tents, enjoying a totally physical, 'boy scout' life, where from time to time the unexpected happened. One day I climbed a tall pine on a bluff – really the furthest bank in flood time – above the Manawatu River and found, very near the top, that I had upset nesting magpies. They worked as a couple, squawking and narrowing on me in converging circles, so if I faced one I had my back to the other – an unofficial lesson in military strategy (theirs), and in the necessity that retreat (mine) must be orderly as well as swift if it was not to lead to disaster.

All three of us read a lot in camp; and I remember sitting in the cab of an army truck camouflaged under trees, reading *Sons and Lovers* in a mood of Lawrentian alertness and revolt. John was also an occasional poet, and already a man of decided (conservative) literary and musical tastes. On one of our later annual training exercises, out from Linton, he persuaded me to eat a live huhu grub. It was hard to swallow; but not as hard as his opinion of a formal but strident sonnet 'On a New Zealand Soldier Killed in Korea' I had published that year in the Australian *Jindyworobak Anthology*, and again in our *Craccum Literary Supplement*: 'It stinks,' he wrote to me. 'It's like a column by Aunt Daisy written for the *Daily Worker*.'

AT THE END OF 1951 I HAD A-PASSES in English and history, a C in geography[*] – six papers, three units, enough for me to complete my bachelor's degree in three years. I had also been enrolled that year in French but hadn't 'kept terms' and so had not been able to sit. My intention had been to go on to an MA in history. This was partly out of sheer enjoyment of the subject, partly from hearing Keith Sinclair and Bob Chapman (they could sometimes work in tandem, though not for long) argue that poets did better if they were not burdened with too much knowledge of the history of literature. They in Auckland, they pointed out, Bill Oliver at Victoria and Colin Newbury in Canterbury, were among the next wave of poets after the Curnow cohort, and they were all historians. It sounded convincing; and of course it didn't occur to me that they were just hoping to secure a bright student for their own department. But I was now swinging the other way, inclining to the idea of going through to an MA in English.

I had spent my first year doing what was required of me in class and written work, but also reading more widely in poetry. Donne's *Songs and Sonnets*, no significant part of any course I was taking, had extended my idea of what poetry could be – tough, passionate, unsentimental, complex, real. There was still something of the lout in me, the rough youth who rode on the back of Ian's motorbike and competed for who would be first to 'go the whole way' with a girl; the one who had done labouring work, biked, shared a tent,

[*] I'm quite sure a C was all I deserved. But there was an interesting glitch that year in the examination paper. There were instructions that had to be converted into a map. If you followed the instructions exactly it produced a map in which the river was running uphill.

a lakeside cabin, and even (once) a girl, with Barry, and been quite at home in the smoko-rooms of freezing works and wool stores. I wasn't about to reject that self; but the lout had sensibility and intelligence, and was capable of refinement; and in Donne's poetry there was space, amplitude, room for us all.

My reading was also establishing T. S. Eliot as part of the inner library I would carry with me always; and there were the beginnings of a knowledge of Ezra Pound. But at the same time I was reading almost everything in what was called 'the Glass Case' in the University Library's English room. These were in fact two or three glass cases containing New Zealand poetry, and the name would later be transferred to the new library building, where the 'case' became an air-conditioned room. You asked at the desk for the keys, and were handed them – if you were lucky by Kay Roberts, the dark beautiful one among the younger library staff. This glass-case reading was not part of the courses offered by the English Department, but now constituted one of my most pressing engagements with the printed word. Without being quite aware of it, I was preparing myself for a time when these books, this rich corner of literary history in the English language, would become an important part of what any self-respecting New Zealand English department would offer.

But to go on to an MA in English you needed a European language to Stage II. So I would have to pass French I (two papers) in my second year, French II (three papers) in my third. The 'ear' person who, because he had learned the language the wrong way round, had to 'see' French words in his mind's eye before making sense of them, would be approaching these papers like Byron on horseback or swimming, hoping no one would ask him to dismount, or come ashore, and reveal his club foot.

IN 1952 LOUISE HENDERSON WENT back to Paris where she spent most of the year working in the studio of one of the original Cubists,

Jean Metzinger. Diane and I spent more and more time together, at the university and at her home. We did what students do, worked together, went to parties, to concerts, movies, acted in plays and revues. There is a photograph of us at the Civic Wintergarden cabaret where, once or twice, we went dancing; another, a street photo, of us with rhubarb-/hemlock-survivor Rob Dyer in Quay Street. There is a studio portrait of Diane looking like a French *ingénue*; a tousled, wind-blown snap of her without make-up or pose; one of her in costume for a play in French – *Le Malade Imaginaire*; and one of me dressed for a part in *Lady Windermere's Fan*.

There were certain things that seemed significant to us, even momentous: the opera *La Traviata*, for example, with that melody in the overture which emerges so much later, and then only in a few heart-wrenching bars, in Violetta's dying 'Love me, Alfredo' in the final act. There was the movie *Les Enfants du Paradis*, with its final scene in which the beautiful Garance and the mime artist Baptiste are lost to one another for ever in the Mardi Gras crowd. There was *The Great Gatsby*. Alfredo and Violetta; Baptiste and Garance; Gatsby and Daisy – it might seem on reflection that we knew what lay ahead. I enjoyed the music, the cinematic beauty, the eloquence, that was wrung from those tragic stories; but for myself and our future, I was incurably an optimist.

In August, on my way to the winter tournament in Christchurch, I wrote to her, in pencil and in French, on a New Zealand Railways suggestion card while waiting to board the ferry. I complained about the cold and the wet, described a desultory day filling in time with fellow-students (we had seen *Blood on the Sand* at the Roxy Cinema), and concluded that I loved her *de tout mon coeur. Et si ce n'est pas assez, je ne sais pas dire en Français que ce n'est pas tout.*[*] I went on to score some good goals in the soccer tournament in Christchurch, and to hear Ngaio Marsh adjudicating in the inter-

---

[*] 'With all my heart. And if that's not enough, I don't know how to say in French that it's not all.' Letter lent to me by the recipient in December 2008.

university drama competitions, striding among us in her tweed skirt and sensible shoes, strict but charitable, and baritone.

There was love – lots of it. Diane was fearful, uncertain, erratic, and passionate. I was fearless, certain, unwavering, and passionate. The problem of whether and when to take her to meet my parents was never mentioned, and I put it away for the future – a pity, because she and my mother, both only daughters with one foreign parent, both strong egos and capable of great charm, would have interacted in ways that could only have been interesting. There were rocks everywhere, but I thought we would get through them and cruise on into eternity – and we might have done that if another of those 'distractions' (as I have called them) had not turned up, again with a car, a bank account, a family business and the air (though not in French) of *un homme qui sait se conduire*. He invited her out. We, she and I, were modern, enlightened, and agreed this sort of thing should happen. It happened again . . . and again.

Some time I think early in 1953 I grew uneasy and issued an ultimatum. It was time she stopped going out with him – or, alternatively, with me. While she made her choice between us (and this was really to show I meant what I said), I would be absent at an annual camp with the Signals corps. I don't remember dates or details, only that she was given time, and the demand that she make up her mind. I was confident – not from *self*-confidence, but from what she herself had told me – that the outcome could only be in my favour.

I have said I want this account to be as truthful as I can make it; but writing about amorous engagements with, and disengagements from, people who are still alive can seem a trespass. So I will approach this part of my story by a circuitous route, which requires me to go ahead one or two years, when my brother-in-law, John Datson, secured a vacation job for me in the foundry at MacEwan's Machinery in Penrose where he worked as the company's buyer.[*]

---

[*] In *The Writer at Work*, University of Otago Press, 2000, pp. 85–86, I wrongly date this at the end of my first university year.

My work, making sand moulds, involved operating a heavy, jolting machine that shook the damp sand down and made it firm for the molten metal. Once or twice a week, the furnaces were fired up and a 'pour' was done. Next morning the cast-iron pieces, having cooled overnight, were broken out of the moulds and taken away for polishing, whereupon the whole process began again.

In the smoko-room there were a few shelves of grubby paperbacks with lurid covers, clearly chosen as entertainment for unsophisticated manual workers. Among these, however, I found one called *Conjugal Love* by Alberto Moravia. It had the usual lurid cover; but I soon found I was reading a novel very different from all the rest; and different, too, from the modern English-language novels that figured in my English literature courses. Stylistically it was striking, highly visualised, in the Italian manner, and 'intellectual'. It was my first encounter with what would later be called 'meta-fiction', where the story is partly about itself as story, and how it came to be written.

But what is relevant here is that in this, and almost everything of Moravia's I read subsequently (and I went on reading him over many years), there was a first-person narrator, and an underlying concern about 'provenance' – how what is told is known, who knows it, and whether the story teller can be trusted. Later I would find essays in which Moravia argued that in the twentieth century, now that 'God' as previous centuries had understood the word, was dead, there could be no 'eye of God' novel; no ubiquitous, all-seeing, all-knowing narrative voice. The story had to be dramatised; it had to have a human source, and that source had to be located, identified, and itself be part of the story.

This focused an anxiety of my own in my attempts to write fiction; and in my first two substantial published stories, 'A Race Apart', written about 1958–59, and 'A Fitting Tribute' (1963), I not only had first-person narrators, they were distanced from myself in that both were female – the first a middle-class, middle-aged Englishwoman; the second a very young Kiwi solo mother.

Neither of those stories was derived directly or obviously from events in my own life; but my third, 'A Quality of Life',[*] was. I tried to remove it from myself by various kinds of disguise. The events take place on a mythical South Pacific island called Nova. It is narrated by a man in his middle fifties, already a grandfather, famous in his homeland, and successful beyond, as a novelist. I was, at the time of writing, none of these things, and imagined that this smokescreen, together with the meta-fictional element (the story is about a novel the writer has completed and is now burning in his garden incinerator) would protect me, and those I was writing about. Whether the story was successful or not (a quite different question), it was naïve of me to think speculative connections with real events and real people would not be made, and Eric McCormick, in his role as elder statesman of New Zealand letters, took it upon himself to reproach me for what amounted to fictional home invasion. All I could say by way of defence was that the story mixed things which had happened and things which had not, and no one, not Eric (Louise's friend), not anyone but those involved, could possibly know which was which.

Early in the story the narrator describes how he has come upon a poem (it is by W. B. Yeats, but the story doesn't say so) containing the lines

> And I took all the blame out of all sense and reason,
> Until I cried and trembled and rocked to and fro,
> Riddled with light.

He goes to the library to find out more about the poem, and learns that it was written when the poet had just heard that the woman he loved was to marry someone else. This causes my narrator to remember his own feelings under similar circumstance in his youth, and sets him writing the novel which he has just completed, and

[*] *Five for the Symbol*, Longman Paul, 1981, pp. 113–38.

which he is now burning in his garden because he has realised that truths discovered in the course of writing it can never be told.

So 'A Quality of Life' was fiction. But it did contain, in a tone that walked a fine line between tragedy and comedy, certain emotional truths derived from life:

> One night when I was walking home from Veena's house, full of my hopeless passion, having just kissed her and failed to extract from her any guarantee that the deep love she professed to feel for me would last out the night – walking under a clear sky watching the moon come and go among the branches that overhung the street I was suddenly conscious that all this would pass, that she would not marry me, that I would not die of grief or even carry away from our affair a wound or impairment that anyone would be able to detect. That love is blind is not merely a cliché; it is untrue. There at the dazzling centre of my passion I saw the future with perfect clarity, and in the wisdom of my seared soul I spoke calmly and with authority to the lesser mortal I might become: 'Don't mock.' That's in essence what I told myself. 'When it's over, and you are over it, don't grow to think yourself superior to the man you were. Respect him.'
>
> You may laugh, then, reader – it is your right. But I may not.

Diane's engagement was announced in mid-1953 and she was married early in September. I remember well the afternoon of her wedding, my feelings of hollowness, of disbelief, of regret. I doubt that I gave any thoughts to the possessor of the car, the business and the bank account. If I did, they would not have been friendly; I would not have wished him well. But I'm sure my thoughts were all of her, and of what we had lost. It was happening in a Presbyterian church in Remuera, followed by a reception at the Henderson house, attended by many of our student friends. Understandably, I had not been invited. Rob absented himself, but did not miss the opportunity to deliver Diane advice: 'Happiness', he wrote, 'is never wondering whether what you have done is right; whether you have the best of what is offering; that is the part only of a child. You have been a little like that, but you are older and more poised now.' He wished her well ('Good fortune tend thee') and concluded, 'I hope you will never again have need of me and that we will always be friends.'

How had she needed him? What was the help he had given? He didn't say. To me he had already written (kindly, but not meaning it), 'Actually, you were much too good for her.'

> And I took all the blame out of all sense and reason,
> Until I cried and trembled and rocked to and fro,
> Riddled with light.

It's interesting that all these years later I cannot find any confirmation that Yeats wrote this poem, 'The Cold Heaven', after receiving word that Maud Gonne would marry someone else. That is a piece of insecure intelligence I must have picked up somewhere, or invented. Harold Bloom calls it 'the freest complaint of Yeats's defeated love for Maud Gonne' – which is near enough. He also calls it 'a communal voice', remarkable for its 'fullness in presenting the self's unguarded encounter with its own remorse.'

SEVENTEEN
THE QUEEN AND SOME OTHER YOUNG WOMEN

In the meantime some less important things had happened. In 1952 a King had died. At the end of that year I had passed English II and History II (three papers each), and French I (two papers). In 1953, around the time I was learning to accept (if I did accept) that it was all over between me and Diane, Ed Hillary back at base camp with Tensing Norgay told their British mates, 'We knocked the bastard off.' A day or so later a new queen was crowned. Our Prime Minister, Sidney George Holland, in London for the coronation, was described by the BBC commentator as being in 'such a state of loyal ecstasy' he seemed unable to contain himself. The *New Zealand Listener*, usually dependable in its choice of poetry, gave a whole page to a sort of anthem by one Walter Brookes, the verses surrounding a large and elaborate EIIR, and interspersed with heraldic illustrations.

> Lord who unto this day
>   Wast England's guard and stay,

Whose hand was seen
In days with sorrow fraught,
In days which came to naught,
Our guide in deed and thought,
Save our new Queen!

– and on in that manner for twelve unfaltering verses. There was talk in Britain, and it echoed out across the 12,000 miles between, of 'a new Elizabethan age'.

Lacking Diane, I had looked around for a new friend. In French classes there was a student, Thelma, with beautiful thick red hair. In a moment of half-serious levity Diane had once told me she envied that hair, and that if I ever went out with it she would be intensely jealous and deeply displeased. Thelma and I were soon close. It was meant to be revenge but became a real friendship. We read poetry together at her house and listened to recordings, especially of Stephen Spender reading his own work. Sensitive, faintly quavery, faintly absurd; sincere, posh, authentically himself – it was all there in the Spender voice:

I think continually of those who were truly great,
Who, from the womb, remembered the soul's history
Through corridors of light where the hours are suns
Endless and singing. Whose lovely ambition
Was that their lips, still touched with fire,
Should tell of the Spirit, clothed from head to foot in song.

It was strangely Shelleyan from the man who thought 'Epipsychidion' collapsed; but you would not look to Spender for anything as mundane as consistency.

I bought his *Ruins and Visions* (marked down from nine and sixpence to seven and sixpence). Next came his autobiography, *World Within World*, and Thelma and I read it together, matching up its confessions, uncertainties and tentative triumphs with the poems. I took some comfort from a scene in which the young Spender approaches his equally young but unequally formidable fellow-undergraduate at Oxford, W. H. Auden, asking whether he, Stephen, is really 'any good' as a poet. Auden confirms that he is. 'We do not want to lose you for poetry,' Auden tells him. Foolishly, typically, Spender asks, 'But why?'

'Because,' comes the cold reply, 'you are so infinitely capable of being humiliated. Art is born of humiliation.'

We read some of the best-known of Auden's work too; but I was trying to escape from the kind of forms that move always towards a tight ending, the final rhyme closing the door on the experience rather than opening a window beyond. Better for me at that time was Louis MacNeice's *Autumn Journal*, and I tried my hand at that sort of ongoing loose-limbed diary poem:

> Sunday morning, and I wake to hear the rain –
> Steady beat on the roof and in the street,
> Water splashing from a broken drain
> And shaking the blossoms outside my window;
> And over it all, faint above the steady beat
> Church music rises from the radio below –
> 'Abide with Me' quivers on the heavy air,
> And still the steady beat inviting return to sleep.
>
> And I think how easy it would be to believe again,
> To lie here sending prayers like arrows
> Into the heart of God; to thank him for the rain,
> To ask forgiveness
> For what time has rendered irretrievable now . . .

It was not true that it would have been 'easy . . . to believe again' (and when had I ever?). I suspect Diane was still lingering in the line about 'what time has rendered irretrievable now', for which 'forgiveness' might be asked. But at least the writing was relaxed and the tone of mawkish lamentation gone.

I was also discovering that deliberation, regular application, hard work, though they were as necessary as the athlete's or swimmer's training, would not in themselves produce real poems. There was something else, mysterious, and never predictable. It had been called 'inspiration', or the Muse; and it was often doubted and derided, usually by academic critics who thought poets 'made it up' in order to excuse silences or to render the process more interesting. It was, I was finding, real. I could decide to 'write a poem', and would now and then succeed well enough, and often fail. But there were very rare moments when a poem – even a poem with a complex form and rhyme scheme – would seem to write itself. Nature, as Matthew Arnold says, will now and then 'take the pen from the poet's hand' and seem to do it for him. It was here my interest in Zen thought and practice found a place. I thought of it, not as a tapping of the unconscious (as it was frequently explained), but as a speeding up of the consciousness. Consciousness outran itself, and outran memory, so it seemed almost as if at one moment there was not a poem, and then there was one – though the marks on the page gave clear evidence of work. 'Night Watch in the Tararuas' was written in that way. It is very much a poem of its time, tight and complex in form, owing something to Donne and something to Baxter; yet it was written with great ease. And a few years later when Frank Sargeson commended the work I had put into it, and pointed out the auditory play in the phrase 'the knife-edge knowledge of death', I had to conceal from him the fact that I had never noticed the echo. It had happened, 'naturally', in the state of aural grace out of which anything good I was capable of in poetry came.

Thelma was clever, a good talker and listener, inclined to be salty, disdainful of sentiment and nervous of sex – a good companion, an intellectual friend; but there was something apart from literature and intellectual things that bonded us. We were both, we agreed, and especially together, terrific ballroom dancers. I have never danced with anyone so intuitive, so perfect. We went to public dances (the Wintergarden cabaret usually), not for the before and after; not for anything but to dance. I still remember it with a kind of exhilaration. Thelma was slim, pale-skinned, of immigrant Scottish parents, with that mane of red hair swinging out behind in the turns, or falling in a russet cascade when I held her around the waist and she leaned back against my arm.

Marilyn Duckworth in her autobiography comments that when looking back to one's youth quite short periods seem to have lasted a very long time; and I think my dancing days with Thelma possibly lasted not much more than one term. I am able to find only one sheet (page 6) of one letter from her, undated, and in this she concludes, 'Perhaps it's just one of those warm fragrant nights – perhaps it's the mood – I don't know except that I begin ever so slightly to miss you.'

Perhaps it was more than just the warm fragrant night. I had met blonde bosomy Susan, English-born (she would go back there later), confident, noisy, middle class and jolly, a new friend, another *kind* of friend. There is a letter from her written from her parents' farm in Waimauku during the May vacation. She and I have met as participants in the capping revue and have spent 'a hectic week together'. We have hitch-hiked right around the top of the harbour on the tray of a truck collecting farm vegetables for the market, and partied, and embraced in the dark of a warehouse smelling, like the Psalms, of dried fruit and almonds. 'O darling wasn't it crazy, but wonderful? I miss you too much to be good for you. [. . .] I have to go to bed. I wish you were here my darling, 'cos I love you.' There is a lot more of that sort. Two or three months later she is writing the kind of letters one writes when the 'crazy but wonderful' time is over and you don't want it to be.

THIS WAS SUPPOSED TO BE THE FINAL YEAR of my BA – English III and French II (three papers each) and Philosophy I (two papers). A European language to Stage II was a prerequisite for going on to an MA in English. Otherwise I would simply have finished my BA with English III, History III and Philosophy I, and done the MA in history.

I was in Linton undergoing with the usual reluctance my compulsory annual holiday[*] with the military when I got the news that I had passed Philosophy I, English III (with an A), and failed French II. The failure seemed extraordinary – hardly possible. One paper was a period of French literature, where I knew I could do well; and a history of the French language, for which I had prepared with care. Another was set books, and again I felt safe, well prepared and good at translating from French to English. That left paper A – 40 per cent French into English where I thought I should be safe, and 60 per cent English into French where I knew I was not. In this I worked too slowly, conjuring up the forms of irregular verbs, the subjunctives, conditionals and reflexives, the verbs that took *être* and the ones that took *avoir*, unable to be quick and spontaneous. The ear person, who had learned by sight off the page, didn't at that time understand what was wrong, or know how to unlearn and begin again. Still, I had prepared myself so carefully I found it deeply puzzling – or would have, if the marker in that crucial paper A had not been the egregious Dr West.

There is now a seat – a sort of park bench – with a plaque memorialising Dr West in the courtyard outside the building in which, during my last years as professor of English, I had my office.

IN MEMORY OF
DR ALBERT WILLIAM HARVEY (DICK) WEST
1905–1988
FIRST NEW ZEALANDER TO GRADUATE WITH A
DOCTORATE IN FRENCH FROM THE UNIVERSITY OF PARIS
OUTSTANDING TEACHER SCHOLAR PERSONALITY
AT THE UNIVERSITY OF AUCKLAND 1942–71

---

[*] Army archives show I was in camp (Linton) twice in 1952, for three weeks in February and a further three weeks in November.

I have sometimes thought of dousing it in petrol and setting fire to it. I am doing it now, symbolically.

Dr West, 'Dickie' as he was known to his students, was an awkward stiff-shouldered man with a big voice and strange mannerisms, famous among the young women for what the feminists of the 1980s called 'ogling'. I don't think he seduced his female students; the idea that any of them would be willing was unthinkable. He just yearned, and it showed; and this was innocently exploited by young women requiring extensions on overdue essays. It was widely known and acknowledged in student conversation. I don't recall that anyone deplored it. It was just 'Dickie', and Dickie was a relatively harmless absurdity.

A walk-on part in this drama belongs to my fellow-undergraduate Emmie Moore. Emmie was lovely – tall, slim but ample, blonde, an easy, outgoing personality, sporty, boyish, a more glamorous Jean Lamont. Then or later I always thought of her in conjunction with John Betjeman's 'A Subaltern's Love Song':

> Miss J. Hunter-Dunn, Miss J. Hunter-Dunn,
> Furnish'd and burnish'd by Aldershot sun,
> What strenuous singles we played after tea,
> We in the tournament – you against me!
>
> Love-thirty, love-forty, oh! weakness of joy,
> The speed of a swallow, the grace of a boy,
> With carefullest carelessness, gaily you won,
> I am weak from your loveliness, Joan Hunter-Dunn.

Emmie and I were friends only in the classroom, cloisters and caf, and possibly once or twice on the court outside the student union; but to the burning, stiff-shouldered Dr West, our sitting together at the back of his classes must have set off intolerable imaginings. He had seen me about for close on two years with the divine Diane. Now, dog that I was, I was making Emmie Moore my next victim.

At the end of one of his lectures he waited while the class filed out. As I passed towards the door he detained me. We, Emmie and I, had been talking in his lecture and doing something with a piece of paper. Had we been playing noughts and crosses? I said no, I thought we'd been doing a composite doodle while listening to his fascinating lecture. I wondered why, if we had both disturbed him, only I was receiving the rebuke, but I didn't ask that question, and I apologised. He went on grumbling in an undertone, and I went on acknowledging fault, while the new class came in for the next lecture. Suddenly gathering his gown around him, with the sort of dramatic movement he was prone to, he swept to the door, stopped, turned back, and shouted, 'And in future, Stead, *you leave that girl alone in my lectures.*'

I was left at the front of the newly filled classroom, all of them looking at me and wondering what I had done. It was a good trick and I should have let him have his triumph; but it was below the belt, I was embarrassed, and I pursued him to his office in the tower.

He was not courageous at close quarters. I suppose pursuit was unexpected, and I was indignant and *féroce.* Possibly he felt threatened. He listened to my complaint, and said nothing.

Our next encounter was in a conversation-class. I was now careful to put space between myself and Miss Joan Hunter-Dunn. Dickie took up a position at the front of the small lecture room with one foot on the front desk, leaning forward with his hands on the bent knee. The desk was too high for this to have quite the effect intended. Rather than nonchalant, he looked uncomfortable. Nonetheless he held the pose. After a few innocuous exchanges with dependables about the weather, he turned his beam on me and asked with the heaviest sarcasm, '*Dîtes-moi, Stead, qu'est ce que c'est qui fait* un grand homme?'*

The animus was so patent it produced a small shot of adrenalin, and an instant reply. '*L'occasion, Monsieur.*'

* 'Tell me, Stead, what is it that makes *a great man?*'

It still seems to me the perfect answer, because 'occasion' in French means what it does in English, but it also has overtones of chance, opportunity and luck. I should have been (as I well might have been) tongue-tied. It would have suited him better.

When the news of a failure at French II reached me, I had to revise my plans. I could not go straight on to an MA; and since I had been receiving a government teaching bursary, I would have to spend a year at teachers' college while completing the BA. Back in Auckland, the picture of how I had failed became clearer. In those days you didn't pass individual papers, you passed units. So an average of 50 per cent over the three papers for French II was a pass. I had easily averaged the necessary 50. But there was another rule that you must not get less than 38 in any one paper, and Dickie had marked me down so far on his paper, it didn't matter how well his colleagues marked me, on that technicality I had failed not only his paper but theirs as well, and the unit.

Byron's club foot had been amputated at the hip.

THE BAD NEWS CAME TO ME IN LINTON in November, in a letter from Kay:

> I am awfully sorry. I wish I could write a message of comfort. The only thing I could think of was that you don't have to wonder hopelessly that you shouldn't be at Varsity at all . . . It's just a horrible nuisance really, isn't it? So much for my clumsy but very well-meant condolences. I read a little bit of Pound the other day that reminded me of you in the army:

> > And I am homesick
> > After mine own kind that know, and feel
> > And have some breath for beauty.

Kay Roberts, the famously beautiful and formidably literate young woman in the university library, was one of two new friends I had acquired during the second half of 1953. The other was Jill Evans. They had been at school together, and seemed at first to come in a single package. Kay was known to have a handsome boyfriend, a kinsman of Rob Dyer's, a King's College lad called Lawrence who went among his friends by the name of Rupert and whose parents had a sheep farm on the Awhitu Peninsula. Later I learned that, to give herself a rest from him, Kay had sent him to Australia where, after staying with her sister and buying a rifle, he was hoping to shoot crocodiles.

Jill seemed non-specific in her male attachments, though there were always some about. She was a singer, with a fine, true, lyric soprano voice; a natural actress, too. I have an enlarged photograph of her, which she has signed as a movie star might, 'Best wishes, Jill Evans' – but in a rather untidy hand with ink blots. If the contents of a woman's handbag, or equally her handwriting, should be considered the mirror of her soul (which would be unfair), Jill must have been beyond salvation. On the other hand if she could have sung at the Gates to Paradise, the handbag inspection would have been overlooked.

Jill and Kay were both verbally quick and clever, both intensely irreverent, laughed a lot, pretended when together not to be serious about anything, and made a startlingly fine-looking pair – Kay dark-haired, olive-skinned, with fine eyes and a lovely mouth; Jill slim, sandy-red-haired with keen, eager features. I found them intimidating but persisted, and seemed to be accepted, at least on probation, though not particularly by one or the other.

By November, when I went into Linton Camp, the friendship was close enough for me to be writing to them both, and they to me. When I came out I took a Christmas job – long hours again – with Jill in the mail sorting room in the Central Post Office, and sometimes (or was it only once?) I went home to Northcote with her by ferry. This was before there was a harbour bridge, and rather than take the road from the wharf to her house we walked around the bays, stopping at intervals, lying down to rest under bluffs from which the pohutukawa, just then coming into bloom, hung out recklessly. Where did I sleep? I asked this question recently, and she said she thought she put me in the garage, to sleep in the family car. I have no memory of it, but I believe her. Later Kay was with us there. It seemed a very romantic time, as if the harbour water was always a tranquil mirror for a moon that was always full. The three of us seemed to share everything, even once or twice a bed, though more or less chastely. Jill's mother, finding us thus compromised in the middle of the night, remarked darkly, 'It won't be the same in the morning', and left us to it.

Kay at this time was being vigorously pursued by our fellow-student Ken Piddington, son of the professor of anthropology and destined for a distinguished diplomatic career; and I once spent an uncomfortable night with him in the Men's House Committee room, being woken at intervals and asked not to spoil his chances with Kay because his intentions were entirely serious and matrimonial. This future Commissioner for the Environment had biked all the way out to Henderson to fix Kay's family's corrugated-iron water tank (Te Atatu Road at that time had no mains supply); and I didn't tell him that the repair had lasted only half a day, nor that I had made a much more favourable impression by giving Kay, while we were dressing to go to a ball, the structure and outline for an essay she had to write.

At the end of 1953 her newly crowned Majesty came to New Zealand – the first reigning British monarch to visit. She was stationed first at Government House, Auckland, next door to the university, and was there on Christmas morning when news came of the Tangiwai disaster of the night before.[*] Her Christmas broadcast had to be rewritten to incorporate sustaining and consoling words about it ('Mey husband and Ey . . .'), but since New Zealand

* See p. 43 above.

time is twelve hours ahead of Britain, that was perfectly possible. In Government House gardens that morning a group of Auckland schoolchildren sang her Christmas carols. One of them, a portly boy called David Lange, would many years later meet her in his role as New Zealand's Labour Prime Minister.

I took my little sister, just about to turn five, to see the Queen as she passed along Princes Street in an open car. I sat Frances up on my shoulders, as Dad had done for me to see the funeral of Peter Fraser. This was also, in its more banal way, a moment of history, because there would be a slowly, and then not-so-slowly, diminishing return of fervour for the British royals as New Zealand grew up and grew out of its colonial mindset. I took Frances because I knew she would find it exciting – as one would take a child to the annual Santa Parade – but I didn't share the fervour, nor affirm the symbolism. This new Queen, harmless in herself, destined to be effective because able to seem entirely characterless, still represented the empire and the British class system, which no self-respecting young New Zealand intellectual could want his country to go on being part of. To see the huge New Zealand crowds in effect reaffirming those things was embarrassing. One felt ashamed, and looked to the writers, and especially the poets, Fairburn, Mason, Curnow, Glover, Baxter, for an independent voice, an end to this ancillary status.

The literary nationalism of that time was salutary, sanitary, necessary. It challenged what prevailed in the media and in New Zealand's common conversation. It took courage and it gave offence. I remember that when a British peer was reported to have described the Queen as 'dowdy, frumpish and banal', New Zealand seemed collectively to receive this, not as an amusing piece of gossip from afar, but as if insulting to ourselves, wounding, a punch in the stomach.

I WAS BY NOW BEGINNING TO BE A published poet. Looking back at my work of those years, published and unpublished, is not full of surprises at youthful brilliance. In fact the British peer's 'dowdy, frumpish and banal' would not seem an unfair description of much of my early writing. Now and then there is a stanza, or a short poem, that stands out for feeling, or technical management. Recently I found this from that time:

> I walked the lake's bright shoreline winter made
> Leafless, and in that thin, exacting air
> Thought how the sun that round me only played
> In black and white on sullen, lifeless things,
> Oceans away found colour in your hair
> And warmed your blood with your imaginings.

That long single sentence running easily through its interlocked rhyming pentameters signalled things to come. But mostly I was still finding my feet.

The new year, 1954, was my teachers' college year, the year of marking time while I completed French II. It was also Kay's year, the year when Kay and Karl became K & K.

Kay came from Henderson, in those days a village on the western edge of Auckland under the Waitakere Range ('the Waitaks'), where people from Croatia's Dalmatian coast ('Dallies'), and the Lebanese Corban family, were establishing what became the New Zealand wine industry. This is the 'Loomis' of Maurice Gee's novels. Kay was at school with Maurice and, like him, learned to swim at Falls Park. Her father was Henderson's town clerk.

Her family were conservative, English father (recently dead, at the age of 53), mother New Zealand-born of Protestant Irish parents; National Party supporters all. Kay was in revolt, the rebellion signalled first in sending 'Rupert' on his Australian croc hunt, and now in announcing she was going to marry a pinkish student-poet who had just failed to finish his degree. Checking there was no one about to hear, her farmer grandfather, Uriah McClinchie, said to me out of the side of his mouth and in the accent of the Rev. Ian Paisley,

'Why don't ye get y'self a proper job?' Her oldest sister, married and affluent in Australia, and trying to put a good spin on what was about to happen, wrote, 'What if you do have to skin along for the first year or so – doesn't matter so long as you get on.' Her middle sister, married in Auckland and already mother of one, told me at our first meeting that I should not be a full-time student; she had been part time, and that was better. Their mother, who must have known Kay and I were lovers, and was frightened of possible outcomes, was keen for us to get on with it, and accommodating. My own mother, who had shed possessive tears at the news, was silent and displeased.

I ask Kay (this is 55 years later) what she remembers of that time. We are in the car, coming back from swimming at Kohimarama. She remembers wanting to see me, and the thought coming to her that she should go to Lewis Eady's music shop – and there I was, in one of the booths, trying out the classical records I couldn't afford to buy.

I remember our taking the lift to the roof of Radnor Apartments over the road from the university and the joy of finding a secret place where we could be alone together, out of sight; and a 'sickie' taken at Cheltenham, in the water and among the lupins.

We both remember being rained on making love in the pines above Waikumete . . .

She says, 'I didn't want to marry you.'

'So why did you?'

'You wanted to. Mother wanted it.'

'You could have sent me off to shoot crocodiles.'

'You would have refused. And I didn't want to lose you. I just didn't want to get married.' When I question this she says, 'You were still in love with Diane.'

I remember how, parting, we used to say, 'Don't get run over' – a mantra, but hiding so much feeling, such anxiety at the thought of loss.

'Not true,' I tell her. 'That was over, and I was over it.'

HERE IS HOW I THINK I SAW MYSELF: Right through the three years of my BA I was troubled by arguments about the freedom of the will. In my first year, writing an essay about Shakespeare's *Macbeth*, I annoyed my Irish tutor, Jim Walton, by taking an unorthodox path past the usual moral arguments into the question of free will. What was Shakespeare trying to represent in the supernatural figures who set the action in motion? Are the witches Macbeth's will? Is he free to do other than he does?

The subject came up in history too, where a question like, 'What were the causes of the First World War?' implied a whole complex equation of acts of will for which responsibility might be assigned.

It was there quite specifically in my third year when I did Philosophy I. I got only a C for that, though I had given careful thought to the problems posed, and was sure I deserved better. Later, when I came back to the university as a member of staff, Bernard Pflaum, who lectured in ethics, came up to me in the common room and said, 'Why didn't you tell me you were a brilliant young man? I would have given you an A.' This was only half a joke. Pflaum, a Jewish refugee who also told me he read only the beginning and the end of Stage I exam answers, had taken a strong line on the freedom of the will and moral responsibility, and didn't waste too much time on the subtle doubts of Stage I students. If you were worth more than a C, that would emerge later on.

I always felt the conjunction of 'free' and 'will' was the moralist's sleight of hand. We all knew what it was to make an 'act of will'. But logic seemed to challenge, or at the very least demand to know what was meant by, the claim that it was 'free'. The act was a product of the actor (who could not choose to be someone else), the moment and the circumstances. It was a product of its history and its 'now'.

Even in French literature the problem had come up in relation to the Existentialists, who aspired to *l'acte gratuit* – an action so 'gratuitous', so out of character, so *not* the natural outcome of its time and place, it would prove, and assert, your individual existence and your freedom. But the wish to commit such an act itself became part of the total of circumstance, the history from which I could see no escape. It was socially necessary that we should all behave and speak as if we possessed freedom to choose and were responsible for our actions. But 'socially necessary' was not the same as 'philosophically true'. This was simply society's contribution to the determining nexus.

This crux is at the centre of the poem that gave a title to my first collection, *Whether the Will is Free*. The speaker is watching a girl beating time to music, and seeing outside the window a dog, and a bird hopping on snow:

> [. . .]
> Whether the will is free the shiver
>
> Runs in me that ruffles the feather;
> Whether the will is free the beat
>
> Of the doved hand, the dove moan,
> Chords my mind to the gramophone.
>
> [. . .]
>
> May be I'm the girl, the bird, the stream,
> The hungry dog in this iron time,
>
> Not hell-bound or heaven-bent,
> Willing to get to where I'm sent.
>
> Under its ice my small life crawls
> Pecking and snuffing at grey walls . . .

Hell-bound / heaven-bent in the sense of hurrying to get some-where? – or bound by fate and bent by it? Willing in the active or the passive sense? These ambiguities (as in the word 'determined', which can mean 'intent on' or 'destined') were alive, deep in the language itself. So Yeats's 'And I took all the blame out of all sense and reason' was intelligible without any acknowledgement of 'free will'. It was the ancient recognition that if the gods curse you, though you have done no wrong, nonetheless the blame belongs to you; and if they bless you, likewise the blessing is yours though you have not earned it.

It is an affirmation. I had been cursed; and now I was blessed.

KAY DID NOT WANT TO MARRY. Helen Clark wept on her wedding day, not because she didn't want to live with Peter Davis (she was living with him already) but because she felt the necessities of politics were pushing her into falsity, compromising her honesty and self-respect. The British biographer Ann Thwaite, my exact contemporary, who married the poet Anthony Thwaite in the 1950s and remains married to him, said to me once, 'In our day we married to have sex.' It was a licence to live together. That was why the paraphernalia of it, the white dress, cake, presents; God, clergyperson, and promises; the speeches, the pushing together of Montagues and Capulets in smouldering bonhomie – all of it – was so repellent to pathologically honest Kay.

Nonetheless, she defended our plan against suggestions from across the Tasman that it shouldn't happen, that we should 'wait'. 'I had a letter from Aileen [oldest sister]', she wrote to me, 'crying quits and agreeing with me on certain points at least. I shall write a letter of cautious conciliation. Not giving an inch though.' But she worried about her own role in the future:

> I think I must have something to steer towards apart from marriage, as you have in your writing [. . .] so that we can be partners working side by side towards something apart from ourselves. I am afraid of spoiling the balance by turning towards you instead of going

along beside. Like parallel lines going smoothly till one goes off, either inwards which would be me, or outwards which might be the way you would react if I *did*, and it is ruined. Do you understand? I need a direction. Do you think reading and finding out about things would be sufficient? – I don't think I am a creator. Without you I am more exposed to other people, particularly those here, and I buck increasingly against the idea that to be a wife and mother is an end in itself. No one suggests that a man should be nothing but a husband and father. This isn't feminist talk. It's women I'm against, because I think they are too lazy and complacent to think beyond the home. I think if I get like that we won't be happy.

We've thought all this before of course but it has become clearer to me suddenly. [. . .] Help me, won't you. In some ways it's hard to be a woman – that is if you're aware of these things.

'This isn't feminist talk', she wrote; but it was – just a decade ahead of Betty Friedan and Germaine Greer, and in a tone that was more reflective, less strident.

These letters came to me in November 1954. I was back at Linton, doing my final annual camp, and once again waiting for my result in French II, once again with confidence but this time better-founded, since Dr West had handed over the crucial paper to another, Mr Gransden or Dr Bennetton (or possibly both – memory is uncertain). A telegram came from Kay saying I had an A-pass in French II; and then a letter: 'Congratulations, darling, you knocked the bastard off. Your marks were 62, 79, 84. Isn't it marvellous to go out with a flourish. Everyone here is delighted and sends congratulations. Balls to West!'

OUR FRIENDS PATSY THOMPSON AND John Dutch were to be married towards the end of November. I had been told a wedding would not be sufficient excuse to get me released from camp in time to be there. I had had an early release from the previous camp and was owing three extra days' service that would take me just beyond the crucial weekend.

I was put on overnight guard duty in and around the guard room and company office. Idly filling in time in the middle watches, I found in an unlocked filing cabinet the letters that showed the extra three days I owed the New Zealand Army. I gave it only a moment's thought, and removed them. Next day I wrote a letter pointing out that my time would be up, my service complete, on the Friday.

Major Pope, our dim but diligent Cold Warrior CO, surprised me. He remembered the missing papers, suspected me of theft, but how? My recent guard duty didn't occur to him. He was convinced I must have done it in broad daylight, under their noses. He was full of bluster, threat, displeasure, and perhaps (though probably not) a sneaking regard. I remained silent, and he let me go.

I apologise to his shade, but my presence in the army served no useful purpose – certainly none to him – and if it helps, a poem could be said (indirectly, and with a slight alteration of the circumstances in the interest of brevity) to have come of it half a century later, one, incidentally, read by Garrison Keillor on his wonderful programme *The Prairie Home Companion*:

You

Our friends' wedding:
I'd lied, called it a funeral
to get army leave
so I could be with you.
It was a surprise, a present
and your blush of pleasure
cheered me like a crowd.

So here we are on the step
above 'the happy couple'
who will one day divorce –

looking into the future
which is now.

Ten friends together
in that photograph.
Fifty years on
and four are dead.
Who will be next?
Who will be last
and put out the light?

It's time to tell you again
how much I loved the girl
who blushed her welcome.
Forgive my trespasses.
Stay close. Hold my hand.

EIGHTEEN
THE PURPLE TIE,
THE WEE NARCISSUS,
AND THE WEDDING

The Grandmother without the Voice was not the Grandmother. She died in 1954 after some years of silence and slow physical and mental decline. Mum, herself once again the mother of an infant, deserves honour for the way she had managed to nurse her mother, see to her meals, get her in and out of a wheelchair and push her daily to the front veranda where she could sit looking at the garden, unweeded, tousled, running to seed, but profuse with flowers – the lavender on one side of the path to the lower garden, the huge rosemary on the other, the pergola sagging under the weight of roses that shed their petals on the path. In spring there was the mimosa (Australian wattle) in brilliant flower, the clematis that grew under the kitchen window (said to have been planted from Mum's wedding bouquet), and down by the front gate the lilac trees that bloomed for my birthday. Close to the veranda, just out of sight but scenting the air, were daphne, jasmine and verbena.

Kay was in the house during the Grandmother's last hours. I had always imagined 'the death rattle' was something heard at the last moment, signalling the expiry. I hadn't realised it was something that went on, stertorous and desperate, for many hours, the body, programmed to struggle on, fighting for the life which the ghost has already given up, the sound accompanied by the smell of death in sour competition with the smells of a life that has passed its use-by date.

Her body was taken away by the undertaker and then returned to us, bright as a button, to lie in state in the front room with the grand piano. Given a free hand with the make-up she couldn't have done better herself. If there was a Heathen heaven for her to go to, I knew she would be there, the ticket paid for by her years of unstinting love, the entertainment an ongoing Hollywood musical with Fred Astaire and Ginger Rogers, set on a Pacific island, and with a Swedish sea captain for eternal company. She was buried at Waikaraka Park, right at the far edge of the cemetery looking out on an inlet of the Manukau Harbour. It seemed right she should be in sight of the sea. Recently Kay and I hunted for her grave and didn't find it. It seemed a reclamation had extended the cemetery out into the harbour, causing me uncertainty about where we should be looking.

When I was writing *The Singing Whakapapa* we searched unsuccessfully for John Flatt's grave in the cemetery beside the Te Aroha Racecourse. Now the grave of her other grandfather, Martin McDermott, has lost its Symonds Street stone and is indeterminate. Her father's has vanished under the Grafton motorway extensions. Her mother was left in an almost unmarked grave on a remote Pacific island. Friends recently tried unsuccessfully to find her husband's grave on Noumea. All vanished, or vanishing, which is only (once again) a speeding up of the process. In these pages I have given their names a little more life, a few more years to fade until it is not a matter of concern; until there is no one to whom it matters.

1954 SHOULD ALSO BE MENTIONED AS the year when my old enemy the grand piano and I agreed to differ for the last time. I told Mum I was going to take lessons again, and that I had chosen her to be my teacher. There was amusement mixed with a slight undertone of ferocity on both sides. She agreed, but gave not the least encouragement or sign of thinking any progress would be made. She was right – I knew as well as she did there would be none. But I was quite clear. I was going to assert myself, in all my shining pianistic incompetence, and she and the instrument would just have to make the best of it.

I went back to scales and exercises. I could hear, and feel, the delicacy in the simple ones, and then the incompetence creeping in as they got more difficult. Never mind. That's how it had to be. As for a 'piece', Mum, seeming to understand what I was doing, skipped over the simplest stuff and went straight to Mozart – the *Rondo alla Turca*. I learned it. I played it. I listened to myself playing it. I heard all its faults, its clumsiness and unsubtlety, its awfulness. But to do the impossible – that is, to do it well – was not the object. It was just to bloody *do* it.

I did it, and closed the lid on my past, and never touched the piano again; but I have never stopped listening to it, marvelling at what it can be made to do, noticing what is exquisite, powerful, delicate, deeply felt and, no less, what is less than perfect (including the occasional wrong note), in performances, always enjoying, but never quite without a faint flavour of regret.

The Muse, on the other hand, seemed to reward persistence – in Australia first, then at home. I had poems in the *Jindyworobak Anthology* of 1952 and '53 ('the Jindy' as its editor called it in letters); encouragement from *Meanjin* and the Sydney *Bulletin*.[*] Louis Johnson took poems for his *New Zealand Poetry Yearbook* and for the periodical *Numbers*, Noel Hoggard for *Arena* (and my first

---

[*] I had poems accepted for *Meanjin* in 1955. In 1956, when I was living in Australia and the *Bulletin* featured 'Poets from the Six States', I represented New South Wales.

short story, 'Girl Under the Plane Trees'), Monte Holcroft for the *Listener*, and finally Charles Brasch for *Landfall*. The acceptances were not immediate. I tended to like whatever I had just written, and to send it off half-cooked, and sometimes raw. But something turned around in 1954. There was a change of tone in the letters back. Editorial resistance turned into editorial encouragement. Robert Thompson, editing a series of booklets for Noel Hoggard's Handcraft Press, sought one from me. (Brasch advised against, and I accepted that.) Louis Johnson invited me to visit when I was in Wellington for the winter tournament, and sent a street map. Frank Sargeson accepted an invitation to come and give a talk to AUC's Literary Society. Brasch, on a visit to Auckland, arranged to meet me. I won a College Prize for poetry judged by Professor Musgrove, Allen Curnow and Keith Sinclair (and Musgrove had also consulted Fairburn); and in the following year the same poem, 'Night Watch in the Tararuas', won an international prize ($100 US – a lot of money then) for undergraduate poetry.* Frank Sargeson, seeing work of mine in the *Poetry Yearbook*, wrote encouraging letters. He and Louis Johnson nominated me for membership of PEN.

Throughout 1954 I was gathering material for an issue of AUC's student literary annual, *Kiwi*, but it was not destined to appear (produced beautifully, but late, by Bob Lowry) until 1955, by which time my fellow-editor, Rob Dyer, was already in Oxford. I included Sargeson's talk in it; and what I think may be Maurice Gee's first published story. At least I claim that it is, and that I am, therefore, his first publisher. I remember that there was an obscurity about it that was only cleared up for me years later when I read his novel *Plumb*.

Auckland's intellectuals, writers and artists used to meet and be seen at Somervell's coffee bar in Queen Street, and it was there

---

* I.e. the poem had to have been written while the author was still an undergraduate. Thanks to Dr West, I qualified.

I read to Kay and Jill one of the letters I'd had from Sargeson. 'My version of the Second Coming', he wrote,

> is a sort of Ibsen who will be big enough to force recognition from our provincial public – prove to it that a poet with his pencil and paper can be as good as and better than Hillary with his oxygen and nylon rope. [. . .] Let's have the poetry – but I do hanker after the long poems and plays (Ibsen called all his plays poems). It's up to some young poet to take a hint from Curnow and Cresswell – I mean <u>not</u> to wait until the first fine careless rapture is all over, before getting around to what they should have been attempting in the hay days.

He also suggests that if the student Lit Soc had enough money it should invite writers from other centres:

> . . . much better than having poets and writers permanently on the premises – probably bad for them, and bad for pupils who show signs of brilliance and originality in excess of their masters?

I was flattered by this (handwritten) attention and, not yet expert at reading between the lines of literary letters, did not recognise, as I do now, (a) that Sargeson was himself writing Ibsenish plays and (b) that he was sniping at Allen Curnow. Even if I had, my pleasure would hardly have been diminished, and might have been enhanced.

I was still uncertain of myself, afraid of false 'arty' posturing, and prone to equally false postures of toughness, ordinariness, Kiwi-jokerdom. The young poet can be at times a weathervane, an intellectual-fashion barometer, and it was something in the literary air of the time, both in New Zealand and abroad – partly the Modernist revolt against Romanticism, so one read Donne sooner than Keats and Shelley (Kelly and Sheets as Auden called them); and partly a reflection of a surviving 1930s leftist ideal of the worker poet, so young authors, asked for a brief bio to accompany publication of new work, listed their vacation jobs as if to give the impression that they were manual labourers who turned in a sweaty sonnet or two at home from work in the evenings.

All these elements come to me as I try to understand my own strange behaviour during my first meeting with Charles Brasch. Brasch figured in literary conversation not only as the founder and editor of *Landfall*, our principal literary magazine, but as the local Maecenas – a poet, but also a wealthy benefactor of the arts, an arbiter of taste and refinement. I was bound to feel uneasy, and bound to behave foolishly. Charles rang and suggested we should meet in the Auckland Art Gallery, and proceed from there to coffee at Somervell's. His voice was cultured, no doubt a very nice voice but it suggested all kinds of things I couldn't be, or match, and I would probably have described it as 'fruity', or 'prissy'. So I would be able to identify him he murmured, 'I shall be wearing a purple tie.' It was not just the delicacy of tone, or the colour purple, that made me uneasy; it was the middle-class English 'shall'. No New Zealander uses 'shall' in that context except by conscious decision, and for an effect.

I put on a lot of clothes and an overcoat, and sat opposite him over coffee talking in a bullish way about playing centre forward for the university. Allen Curnow, writing at another table, came to join us, and I think at that point I relaxed a little, feeling that Brasch, irritated by the uninvited guest, was now less closely focused on me. His record of this meeting in his journal is less than flattering, though it is, one discovers, in its pained and obsessive attention to personal appearances, typical. He says C. K. Stead, a young man who has been sending work to *Landfall* for perhaps two years, 'has recently been writing verse quite assured and forceful and rich'. He describes me as having 'a long vertical pale face with a roman nose and rather ugly projecting chin and jaw'. He even draws a picture of the 'projecting bow' of the teeth – 'almost this plan', he writes, 'though less elongated' – which might have helped with identification if I had died in a fire soon afterwards and been burned beyond recognition. He adds, 'But I might revise my impressions', and moves on to record something I said about 'not writing easily' and the fact that we were 'interrupted' by Allen Curnow who 'came over and took charge'.

In Wellington for the August tournament I was billeted by a Scottish immigrant family in Ngaio: 'This morning' (I wrote to Kay) 'coming in out of driving rain' [i.e. after the nightmare overnight train from Auckland] 'I was toasted over a fire, stoked with bacon and eggs, shovelled into bed for two hours, and woken to a huge midday dinner. Even the doors in this house roll their "r"s when the wind blows.' I played a match at the Basin Reserve next day and, soon after that, followed Lou Johnson's directions from Epuni Station to his flat in Lower Hutt, taking with me a small dark-haired clever young man who at that time went by the name of John Kay. Kay had written some diminutive poems, one of which I had accepted for *Kiwi*.

I was grateful for the early encouragement I'd had from Johnson, and he was amiable to meet. But he was wary, too, of the academy and (not without warrant) of my association with Curnow. Johnson was one of a group (including Alistair Campbell, James K. Baxter, and later Charles Doyle and Peter Bland) who felt excluded, or inadequately acknowledged and represented, by Curnow the anthologist. They rejected what they called 'the South Island myth' – a sort of literary nationalism based on landscape – in favour of what Johnson called 'peopling the landscape', writing urban poetry which would be 'international'; and as I perceived this war heating up, my loyalty was with Curnow, partly for the reasons given in the previous chapter, that we were at a point in our history where an independent New Zealand identity needed to be asserted; but more from a feeling that Curnow was a major poet who was yet to receive the kind of recognition his work warranted, that the battle was disturbing him profoundly, and that he not only deserved support but needed it. This feeling was not altered by my meeting with Johnson. Lou was welcoming, friendly, and no doubt talented; but he seemed such a blunt instrument compared with my Auckland teacher and mentor, all his generosity, if it was meant to win another supporter, went for nothing.

Johnson, strangely, took a strong dislike to John Kay, and in a letter after my return to Auckland regretted I had not been able to come back, as invited, the following Thursday, because there were things he wanted to say to me which could not be said in the presence of 'the wee narcissus'. 'One can count on such characters for amusing scandal', he wrote, 'but not wish to give too much in reply.' Kay was in the process of changing his name to Kasmin, from which the John would soon be dropped; and I always think of Johnson's description when I pass the Kasmin mansion in London's Warwick Avenue, a small part, I'm sure, of what his success as one of the most notable art dealers of the second half of the twentieth century has earned him. This was a 'narcissus' with an eye for beauty other than his own.

AT THE END OF 1954, WITH THE WAY now clear for my return to AUC for my MA in English, and marriage planned for early January, I took a summer job as an orderly at Auckland City Hospital. I was moved about according to staffing needs from one day to the next. There were horrors from time to time, very little boredom, and sometimes great human interest. But one job gave me anxiety. I was stationed at the bottom of the laundry chute in the Infectious Diseases Block, with the task of gathering up linen and towels as they came down, and folding them for collection. Permanent staff had inoculations against various diseases; I had none – so after a day I went to the head orderly suggesting I should be placed somewhere else. He pretended to be very amused at my fears, and amused himself even further by shifting me to the morgue.

The orderly in charge there seemed to be a necrophile who had found his niche. He told me with relish how he was allowed to make preliminary incisions before the pathologist arrived to perform an autopsy. These were the opening up of the rib-cage and sawing the top off the skull.

My duties did not extend to the autopsy room itself, but involved mopping, sweeping and generally keeping tidy the room housing the refrigerated bodies. Each refrigerator had three or four drawers, and the first sight you saw when you opened one of the doors was the pairs of naked feet, the big toes tied together with a strip of white cloth – a fact I later passed on to Frank Sargeson, who used it in one of his novels. Once, the ghoulish orderly, who was always trying to frighten or shock, grabbed a naked dead baby by the head out of the refrigerator and held it out towards me, close to my face. There is an article (or it might be a chapter heading) by G. Wilson Knight about imagery in Shakespeare's *Macbeth* with the title 'The naked babe and the cloak of manliness', and every time I saw it subsequently, my thought went to that moment – myself confronted with the 'naked babe', required to put on my 'cloak of manliness' and show no reaction at all to the fact that it was dead.

The morgue had a door that opened on to the trees of the Auckland Domain. There was no air-conditioning in those days, and the door was kept open for coolness in the summer heat, but there were strips of coloured plastic hanging down which you pushed through to enter or exit. These were to discourage flies. A kookaburra lived in the trees you looked out on – the only one I have ever seen at large in New Zealand.

After a few days I was shifted again, this time to a geriatric ward. It had its horrors too, inevitably; but there were also quite long periods when I had nothing to do and was free to read. There was a bathroom I retired to when no one was calling for me, where I found I could sit reading in the empty bath with my legs draped over the side. I was at this time reading everything I could find of T. S. Eliot's critical prose, looking for anything that gave information, direct or oblique, about his own experience of writing poetry. My reason for this was that I had noticed all the critical commentaries on his work took as their guide the remarks he had made which suggested that his poetry was the result of a 'classical' intention, a plan, and that any 'difficulty' or 'obscurity' was only the result of missing 'links in the chain' of meaning. Consequently critics like Cleanth Brooks, George Williamson and many others (and Eliot was at that time more cited, discussed, lectured on and written about than any other living writer) all obligingly discovered and filled in the missing 'links', producing an effortlessly intelligible Eliot remote from what seemed to me the realities of his poetry, which was full of mysteriousness, obliquity, surprise and accident.

I was hunting for corresponding accidents in his prose writings, which would give more authentic insights into how the poetry came to be written – and I was finding them. Sometimes the statements were themselves obscure and needed interpretation; but I felt I was understanding Eliot, and the true nature of his poetry, better than any of his current commentators were doing. His poems, and in particular *The Waste Land*, were not conscious constructs, but were aggregations of poetic moments, accretions of random intuitive image clusters, all springing from some central preoccupation, obsession or emotional node, and depending less on the intellect than on the sensuous eye, the quick (spontaneous, opportunistic) wit, the ear for mellifluous language and the gift for tone. These aggregations, once achieved, had to be organised by the poet, arranged into some semblance of order, but they were the result of no plan in advance of the fact; and by suggesting they were, Eliot had misled his critics.

Once I knew what I was looking for I found it everywhere, but nowhere so explicitly as in a lecture, 'The three voices of poetry', given just the year before, and published in a 24-page booklet which I found in Progressive Books, the leftist bookshop in central Auckland. Here all pretence at 'classical' planning, conscious control and the suppression of 'links in the chain' of meaning were gone, in favour of an all-out old-fashioned Romanticism, the poet as victim of a 'creative germ', an 'embryo', a 'thing', a

> bodiless childful of life in the gloom
> Crying with frog voice, 'What shall I be?'

The poet, Eliot explained, is 'oppressed by a burden which he must bring to birth'; he is 'haunted by a demon against which he feels powerless'; and, when the work is done, when the 'relief' has been found for this 'acute discomfort', he is likely to 'experience a moment of exhaustion, of appeasement, of absolution, and of something very near annihilation, which is in itself indescribable'.

These were statements I could relate to the poems as they lived on the page, not as they died in the pages of academic commentary. So in a quiet bathroom in a geriatric ward in Auckland Hospital was developed what was to be, a few years later, the single most fruitful perception of my critical study of Modernism, *The New Poetic*, a book which would have a publishing life of half a century, and which both Seamus Heaney and Paul Muldoon would say made it possible for them to understand and come to terms with Eliot's work.

But I had a few things to accomplish first. One was to make a good fist of the MA and, by that means, to get away to an overseas university.

WHATEVER SPOKEN RESISTANCE, OR unspoken reluctance, there had been to the idea of a conventional wedding, there is no sign of it in the photographs. Not all the usual suspects were there, but many of them. Rob Dyer was already in Oxford, and John Edwards in Cambridge. My three Catholic friends, the poets Phil Rau and Peter Goddard and the golfer Kevin Treacy, were at the reception but not at the ceremony, Catholics in those days being forbidden to attend Protestant services for fear of religious contamination. Kay looks beautiful in white on the arm of grandfather Uriah McClinchie, in his three-piece suit and gold double watch chain. Kay's mother looks relieved, mine displeased, Dad cheerful, little sister Frances excited. Sister Norma is there with John. A cluster of elderly aunts smile and seem happy enough. Jill Evans is bridesmaid, and a new friend, Dennis Boshier (later a professor at the Auckland Medical School) best man. University friends assemble like a football team around the bride's bouquet, held by tank-repair man Ken Piddington, noble and smiling in defeat. Barry Catton is there, soon to take off on his big OE. The couple are seen first, newly married and in their wedding attire, then mysteriously changed into other, still formal but less so, clothes for the 'going away'. Where they were 'going away' to was always, of course, a secret, so we didn't have to tell everyone we were going nowhere except home to our flat on Takapuna Beach. Kay's old school friend Yvonne drove us there in her father's car. Her recollection is that I cooked while she and Kay swam, and that the landlady's middle-aged unmarried son, who also went by the name of Karl, showed signs of anxiety that she should be hanging about when, clearly, we should be getting on with the consummation. Perhaps he hoped to listen through the wall. If so, the next year would provide him with no end of opportunity.

NINETEEN
ANNUS MIRABILIS
. . . AND SO ON

Nineteen fifty five seemed to K & K a kind of *annus mirabilis*. Our flat was a glassed-in veranda, like a railway carriage, a small part of it the kitchen, the rest the living room; attached to this was just one room of the house, our bedroom. Across a small white paved courtyard with a cabbage tree at the centre there was a smaller two-room flat, and another rented room, the flat occupied by our friends Patsy and John Dutch, the single room irregularly occupied by Jack Lasenby when he was in from the bush. Between these two was the single lavatory shared by all four (or five) tenants. Another outhouse contained a bathroom and a washhouse (laundry), also shared. It was unconventional, and I suppose slightly shocking to our families. It seemed fine to us, though at night Kay used to wake me if she had to cross the yard in the dark.

Because the living room was really a veranda the inner wall was white weatherboard. Somewhere we acquired island matting, used in those days for packing bananas, and tacked it over the weatherboard with batons of half-round. Louise Henderson had given us a painting for a wedding present,* one of the very best of her cubist phase, a cow's skull in greys, deep blues and black, which looked wonderful against the matting above a divan bright with cushions. Norma and John had given us a bookcase and we had bought ourselves a unit of cupboards and shelves in pale pine for china and pottery. We placed the bookshelves and the unit back-to-back, breaking the railway-carriage effect and dividing off a small area at the far end, looking out to sea, where we had a table and four chairs. Our view there was across a pohutukawa-flanked lawn to the beach and, beyond, over the Hauraki Gulf to the island of Rangitoto. Down that five-mile wide corridor of sea, past Rangitoto's pepperpot lighthouse, the ships came and went to and from Auckland's Waitemata Harbour. The sea was always in earshot, from a quiet flick-and-suck of small waves to, at rare times of storm and big winds, something close to surf. Near and far, the islands of the gulf, depending where and when you looked, but especially in the late afternoon, gave a sense of the great reach of that blue plane of water. At evening, when a ship left, we watched it sail into the gap that represented the open sea where it seemed to sit with its back to us, diminishing in the westerly light, sinking, going down like a small white sun over the rim of the world. At night we walked along the sand with Patsy and John, arms linked, chanting our favourite and most chantable poems, especially Dylan Thomas's 'Poem in October', and any one of many by Gerard Manly Hopkins. Thomas, a familiar radio voice at the height of his fame and popularity, was just recently deceased from eighteen straight whiskies in New York; and we and the Dutches were to meet up in two or three years' time in England and visit his grave in Laugharne, at that time still marked only by a white wooden cross.

---

* Louise was not, of course, a guest, and this extraordinarily generous present came, unexpected, with a message in Louise's inimitable English in which blessings and regrets were strangely tangled.

Patsy and John, whose wedding I had escaped from military duties to attend, were the couple (as the poem 'You' has it) who 'would one day divorce' – but that was a long way off. Kay had been at school with Patsy, and had known John and his brother at the Glen Eden Tennis Club. The son of a Pakeha mother and a Maori street preacher father, John had run away to Australia before reaching school-leaving age, had worked as a jackaroo on cattle stations, and come back to New Zealand hoping to be a writer. He was in deep rebellion against his family's religion, but knew the same revivalist hymns I did, and he and I used to sing them, never with serious or faithful intent, always with irony in the mind if not in the delivery, but in good voice, John slipping easily into harmony. He and Patsy had already made bookings for London with a shipping line; but we had their company for the first few months of that year.

Along the beach, in a house beautifully designed by a young architect, Bruce Rotherham, lived Hazel and Felix Millar, Hazel, an un- (or under-) employed soprano, Felix a teacher of the violin who would later switch instruments and play principal viola for the Auckland Philharmonia Orchestra. I had seen him just once, a few years before, when Yehudi Menuhin gave a recital in the Auckland Town Hall and Felix turned the pages for him, the two so alike many thought Felix must be the great violinist's brother. Hazel and Felix had converted their beautiful house into a restaurant, 'FELIX'S', advertising that while eating you would be entertained by 'Felix and his Gypsy Violin'. One evening Kay and I, sitting at our dinner table nook, saw Hazel walking on the beach hand in hand with a man who was not Felix. Kay, who had only sisters, thought it must be Hazel's brother. I said I supposed so, but knew I would never be seen walking hand in hand on a beach – or any-where – with Norma.

Soon the news spread (we now knew Frank Sargeson, so were privy to all such gossip) that Hazel had run off with the restaurant cook and was hiding with him on Waiheke Island. In due course

Felix found her and brought her home. The cook had by then deserted her and escaped.

Shortly afterwards, as a direct or indirect consequence of the domestic turmoil, the beautiful house burned to the ground. By now Patsy and John had left for Britain. Hazel and Felix moved into their flat with their little dog Fifi, and for the rest of our time at Takapuna they were our neighbours, and sharers of laundry and loo. When both wanted to practise at the same time one would remain in their flat, the other remove to the bathroom; so we could say of our courtyard, as Caliban does of his island, it was 'full of noises / Sounds and sweet airs, that give delight and hurt not'. Felix and I used to play chess in the sun while he talked, *sotto voce*, about his girl pupils and how he 'rooted' them. I tended not to believe these stories. I knew, or thought I knew, that those who talked a lot about 'rooting' were often not successful or frequent practitioners – but I wasn't sure.

One Saturday morning there was a lot of noise and argument in the courtyard. Felix had heard where the cook was hiding in Wellington, had his address, and was going there to inflict pain and physical damage. His friends George Haydn, and a doctor, Pat Hitchings, were trying to talk him out of it, and we were drawn into the circle. Hazel remained silent, holding Fifi, not wanting, I thought, to anger Felix further by defending the cook, and perhaps even pleased at the thought that the man who had seduced and then deserted her was to be punished. In the end, when it was clear Felix was not to be deflected, George said he would go too, to ensure that Felix, who was broad-chested and strongly built, didn't commit a crime that might cost him his freedom, or his life.

Of this bohemian set on the North Shore George Haydn was one of the cleverest and most amusing. He was a Jewish immigrant whose standard joke when asked about his war experience was to say he had been in charge of the rowlocks in the Hungarian navy – the equivalent, I suppose, of Shakespeare having Antigonus in *The Winter's Tale* land on the coast of Bohemia, whence he 'Exit[s], pursued by a bear'. George had set up as a builder in Auckland, and built many of the houses designed by Vernon Brown and the Group architects. Bruce Rotherham had been one of Brown's students, and George had built Felix's house, now in cinders, and also the simple bach-style house Brown had designed for Frank Sargeson, the one still preserved as a memorial to the writer. George was married to the sculptor Molly Macalister, whose statue of a tall Maori, with cloak, mere in hand, tiny head, and something puzzling on the shoulder which Sargeson suggested must be a chip, still stands at the bottom of Queen Street greeting tourists as they come ashore from cruise liners.

George drove Felix to Wellington in his own car. They were back in a few days, both silent about what had happened there, though Felix hinted over chess that he had been distracted from his purpose by opportunities of another kind, and the cook had escaped again.

Kendrick and Mary Smithyman, both poets, lived within walking distance. I later came to think of Ken as an Ezra Pound – the only child of elderly parents, who had learned at an early age that his duty was to hold forth, to show brilliance, to keep the social ball rolling and be admired. Like Pound he was a collector of random facts, information of every kind, items of intelligence; and like Pound he did not always have a clear notion of the relative value of these items, one to another, nor the ability to make anything entirely coherent of them. This was his academic limitation, but often served him well as a poet, especially later in his career when he developed the confidence to be anecdotal and to stop hiding his meanings under a bushel. In those early days I always felt if he gave me a poem to read and I showed too soon that I understood it, he would rush away and revise it deeper into obscurity. His predominant style was not, however, Poundian. His first collection, *The Blind Mountain*, was predominantly Audenesque, so much so that some of the poems seemed purer 'Auden' than Auden himself. Ken was chunky, short-to-medium in height, with a small moustache and fine, intelligent eyes. He had a brassy manner under which I imagined there was great sensitivity, kindness and generosity.

Mary was silent, sad-on-the-edge-of-anger, and palely beautiful. She had published one book of poems, *Starveling Year*, which Louise Henderson was not alone in telling her friends was 'better than anything her husband could do' – an opinion she would have had from Eric McCormick. Mary had been married before to a serviceman killed in the war, and sometimes gave the impression that she resented Ken for being a survivor. I felt, too, that the dead husband lurked among the obscurities of Ken's early poems. I had bought *The Blind Mountain* two years before, and seemed to discover a ghost in its darker corners, and the poet's guilt and frustration that he could not compete with the dead.

> But you are buried in your past, and I
> am the one who whistles outside, am late
> to meet you in the horror of the night
> where the importunate horseman goes by.
> [. . .]
> What loneliness disputes in you, what once
> could have been, was not, may be or will
> are simpler than we name and growing full
> keep as the moon a season. No one wins . . .

Mary was already showing signs of the rheumatoid arthritis that would slowly close down on her, destroying her life and in the process probably doing terrible harm to the marriage.

The Smithymans invited us to Sunday lunch. Ken talked a great deal, I less, the two women hardly at all. That was one of the things that seemed to mark off the intellectual community from the rest. In New Zealand at large the women talked and were socially dominant (Bob Chapman described ours as a matriarchal society); the 'breadwinners' were silent or monosyllabic. Among writers and academics it tended the other way – men the talkers, the theorisers, their women in silent support. One to one there was equality; but in groups male and female had yet to meet in the middle.

Ken showed us some poems, read one or two, and we talked about them. There was talk about Felix and the cook; and of a similar case, a local fisherman whose wife had had an affair with an American, a lecturer at AUC. The fisherman had intended to take a violent revenge but instead had accepted payment of a thousand pounds and agreed his wife could remain with the American, who had thus in effect bought her. Everyone, it was said, was content, and the new relationship was working well. There was to be a party to celebrate, and we would be invited.

It was a cooked lunch, with beer. It was only when we were leaving that Mary remembered the potatoes. They were baked, still waiting in the oven to be served. She flew into a rage, blaming Ken for forgetting to remind her. If Ken was embarrassed it didn't show.

ONE OF MY EARLIEST PORTS OF CALL after Kay resumed work at the library was 14 Esmonde Road, Frank Sargeson's house, only a ten-minute walk from our flat. It was late morning, and he came to the door with a face in which the displeasure was meant to be seen. Had he forgotten to put up the sign that said WORKING. PLEASE DON'T DISTURB; or had I decided to ignore it? Surely not the latter. For Frank it was a matter of importance (something I have since come to understand very well) that people respect writing as 'work', employment, 'the office', and that it was not to be treated as a leisure activity that can be interrupted by anyone at any time.

I was backing off, embarrassed, apologising and turning away towards the hole in the hedge that served as the entrance to his property when he relented. It was late morning, he said; he had done his page (he required of himself 'a page a day') and would stop now. I should come in and have lunch with him.

Frank's day was regular. It began early with reading. He worked his way through the English-language classics, poetry as often as prose, and a large part of his conversation consisted of current thoughts about Shakespeare, Milton, Spenser, Byron, Walt Whitman – whoever it happened to be – discoveries and rediscoveries. He had an excellent memory and loved to recall vivid scenes from fiction, Dickens especially. After eating breakfast (he brewed his own yoghurt in his hot-water-cylinder cupboard), and perhaps watering and attending to anything urgently needed in the garden, he began his stint of writing, first revising the previous day's work and typing it up, then slowly composing a new page, always by hand. In the afternoons there was more gardening, shopping, chores, cooking. Evenings were given over to reading again (contemporary work usually, and literary magazines), listening to the radio, and entertaining friends. It was a quite strict regime, purposeful, geared to hard work, the aggregation of craft-knowledge, and productivity. Yet at this time, now into his early fifties, he was in something of a trough, trying to write plays (hence the references to Ibsen in his first letters to me), worrying that he had not published enough to justify the years of effort, and seeming to need the company and support of younger people to give him renewed energy and *croyance en soi*.

Frank was gregarious, entertaining and lively; wicked, witty and waspish. He loved literary gossip and, apart from his tireless local correspondence, exchanged letters with several notable figures abroad (William Plomer and John Lehmann in London, for example; James Laughlin in New York) which meant he knew a surprising amount about contemporary writers that only later emerged in biographies and critical studies. It was from Frank I first heard about Pound's long-term mistress, Eliot's 'mad' first wife, Auden's homosexuality, E. M. Forster's taste for policemen, G. B. Shaw's unconsummated marriage and his habit of paying for small purchases by cheque because he knew people often preferred to frame the cheque rather than cash it – and the fact (or myth) that H. G. Wells had exceptional sexual success because women found his body sweet-smelling and irresistible. But under all the gossip, liveliness and irreverence, there was a total, serious commitment to writing and writers, to books and what he called 'the life of the mind'.

Frank always talked and wrote as if he had made a conscious choice to turn his back on the law profession, in which he had qualified, in favour of a determination to prove that it was, after all, possible to be a full-time writer in New Zealand, even given our remoteness, our diminutive market, our lack of confidence and tendency to look beyond our own shores for excellence. He had made himself into an exemplary figure of literary nationalism. We now know that what lay behind this choice was more complicated, less a matter of free will than a case of 'willing to get to where I'm sent'. As a young man he had been convicted of a homosexual offence, and escaped prison only by letting himself be represented as victim of the older man he had been caught with. So his heroic 'choice' of literature rather than law, of books and bohemia sooner than the bourgeoisie, had been more or less forced upon him. Nonetheless, he had elected to go on affirming this preference, to embrace it, never to go back on it or try to recover what had been lost – and so it had *become* his choice. The man born Norris Davy had become the writer Frank Sargeson – for better or for worse, for poorer or for poorer still, and for life. Exactly how this had come about remained, as long as he lived, a secret.

To his friends Frank's homosexuality was no secret; it was acknowledged, displayed in anecdotes, mannerisms, preferences, body-language, jokes; but in its particulars it was out of sight, something we knew about but which happened off-stage. The friend he really loved, jockey and trainer Harry Doyle, was often referred to in conversation. Harry was (Frank told me) physically 'in a state of grace' – by which was meant that he was one of a rare type of person who didn't need to wash often to remain sweet-smelling – a sort of plebeian H. G. Wells.

Now and then one saw Harry, wearing braces and grinning over the top of his *Best Bets* and his reading glasses, when he came for a weekend – but he was there very seldom; and though Frank would pretend, when he came to write an autobiography, that they had been lifelong, live-in partners, most of that was in the mind – in Frank's mind, not in Harry's – until Harry grew old and feeble and Frank provided shelter for him at 14 Esmonde Road. Even that was not to last. Harry died in an old folks home and Frank, riddled with guilt about his failure to make the dream a reality, would not even go to his funeral, because he knew he could not get through it without making a display of a grief which to those present – family members, members of the racing fraternity – would have had no place, no context to make it intelligible. Yet he told me once that one of his most admired stories, 'An Affair of the Heart' (the one I had been introduced to by Mr Cornwell in the fifth form), about the old mother who fantasises that her dearly loved son will at last return to her, and who never goes to bed until the last bus has been heard departing, was really written out of his own longing for Harry, and the fact that he always waited to hear the last bus leave along Esmonde Road before going to bed.

To anyone Frank believed had the talent to be a writer, he would argue that they should do what he had done, make writing the centre, the primary purpose, to which everything else tended and which everything else served. Even on that first visit this was urged upon me. It was a message I welcomed, since 'to be a writer' was what I wanted most. But now I was advised not to marry, and Ken Smithyman cited (quite wrongly of course) as an example of one whose creativity was being sapped by domesticity. I shouldn't be trapped by sex, Frank told me. There was nothing women could do for me that my mates couldn't do quite as well.

He approached this point obliquely, but in the end the message was quite clear – and when I managed to explain that I was already married, the irritation, though it didn't last, was also clear, not so much that I had done something foolish (though I'm sure he thought I had), but because I had not interrupted him sooner and saved him the embarrassment of superfluous homosexual proselytising.

I looked rather delicate in those days and had, I was often told, feminine hand-movements, and he had probably thought I was what we currently call 'gay' (a usage he disliked); or at the very least that I might be sexually ambivalent – enough to be saved from matrimony. But he would rather not have urged his own views, so frankly and so early, on someone not disposed to share them, or not able now to act on them. In any case he recovered quickly and said I must bring Kay and visit in the evenings.

But while this conversation was continuing, Frank on one side of the counter preparing lunch, including a salad full of good things straight from the garden, I on the other side was taking in the room and the image of this lively gnome with his darting movements and darting conversation, his spatulate fingers which he held up to the light while pausing to wrestle with an idea, his not always logical thought-processes and not always credible theories about the world and its motivations. The room was lined with books. There were two attractive paintings by Keith Patterson, calico curtains, a fold-down desk with a large dictionary open and ready for use, windows open wide to the summer weather and the sills covered with produce – white cucumbers, drying red peppers, ripening tomatoes, sunflower seeds for nibbling and pumpkin seeds for planting. Outside, front and back, enclosed by hedges and bushes, there were his garden beds, which supplied not only food for his own table, but extra to be given away to friends or sold to supplement his income. There was an old army hut at the back, which had been his home before the bach was built. In recent times Maurice Duggan, just beginning to be known as a short-story writer, had occupied it; and then Frank's beloved Renate Prince, a young German-Jewish refugee, a student of architecture whom he had protected and fussed over and still talked about with nostalgia.

If I think of houses that impressed indelibly upon my developing consciousness the notion of a way of life, a whole range of possibility beyond mere suburban comfort and convenience, the first was the European visual elegance of 62 Gillies Avenue, the Henderson household; the second was that famous literary and horticultural precinct, Frank Sargeson's bach at 14 Esmonde Road.[*]

KAY EARNED ABOUT £7 10S A WEEK. I had a bursary once again, £75 for the year which, together with what I had saved from vacation jobs, would give us another £3 10s a week; so we had about £11 a week to live on for that year – more than the basic wage. Our rent was £3. Converted into modern dollars these amounts sound pitifully small, but we were comfortably provided for. We travelled by bus from Takapuna to the Northcote ferry wharf (Kay insists it was to Devonport, and it's possible we did sometimes one, sometimes the other), and walked up to the university.

For my MA in English I was enrolled for seven papers. The Shakespeare was taught mainly by Professor Musgrove, with the textual study of *King Lear* taken by Irish Jim Walton, said to be brother of Ernest Walton who had won the Nobel Prize for physics only two or three years before. Jim had been my tutor in Stage I, and had confused us all at first by seeming to talk about something he called Mordren Portrait, until we recognised that it was in fact modern poetry. By master's level he was making textual studies seem like a branch of physics, as if competing with his famous older brother; and though I enjoyed penetrating its mysteries, I remember now only a little of the terminology – Q and F texts and variants, foul papers, variable speech prefixes, memorial reconstructions and, most particularly 'the untrustworthy Compositor B', who seemed in my imagination to take on a life of his own. Jim published his study of the texts of *Richard III* and *King Lear* that year, and after the completion of term three and examination marking, left to return to Ireland. He had served exactly five years in what he now called 'Musgrove's sweatshop' – the same five years as my own as a

---

[*] It is preserved now as a monument, but the space at the back and to one side has been so encroached upon, and the garden so reduced, the feeling of what it was is hardly preserved.

student. In fact I had been in the very first tutorial he gave in 1951, and Musgrove had led him into the room, fresh from his cabin and still bewildered to find himself at last ashore at the world's end. Now (by which I mean at the end of that MA year) I was among those bidding him farewell at the Auckland Railway Station (the Waltons' ship was to sail from Wellington), including Kay, Allen Curnow, Bill Pearson and our new friend from the MA class, Don Smith.

The other MA papers I enrolled for that year were Milton, History of Literary Criticism, Selected Minor Authors, Victorians, Twentieth-Century Poetry and an essay paper on nineteenth- and twentieth-century poetic drama. The last was supervised by the poet M. K. Joseph – Mike – and I had chosen it rather than the essay paper Allen Curnow offered on New Zealand poetry. It was only as the year went on, and I got to know Curnow better, that I realised he had set up the paper partly with me in mind, and was slightly miffed by my preference. My reason was rather 'worthy', but quite genuine – that all the reading of New Zealand poetry I had done in 'the Glass Case' meant I knew the field extremely well. Taking a course on what I had already made myself expert in seemed a waste. I tried once to explain this to Allen, but I suspect he thought it was some residue of the colonial notion that what was 'local' was not worthy of serious study. He must have forgiven me, however, and at the end of the year gave me such a high mark (92 per cent) for his twentieth-century poetry paper, Musgrove (I heard much later) protested that if the department gave marks of that kind it would lose credibility and its reputation for high standards.

But I had another reason for choosing Mike Joseph's essay paper. I had been fascinated in French II by Racine's *Andromache*, especially by the structure of the play, with its balancing and interlocking pairs of powerful, irrational and hopeless loves – Oreste for Hermione, Hermione for Pyrrhus, Pyrrhus for Andromache – and in the weeks between Christmas and the start of the academic year I had been attempting to write a play in verse, entirely modern in setting and language but built on the same structure of character and event. This was the time when T. S. Eliot had shifted from lyric poetry to verse drama, and his plays *The Cocktail Party*, and then *The Confidential Clerk*, were being produced in West End theatres. The lines in my own play used the same rough measure of five speech stresses, and the same flat, naturalistic inflexions and modern locutions, with the same problem that it was hard, apart from the fact of lineation, to see how it was 'verse' at all. And in any case (as I remember explaining to Allen, as the two of us, lecturer and student, clambered around the soft rocks of the inner harbour below his house) it seemed nearly impossible to give modern characters in modern dress the kind of grand irrational motivations of the French original, which in turn derived from stylised ancient drama. Nonetheless I was trying; and Mike Joseph's paper would take me not only through the various (failed) nineteenth-century attempts to bring poetic drama back to what it had been in the age of Shakespeare, but would give me a chance to study formally the very different attempts of our own (twentieth-) century poets to bring verse back into the theatre – Yeats, Auden, Spender, Christopher Fry who was having a brief season of being in fashion, and finally Eliot himself.

My play (which never settled on a title) must have been finished before term began, because Frank wrote to Charles Brasch about it on 18 March:

> I must mention to you my delight that young Stead has written a five
> act play. I and his young wife listened while he read [it], and perhaps
> I am all wrong but it seems to me something new in New Zealand.
> He is devoted to Racine – hence he has produced something very
> lucid and logical [...] I couldn't help thinking of almost any novel by
> Ivy Compton-Burnett. Classicism I suppose. The verse a sort of not-
> verse, but responding beautifully where the heightening demands it.

The play was duly sent to Brasch who read it, reported that he had been 'carried along compellingly', then had it read (I think by

Rodney Kennedy) and reported a second time, this time negatively: there were 'no climaxes [. . .], no heightening and intensifying'; the story was not worked out 'in strictly dramatic terms'. The language was flat, the characters' feelings not convincing and didn't develop. The play wouldn't work on the stage.

Frank was not convinced, and in writing again to Brasch said he wondered whether 'you may be expecting the play to be what it is not'. I didn't know what to think, and had already told Charles I was 'sick of the sight of it'. 'I have all sorts of doubts,' I went on, 'but thought it was good while I was writing it.' Meanwhile he had accepted for *Landfall* a verse letter I had written to Rob Dyer; and when, after discussing it with Allen Curnow, I rewrote it, compressing the pentameters down to tetrameters, he welcomed the revision.

By now Allen and I were nearer to being friends than just lecturer and student; and I remember very clearly the moment when he came into the caf with the typescript of a new poem and asked whether I could find a moment to read it and let him know what I thought. I felt this keenly as an honour and a responsibility. The poem began,

> Mock up, again, summer, the sooty altars
> Between the sweltering tides and the tin gardens,
> All the colours of the stained bow windows.
> Quick, she'll be dead on time, the single
> Actress shuffling red petals to this music,
> Percussive light! So many suns she harbours
> And keeps them jigging, her puppet suns,
> All over the dead hot calm impure
> Blood noon tide of the breathless bay.

It was called 'Spectacular Blossom' (with the unnecessary subtitle, 'Pohutukawa Trees, Auckland'), and it seemed to me to represent a really significant step on from anything he had done before. After a lull of four years the South Islander was beginning to absorb the north into the fabric of his imagination; and it was to be only the first of a whole sheaf of poems during that year and the next, written out of the first flush of his relations with Jeny Tole, who was to be his second wife.

> Wristiest slaughterman December smooths
> The temple bones and parts the grey-blown brows
> With humid fingers. It is an ageless wind
> That loves with knives, that knows our need, it flows
> Justly, simply as water greets the blood,
> And woody tumours burst in scarlet spray.
> An old man's blood spills bright as a girl's
> On beaches where the knees of light crash down.
> These dying ejaculate their bloom.

This appeal to me as an intelligent reader who could be trusted to exercise charity and yet relied on for critical candour was the start of something that was to last, almost unbroken, for the remaining 45 years (exactly half) of Curnow's life. From that time on he would seldom produce a new poem without showing it to me, or posting it to me if one or the other was away – not for advice (though sometimes a little of that was offered), but I think for what Seamus Heaney likes to call *corroboration*, because Allen was the kind of poet (the best kind) who was continually taking himself by surprise, and so needed an opinion he trusted to confirm that the new poem was what it seemed to him and not an aberration. This also made me for a very long time the best informed (as well as one of the most positive) of his critics.

ONE DAY AS I CAME DOWN THE STEPS from our flat and headed across the courtyard towards the steep drive up to Hurstmere Road a female voice – a lyric soprano or siren voice – called to me from the open window of Hazel and Felix's flat. Not able to see anyone at the window I went across and leaned in. The head of the bed was directly below the sill, and Hazel was in the bed, so she had to look back, over her shoulder so to speak, to see me. She must have heard our door shut, known it was Karl because Kay had already left for work, and called to me. As I leaned in the tie I was wearing fell forward. She reached back behind her to caress it, saying it was lovely. This movement caused the sheet to fall forward revealing naked breasts, and not much room for doubt that the state of undress continued all the way down to her very small feet. Her voice caressed me as her fingers caressed the tie. She should have broken into song and I could have joined her in some duet from Verdi, or perhaps Bellini. My mouth was very dry and there had been instant action inside my trousers. I croaked that I had a lecture, would miss my bus, my ferry, mustn't be late, had to run – and did, on up the path – driven, I suppose I have to concede, less by fidelity than fear.

Thirty years later, in a novel called *All Visitors Ashore*, when I recreated this scene, the Karl character, Curl Skidmore, far from running away up the drive, is seen disappearing head-first in through the window, drawn by the Hazel figure, Felice, where they engage in the raunchiest (and I hope most amusing) sex scene I have ever written. This was, however, a narrative device. Curl's lover, Pat, is to catch them at it. It provides her motive for deciding not to have Curl's child, and for leaving him as she does at the end of the novel.

At least ten years further on again, some time in the 1990s, a phone call came from an elderly and infirm Hazel (since, alas, deceased) who told me she had been reading *All Visitors Ashore* and enjoying it more than anything she had read for many years.

I told her I was pleased. There was a long pause.

'But Karl,' she said finally, 'did we *really* do all that?'

I didn't know which answer would better satisfy her, yes or no, and can't now remember which I gave or how I framed a reply.

TWENTY
FRANK AND JANET
AND KARL AND KAY

F riends and family visited. Jill brought her mother one Saturday and was embarrassed by the faint aroma of sex as we emerged, dishevelled and bewildered, from the bedroom to greet them. Don Smith, my fellow-student in the MA class, came for lunch – by bus, ferry and bus again, all the way from South Auckland. Finding the bedroom blinds down he waited discreetly on the sand, reading the little copy of Sterne's *A Sentimental Journey* he had brought in his pocket. After lunch we walked around the rocks to Thorne's Bay and on to Milford, Don talking about Sterne, about anything and everything, talking and walking being his special talents, along with running. He was tall, handsome, athletic, a half-miler destined to run for Oxford, and for New Zealand in Commonwealth and Olympic Games. A few years on, in England, we would put him together with Jill in the back of our Ford Popular and drive them to the Lake District, an experiment in enforced contiguity that would lead to their marriage, and cement our friendship with both for life.

Kay and I dreamed and talked our way into life together, into a way of life notable (or so it seems when I look back on it) for its purposefulness, intent always on the best in books, music, art, theatre, ideas. There was nothing self-punishing about this; we pursued these things because they were what we liked, not because they were what we thought we ought to like. But we did also, no doubt, think they were what we ought to like – things that anyone with intelligence and good taste would prefer and would choose. I don't believe we were either puritanical or snobbish in this, but imbued, perhaps, with the notion that history had opened doors for us closed to our parents, and that it would be wasteful, foolish and self-denying not to pass through them.

Meanwhile the lapping of waves lulled us to sleep at night, and in the daytime there was the sound of a violin or a soprano voice in the little courtyard, or the drone of bees coming and going overhead from their hive in the cabbage tree. There was swimming – a quick run across the lawn, over the sand and into the water; and those weekday ferry rides across the harbour, enjoyable in every kind of weather, but best of all the night crossings when the sea was calm, the moon was on the water, and our ears were full of the sounds of violin, piano or whole orchestra, some great work from the classical repertoire we were coming to young and fresh.

Frank forgave me for marrying because he liked Kay, enjoyed her irreverent humour, admired her intelligence and her beautiful eyes. He asked us questions about our families, our childhood, our sex life – enquiries that were not 'proper', but never offensive because the interest was so genuine, as if he had been an anthropologist engaged in a study of the heterosexual young of 1955. His eyes were bright, his fingers mobile, and there was an old-fashioned politeness, always apologising for interrupting (and always interrupting). Sometimes I thought he was not strong on logic, and that I was smarter – clearer headed, and better at explaining myself. But then I would be forced to recognise a mind working obliquely towards its own secret destination, and I would be less certain of myself, and impressed by his cleverness. Above all he was entertaining, engaging, affectionate, sometimes sharp, sometimes shocking. Once, when the subject of mothers came up, he said with ferocity that when his died he would 'dance on her grave'. We were both silent, appalled by such an impiety.

In politics Frank, like my parents, had been of the old Left in the '30s and '40s, and remained staunchly with Labour, which, in addition to its creation of a welfare state, and some movement towards foreign policy independence, had fostered the arts, set up the State Literary Fund and a national orchestra, and had even provided some sort of unofficial pension for Frank himself. We were all three of one mind on these matters, embarrassed by Prime Minister Holland when he spoke for the nation, unpersuaded by the rhetoric of the Cold War, and depressed by *Time*-magazine America, so full of its own virtue, blundering about the world making needless enemies of the Left, and giving communism the appearance of having a monopoly on the heroic future. The figures that represented America at that time were, at home, Senator Joe McCarthy, the rabid anti-communist witch-hunter, and, abroad, the inflexible secretary of state, John Foster Dulles. 'Dull, duller, Dulles' was a common joke, but, worse than dull, he was dangerous. His reaction to the French defeat at Dien Bien Phu the year before, and his belief that the colonial gap in South East Asia the French would leave had to be plugged, meant he was already taking the first steps that would lead ultimately to America's war in Vietnam, the war which, as Martin Luther King said, poisoned the American soul, and in which New Zealand would play a minor and inglorious role. [*]

My reading was prescribed by my MA courses, but Kay was available to influence, and for all of that year she read more or less as Frank directed. We visited two or three times a week, Frank

---

[*] In 1954 Walter Nash, leader of the Labour Opposition, had said 'Outside nations, no matter how powerfully they assist the French to subdue the Vietnam or Vietminh people, cannot succeed . . . The only solution lies in the people of Indo-China governing themselves . . . in their own way' – but no one was listening.

often cooked for us, and taught us cooking – a lot of it learned, probably, from Elizabeth David, but he was also good at traditional pot roasts. We would often get home and find a bag of vegetables in the doorway, and a note inviting us to call, telling us he had a piece of gossip to relay or a book or article we should see.

My MA reading was almost more than I could manage, and there was even a time when Frank read a book on Milton for me, *The Chariot of Fire* by G. Wilson Knight, taking notes which I have kept. This was a great kindness, offered and accepted, but there was not a lot I could do with notes from a book I hadn't read myself, even though about poems I *had* read. Looking at them now, however, I see they give an impression of Frank's conversation. He writes first that Knight's book springs from passionately held beliefs, 'but he puts them forward in prose which is much more eloquent than precise'. Frank suggests it to have been a disadvantage

> that his book was rapidly composed when Hitler was threatening to invade England, a circumstance which means [Knight] readily accepts Milton's view of England as a 'Messiah nation'. He (p. 141) talks of 'British conscience' as opposed to 'Machiavellian Europe', surely a notion which is dangerously unsound.

Soon Frank is into the question of Milton's theology, his 'Arianism' – Christ not as god but as divine similitude. Knight has stressed the powerful contradictions in Milton between belief in the kingship of Christ (and, incidentally, of kings), and yet the kingship that is in every man, which may in certain circumstances license a Cromwell taking the head of a Charles. This contradiction, or unresolved tension, which Knight has suggested is in all three of Milton's major poems, and essential to their greatness, reminds Frank of something from his own reading and produces the following typical aside:

> (Note. A Gorki story about Tolstoy appears to be relevant here. Tolstoy saw a soldier approaching in the distance and with disgust

spoke of the waste of war and the demoralisation of healthy young peasants by putting them into uniform. As the soldier passed however Tolstoy looked at him appreciatively and muttered, 'A magnificent animal'. You thus have two Tolstoys – Tolstoy the preacher and Tolstoy the great artist. This may be compared to Milton's attitude to Satan.)

It's a good example of how his mind worked, especially relishing the moralist suddenly overtaken by the artist.

A lot of Frank's reading was poetry. He revered the great poets, and would like best of all to have been a poet himself. (The same was true of Janet Frame.) There is a moving passage in his autobiography where he describes his sad youthful recognition that he would never write poems like Keats's; but then he reads a passage in the poet's letters describing an old Scottish lady, and recognises that in gaining a great poet the world lost a great novelist.

> I was moved at last to such a state of heart-knocking excitement I felt driven from my room to the streets outside where I walked for hours which I am never likely to forget [. . .] and I returned to my lodgings with the conviction that I was going to repair the loss by writing the sort of novels the poet might have written.

This recalls a moment of youthful *naïveté*; but it also represents his underlying seriousness as an artist whose medium was language and whose genre was fiction. Always for Frank poetry and the history of poetry (what F. R. Leavis called 'the great tradition') were there, providing a kind of linguistic loam for all writers, a bank of examples of excellence, freshness, range, unpredictability, individuality. He loved especially, and liked to quote, Auden's sonnet 'The Novelist', both for its description of the poets 'encased in talent like a uniform' who 'can dash forward like hussars'; and for its account of the novelist, who

Must struggle out of his boyish gift and learn
How to be plain and awkward, how to be
One after whom none think it worth to turn.

For, to achieve his lightest wish, he must
Become the whole of boredom, subject to
Vulgar complaints like love, among the Just

Be just, among the Filthy filthy too,
And in his own weak person, if he can,
Dully put up with all the wrongs of Man.

My own reading had to include one further play each week to be discussed with M. K. Joseph. Mike was always very gentlemanly, and when I appeared to have finished giving my preliminary account of the play, he would wait a moment or two to be sure there wasn't anything I wanted to add; while I, slightly nervous in these one-to-one encounters, tended to rush in to fill any silence with a few further statements. Consequently it was as if I never stopped talking and he never started.

It was during the work for this paper I recognised that the nineteenth-century poets' failure even to begin to match Shakespeare in theatrical writing (which was their ambition) came from writing 'poetically', thinking always of the page, rather than practically, in terms of the theatre; not letting the 'poetry', the fine writing, the heightened moments, come as or when they would, almost as a by-product.

ONE AFTERNOON EARLY IN THAT YEAR, when I made what was meant to be a brief call to borrow or return a book, Frank insisted I sit opposite him at the counter that divided kitchen from living space and tell him what I thought of a poem he would read me. I don't possess a copy of what I was asked to 'judge', but I suspect

it was the same he sent, some months later, in a letter to Charles
Brasch:

> Buy a caterpillar that is wound up
> and crawls with rippling back
> across your day and night
>
> the wind breathed a blow away spell
>
> the wind is warm, was warm
> the days above burst unheeded
> explode their atoms of snow-black beanflower
> and white rose
> mock the last intuitive whodunnit whodunnit
> of summer thrush
>
> it said to the plant
>
> the sun pinned on the pocket of my land
> taking underground green all willowed
> and white rose
> and beanflower
> and morning mist of picnic of song
> in pepperpot breast of thrush.

What did I think? I didn't know what to think. It didn't sound
and, when he gave me the sheet of paper, didn't read, quite like
a poem. It had no structure, no shape, but it was full of striking
imagery and flashes of brilliance. That is what I thought; and I suppose, it is almost true to say, that is what I would go on thinking
about the work of Janet Frame. Because what Frank now explained
was that 'Miss Frame', whose short stories he and I had both read
and admired in the *New Zealand Listener*, had recently been
released after spending most of ten years in mental institutions.

Her sister and brother-in-law had brought her to visit, Frank had asked her what she wanted to do with her life, she had whispered (not lifting her eyes to meet his) that she 'wanted to write', he had offered her the army hut in his back garden to live and work in, and she had accepted. *Voila!* In the time it takes to write a longish sentence literary history had been made. The future Nobel Prize nominee* was writing a novel (it was *Owls do Cry*), and had shown him the opening pages from which he had extracted these lines, typed them as a poem, and sent them to John Lehmann for *The London Magazine*. It was an offer Lehmann found he could refuse, though with comments much like my own about unstructured brilliance.

Next time we visited, Janet was at first nowhere to be seen, but after half an hour made an entry, very quietly, and sat in the shadows saying nothing at all. What could she have chosen to do that would have made a more memorable impression? If you ever find yourself, dear reader, wanting to be remarked upon and remembered, enter late, and silent, and say nothing! I'm not sure that Frank even introduced her. It was understood that she was so shy she must be given time to get used to us. It took a few visits, but soon it was as if we had known one another since childhood – and sometimes as if we had neglected to leave it behind. Recently I found among my old MA lecture notes a sheet in Kay's handwriting. It contained a fake 'poem' made up of the lines from the index of first lines at the back of a poetry anthology. This was a game the four of us played, one acting as amanuensis, each contributing in turn, adding a new line, one that gave a new meaningless meaning (preferably one that was funny, and occasionally obscene) to the growing 'poem'. The results would have graced the pages of John Ashbery. Years later, when I came to look again at Janet's collection

---

* There are of course no publicly acknowledged nominations for the Nobel Prize in literature, but word goes around in Stockholm, and it was 'authoritatively rumoured', several times in the 1990s, and again in late 2003 when she was dying, that Janet was on a short list and seriously considered.

The Pocket Mirror, I recognised one of the poems there as the result of one of our games:

> In our town people live in rows
> – the raging and the ravenous
> the tiger in the tiger-pit
> 'Shall I write *pretty* poetry?'
>
> I have with fishing rod and line
> caught a cosmic Leviathan, that monstrous fish.
> Damn it all! This our south stinks peace!
> . . . I idly cut a parsley stalk
> [. . .]
> At Dirty Dick's and Sloppy Joe's
> *in our town* people live in rows.

– lines which mix Eliot, Yeats, Pound, Hardy, Auden and probably others.

Janet was devoted to poetry. She was adept at word-play, inventive, clever, funny. In fact she seemed to me always on the edge of laughter, and I came to see this as springing from her perception that everything, all human structures, were precarious, capable of falling into ruin in an instant, and that consequently our social conventions, which required us to treat them with respect and behave as if they were secure and authoritative, were groundless and absurd. In one way Janet was very conventional. She did whatever was expected of her, was even, herself, what she mocked in her writing – 'a lovely girl no trouble at all'. So in Frank's company, and in her writing, she echoed his ideas, his kind of social rebellion, his bohemianism, NZ Lit's strike against bourgeois conformism – just as, in more conventional company (as she grew capable of dealing with it) she was herself conventional: shy, smiling, modest, never giving offence or putting a foot wrong. Like Auden's novelist, she knew how to be just among the Just, 'among the Filthy filthy too'.

But the laughter that was always threatening really mocked not only herself and her own conformism. It called into question all structures, social, political, religious, personal. She had been, in her mind and in reality, too close to the edge ever to think anything deserved more than the pretence of assent. Some of us felt free to reject the idea of God, supernatural authority, the numinous, the divine. At heart I think Janet went much further: she was a meek anarchist, an intellectual suicide-bomber, who rejected the whole human order, and whose work, structureless, directionless, brilliant, with flashes of genius, offered not hope but a black hole.

We made a strange foursome: a 52-year-old talisman of New Zealand literature who concealed, under a change of name, a past conviction for a homosexual offence; a 31-year-old writer of genius whose mental state had been officially diagnosed as schizophrenic; and a rather conventional (except that the woman was the 'breadwinner') young couple, student-poet and librarian, aged 22 and 21. But when we were together during that year it was a mix that seemed to work for us all. We stimulated one another and were fond. Frank extracted new energy from it. Janet was writing the novel that would be one of her most successful. My studies, and Kay's work in the library, went their way as such things do; but I think she and I felt as if we were inadvertently enrolled, as well, for an extra-curricular course that might have been called 'Off-beat and Unexpected 101'. Many years later, in the second volume of her autobiography, Janet romanticised that year, and us, 'the golden couple', 'drawn with Frank into my web of worship':

> Their intelligence, their beauty, their love brought joy to Frank, who was often depressed by the neglect of writers. [. . .] The friendship of Karl and Kay filled my life, giving me at last a place in my own years.

Almost simultaneously (early 1980s), I romanticised our strange friendship in my novel *All Visitors Ashore*, Frank as Melior Farbro the painter in love with 'little Kenny' the trade union activist, and

Janet as Cecelia Skyways, the writer who addresses fanciful flyaway letters to the Blessed Virgin and to the Prime Minister, and engages the spider she calls Bodhidharma of the Web in Zen conversation.

There was truth in our romanticising – a kind of truth, a good kind. 'Though I speak with the tongues of men and of angels and have not charity, I am become as a sounding brass or a tinkling cymbal.'

AT SOME TIME DURING THAT YEAR Kay found she was pregnant. It had happened on an overnight visit to her family at Henderson when (like Cherie Blair at Chequers) she found she had left the equipment (in those pre-Pill days it was a contraceptive diaphragm) at Takapuna. We thought we had mastered the 'safe' time of the month, but nature's mastery of the unsafe time was superior.

It was inconvenient but didn't seem to me a disaster. That was my first reaction: we would cope. But Kay was firm. She had seen her sisters with babies, knew what it involved and that she was not ready for it. The time would come, but not yet. There were things she wanted to do, places she wanted to go. We had been receiving letters from Patsy and John in London, and she reminded me how we had walked along the beach at night, planning to meet them there – travelling on a scholarship if I could get one, or if not, just making our way on our earnings, as they were doing. I was, as so often, willing to be where I found myself, or to go where I was sent; but it was obvious she was right, we had things to do that would be much more difficult, hardly possible, with a child. Abortion was a frightening word, not only illegal, but dangerous. But it was her choice to make, and she was unwavering. So, though terrified, I agreed – if it could be done we would do it. The concerns I felt were not about morality, but about Kay's safety. Later, of course, when terminations under certain circumstances became legal, the argument against them took a strident moral tone. While the law forbade it, and desperate young women died from time to time in the back streets, those who would later call themselves 'pro-life' were silent.

We had heard from Frank about a literary wife who had recently had an abortion. Kay said we must ask him. He confirmed that he knew of a network of women who helped one another in such crises. He put us in touch with Irene, wife of Bob Lowry, the printer who around that time was at work on the issue of *Kiwi* I had edited with Rob Dyer. Irene arranged another contact who, in turn, was in touch with a third. It would cost fifty pounds – a large sum – but I had recently received a hundred dollars US for my prize poem in America, and that would cover it.

So appointments were made. We crossed into town, went to one address, were driven from there to another in deepest Newton Gully, and from there were led on foot through small back gardens (gone now, alas, under motorways). There were bits of corrugated-iron fencing, a small vegetable patch, a miniature glass-house, a pile of bricks from a half-dismantled chimney, an outdoor 'dunny', a copper-turned-incinerator, all half-seen in the half-light. At the back door of one of these back-street houses we were met by a woman who introduced herself as 'Brownie'. Her hair was the kind that spends its nights in irons. Her lips and nails were bright red. There was a cigarette implanted at the corner of her mouth, to burn there rather than to be smoked. Indoors there were signs of the affluence crime can bring – armchairs too big for the rooms, a gilt mirror, three china ducks up the wall, and what land-agents in those days called 'wall-to-wall and vens'.

At that point I would gladly have fled but Kay remained firm. She was blindfolded and led away into a bedroom. Sick with fear I waited while hideous carpet fought it out with hideous wallpaper. I asked Brownie whether Kay would suffer pain and she produced a mantra which for a moment struck terror. 'When you pick ripe fruit it comes easy. If it's green . . .' And a shake of the head.

I recovered only by reflecting that having a full-term baby was not remotely like picking ripe fruit. Kay emerged, pale but not distressed. Whatever is done in such circumstances had been done. There was no pain, Kay said, only momentary discomfort, and a strong smell of chlorine.

We paid the money and went back to the ferry, and home, holding on to one another and wondering whether we had been duped. That night the bleeding began, and went on. There was a great deal of it. Felix Millar lent us an old china 'jerry' stained with Friar's Balsam which he used to clear his sinuses. I waded into the sea with it, thinking of Macbeth:

> Will all great Neptune's ocean wash this blood
> Clean from my hands? No, this my hand will rather
> The multitudinous seas incarnadine,
> Making the green one red.

Now I did feel a sense of sin, not that a pregnancy had been terminated, but that I had been party to something that might kill my treasured Kay. Next morning the bleeding continued. Felix's doctor friend Pat Hitchings was called. He turned out to be Catholic, and censorious. He sent Kay by ambulance to Greenlane Hospital, where she was spoken to in the tone reserved in those days for 'bad girls'. But a dilation and curettage were performed. It was all over. We breathed again. We were both shaken, but a load had been lifted.

THE AUC LITERARY SOCIETY CONTINUED. We invited Frank to read to us, and on another occasion Bill Pearson, who was known to have written a novel, *Coal Flat*, as yet unpublished. Bill was a West Coaster, recently returned from London after completing a PhD there. Ten years my senior, he was one of an extraordinary group all born in 1922, including Keith Sinclair, Bob Chapman, Maurice Duggan, Kendrick Smithyman. Bill was best-known for a long essay, 'Fretful Sleepers', which had appeared in *Landfall* in 1952 – a penetrating sociological/psychological/moral analysis of the

New Zealand character and of the difficult place of the intellectual and the artist in our society. I had read it when it first appeared, and had even read parts of it to my parents. I must have been impressed to do that; and I remember which pages I read from, because they contained the word 'vulva', which I had not encountered before, and I registered a slight parental flutter as it passed by, warning me I should look it up. As for the broad argument – Dad seemed faintly bewildered by what I read; and re-reading it now I feel faintly bewildered myself. Pearson was so confident and damning in his dismemberment of the mental processes of 'ordinary' New Zealanders, but then, equally, of intellectual New Zealand and its literary and artistic cliques, seeming to leave himself dancing, alone and purified, not on the head of a pin but on its point.

And yet it spoke to us at the time, and we were stirred. Kay had read it too, it had become a reference point in our conversation and the conversation of our friends. It was another document of the literary nationalism of the time, belonging with Curnow's introduction to his *A Book of New Zealand Verse*, with Sargeson's self-projection as the man who wrote at home and published at home and abroad, and with Bob Chapman's essay 'Fiction and the Social Pattern'.

Bill was socially awkward, faintly truculent in manner but with a kindly eye and good liberal conscience. He had a tendency – not uncommon among writers – to paranoia, but in his case augmented by an astonishing memory (if it wasn't simply a very detailed diary) for who had said what when, and what was intended or implied. When lecturing he found it hard to meet the collective eye of his class, so his glance seemed always to move in a curve that went from his notes to the floor, and then in a great sweep to the farthest corner of the ceiling. Seen from behind, walking, he looked like a sailor in high seas, his arms slightly raised on either side, his torso swaying, a motion that increased with alcoholic intake. In those days he drank beer – a lot of it; or perhaps it was that he needed very little to make him seem less than perfectly sober. I never saw him helplessly drunk. He was never an embarrassment, but always primed. It was probably his 'necessary protection', as cheap wine was for Colin McCahon who used that phrase for a series of paintings; but, unlike Colin, Bill was able, later on, to give it up and survive without it.

Another protection for him in the English Department was Allen Curnow. Allen and Bill, along with Irish Jim Walton and Scottish Tom Crawford, formed a kind of phalanx at this time, two Kiwis and two Celts, against English Musgrove, the HOD whom they distrusted as an Oxford import, a sort of colonial governor.

It was my job as Lit Club student chairman to preside over the readings, and Don Smith's memory is that I was worried before Bill's because he seemed to have taken more of his 'necessary protection' than usual. While reading he clung to the lectern with a grip that turned his knuckles white, but he read on, manfully and audibly. *Coal Flat* is the classic West Coaster's novel, conservative in form, but with the intelligent terseness and economy Bill's prose always had, and only failing in its own eyes because Bill had felt it necessary to disguise the homosexuality of its central character (in effect himself). He read the passage which recounts a meeting of the local school's parent–teacher association. It was well received and Bill was relieved – we all were.

Frank had told me that Bill was homosexual. Bill had none of the obvious outward signs of it, and since Frank tended to see it everywhere, even where it was not, I had taken this information with several grains of salt. In fact he was right, and I suppose this explains what puzzled me at the time, that Frank not only came to Bill's reading, as Bill had come to his, but asked questions which seemed to be full of innuendo, slyly friendly, but causing Bill to bridle. Since Frank's conversation could be at times so oblique as to require translation, it didn't occur to me that under these questions and answers a second level of secret signals was being exchanged.

Margaret Mahy, then a student a few years my junior, and Maurice Gee, a year ahead, were in the audience, together with members of the current MA class – Smith, Jim Traue (who would one day be the Alexander Turnbull librarian), Lois Coles and others. Members of staff attended too. Keith Sinclair, who used to refer to Bill Pearson as 'the little jockey', came to both readings. Allen Curnow was there for Pearson but not for Sargeson.

Curnow and Sargeson were chalk and cheese, especially after Frank caught Allen at the bus-stop when 'Spectacular Blossom' appeared in the *Listener*, and told him that the red stain pohutukawa shed over Auckland beaches in summer was composed of stamens, not petals. Curnow's poem had referred to a pohutukawa as 'the single / Actress shuffling red petals', and since he was most particular, even pedantic, about what he called 'the reality prior to the poem', this information from perky and challenging Frank was an unacceptable invasion of his space. When I praised Allen's poetry to Frank, he would show his irritation: 'Oh, of course Curnow's terrific, but *bugger him!*' When I spoke of Sargeson to Curnow there was never much response. *Chez* Curnow, Sargeson was acknowledged, but there was no personal warmth.

In June my American poetry award was announced. In August *Meanjin* (Australia's *Landfall*) took a Takapuna poem, and Holcroft, saying he 'liked it too much to turn it down on account of length', took one for the *Listener* which Charles had declined because of what he called 'its jog-trot rhythm'. At least it showed that nostalgia for Kaiwaka could still be caught in a framework of interlocking rhymes, the first stanza of which went:

> And could he now go back? – to the milky mornings
> Waking to Daisy's bell, a dance of dogs,
> And the nipping early air in a yard all mud;
> Summer mirrored on the dam; the cut scrub burning,
> The gorse bright yellow until the time for logs –
> Then damp days heavy with the axe's thud.

Don Smith and I called on Bob Lowry at his Pilgrim Press in Wakefield Street to check on progress with *Kiwi*, and were taken to the local tavern for a beer. Soon afterwards proofs came, and then the final product, very handsomely printed. Bob was paid but not thanked, and after a few weeks came a message that I was to call him. When I did he asked was I pleased with the work. I said I was, very pleased. Well, why hadn't I said so? – and he ticked me off roundly for behaviour 'typical of you young fellows'. I was full of apology and praise for the job he had done, but he shouldn't have had to ask for it. It was a good lesson – a reminder that Lowry the printer was a serious artist. Money didn't matter, and time was flexible: but the aim was to produce something fine, and when that happened, praise was due.

I continued to exchange letters with Rob Dyer. He had gone off to Oxford on a scholarship, aged twenty or twenty-one, and had spent his first few months in England teaching Greek and Latin to Eton boys (one, an earl) only a few years his junior – I think with some success. He had sent us Maurice Bowra's *Oxford Book of Greek Verse in Translation* for a wedding present and followed it later with Philip Larkin's *The Less Deceived*, inscribed 'To Karl Stead on the occasion of Larkin assuming the title of leading English young poet and selling out his first edition in 3 months – a gift of many morals'. He also gave an account of seeing 'quite an amusing play in London called *Waiting for Godot*', which seems, at a distance of half a century, rather like reading one of Simon Forman's diary entries about 'a new play by Wm Shakespeare':

It has had hysterically good write-ups but is a little over-abstracted
– about now that the old squire-order is gone the ordinary
people don't know what to do and have no initiative. The two
chief characters are portrayed as the two thieves waiting for the
Messiah, who promises to come on a mythical tomorrow but whose
coming will only result in their crucifixion. Sick in body, clothed in
yesterday's tatters, they lack initiative to put on a new habit and are
tongue-tied before the decaying squire whom they are powerless
to help. They are rather well-characterized. But the joy of the play

is the intellectualism, the squire's slave carrying his heavy bags, fetching and carrying at his master's word. He used to dance and make pretty speeches but now when ordered to think he can only utter half-formed half-understood thoughts.

Rob had written an editorial for *Kiwi*, full of grumbles about the lack of great causes and the consequent shrinkage of poetry into mere 'individualism'. So the praise he handed out to me, as the one among us who had come through as a poet, was distinctly qualified by its larger argument. Similarly ambiguous, even sinister, as if containing a threat, but also, I thought, strangely moving, was the poem he had told me was written in his own persona and addressed to me, which I printed at the end of the book:

Epimetheus Speaks

Prometheus, friend and brother,
Why did the bright gods give you this,
To grasp the spinning wheel of things
And though in pain have glory yet,
While I must build this slow palace of truth
From the deeds I have not done?
All that is and has been I have known,
But for the moment's need
I am, all incomprehensible to you,
Ungifted till the moment's past.
And so, unless the gods may use me,
An instrument of vengeance and of mirth,
I cannot like you ambitiously frequent
The tattling lips of men,
But rest aloof and sage,
While the subtler eagle preys upon my soul
Of all I have not known nor done
Till the hot moment has grown cold.

TWENTY-ONE
ALL VISITORS ASHORE

One day Frank told me Janet had been writing poems. He could read and comment, but she needed someone more like a contemporary to go through them with her, help her sort out what was working well and what was not. He had suggested me, and she was keen. I was quite ready to do this, but surprised that he thought it needed this almost formal approach, and the fixing of a time when she and I could be alone together, undisturbed. There was a strange tone to all this, I thought, but the arrangement was made.

So I found myself one afternoon alone with Janet in the army hut, going through her poems, reading them, having her read them to me, and offering comments. I understood it was our job to be analytical together, and if there were poems that were less than successful, to work out why, and how they might be improved. I also understood Janet's sensitivity, and knew I must tread warily, work by indirection, hints, questions, suggestions. It was a meeting of the shy and the super-shy, but one in which, though she was eight years my senior, I was more able to be at ease and to take control.

I proceeded with the greatest delicacy. There was much praise given, much of it deserved, some just *pour encourager*. Suggestions of possible improvements were kept to a minimum, and reduced, and finally stopped altogether as I felt, more and more, that something had gone wrong. Were we here to talk about her poems, to work seriously together as fellow-writers, or for some other undisclosed purpose? From being warm and shyly welcoming Janet had become quiet, cool, and was now approaching coldness and silence. We were stalled. What was wrong? She wouldn't meet my eye. Her expression was fixed. She seemed angry, insulted. I offered some kind of generalised apology, as if I had stumbled in the dark into the wrong bedroom, and left.

Frank had been gardening around the front of the section, keeping a distance, and the house, between himself and the hut. He seemed surprised to see me so soon, and looked anxious. I told him something had gone wrong, I didn't know what it was. A day or so later, when I ran into him at Hall's Corner and asked how she was, he told me she had locked herself in the hut and refused to come out or to eat for the rest of that day, and had emerged only the evening of the next. But she was all right now. She was a very difficult person. Had I read . . . And he changed the subject.

This locking herself away was something she had done before, once leaving a note on the counter that said 'I AM MAD TODAY'. Relations between them were not easy. Frank was fond of her, admired her intelligence and her writing, believed she had genius. He cooked for her, waited on her and worried about her, but half-resented it. He always needed people to need him, but could never quite forgive their demands on his time and energy. For her part, her autobiography indicates that her degree of dependence on him made her uneasy; and that she sometimes felt in him 'a vein of distrust, even of hatred, of women as a species', and so of herself.

Here is what Michael King writes in his Frame biography, *Wrestling with the Angel* (page 127) about our encounter in the hut:

Among the many 'first' experiences that she was still to have, because of her time in hospital, was that of a sexual encounter with another person. In this area as in others her mentor, a novelist and playwright, was more than happy to create the circumstances in which action might plausibly occur.

Sargeson reported to Stead that Frame would welcome his opinion on poems she was writing. Stead, happy to oblige, and not averse to hints of a dangerous adventure, went along to the army hut.

He then quotes what I made of that encounter in *All Visitors Ashore*, a comic moment of misunderstandings, latent but unexpressed sex, and spilled tea. But like so much else in that novel, what happened and what, thirty years later, I made of what happened were very different.

King's account, and my own impressions at the time and reflections later, accord in one important detail: we both concluded that Frank, with his unorthodox, and I suppose extraordinarily practical, view of sex, and perhaps encouraged by what he had perceived of Janet's interest in me, had decided this was what she needed, and that by putting us together in convenient closeness, he would be providing it – a matter of simple addition, one plus one. But the phrasing of King's account ('Stead, happy to oblige, and not averse to hints of a dangerous adventure') suggests that, even if nothing was said, I was a knowing and willing party to the arrangement. This is quite wrong. I had thought I was there to talk about her poems. However many ways I had of thinking about Janet, the prospect of having sex with her was not one of them.

When Janet, later in life, came to write her autobiography, it was structured around the story of herself as a young woman who, in order to attract the attention of John Money, a Dunedin psychologist, read up the symptoms of schizophrenia and mimicked them. From that mistake followed her whole sad history of misdiagnosis and mistreatment.

Frank, at the time she was living with him, wrote to friends about 'the madwoman in his garden' who had many personalities, some dark, even dangerous. He liked to make a drama of it. But to Brasch he wrote quite seriously that her conversation was full of dark corners that produced in him 'blank despair'. 'There are times when one just can't listen any more – to fantastic misinterpretations, accounts of nightmares, and unceasing talk of death'.* Most interesting, he has a theory about her which is like the opposite, the mirror image, of her own account of herself. She has 'escaped from the Hospital', Frank decides, because her 'very remarkable intelligence prompted her to simulate sanity in order to get free – to give herself one last chance. But it is all turning out quite badly.'

Not that she had simulated schizophrenia, but that, though 'mad', she could simulate sanity!

A few years on from this MA year, when I was called to the Maudsley Hospital in London to visit Janet and to talk to her principal physician, Dr R. H. Cawley, he began by asking whether I thought she was 'mad'. I said no – she just lacked a skin. I meant this quite sincerely. It was not just her intelligence, and her talent as a writer, made me give that answer. If the word 'mad', the notion of 'insanity', means anything (always an open question), it surely has to mean a degree of social incompetence, unpredictability and lack of control far beyond Janet's. But what I did not even attempt to say to Cawley, and never tried to write down until very recently, was my sense of her, at that time when I knew her so well, as *different*. Shyness, hypersensitivity, timidity, fear, all to the point of morbidity – these were extreme, but only different in degree from what one had encountered, and in some slight degree experienced, oneself. But beyond all that there was something intangible I felt very strongly, with a sort of animal apprehension when we were young: something that expressed itself in body language, clothes, shoes, and in the body itself, neck, skin, hair.

* 24 February 1957.

The wonderful thing about fiction is that you are not shackled to facts. To truth – yes, but only a general truth, a truth your readers will recognise as humanly possible, even likely, at least credible. In *All Visitors Ashore* that was the truth I served. Cecelia Skyways is Janet Frame idealised. But who is to say that the fiction is not a better, truer, deeper recall of the 'real', the interior, the magical Janet Frame?

EXAMS WERE COMING AND I WORKED hard, everything else set aside. They were to happen at the end of October and on into November. As Guy Fawkes approached Karl Morton, our landlady's slightly strange middle-aged bachelor son, began to prepare his beach bonfire of driftwood, pine branches and anything else that would burn. It grew higher and higher, a ten-foot tower. There was a ragged 'guy' perched on top, looking like Karl's mother who had no doubt contributed its floppy hat. Karl said it would be the biggest on the beach – the biggest *ever*. His eyes gleamed. I suppose he had made bonfires there all his life, since childhood. This was the old Takapuna, with the feel of Bruce Mason's *The End of the Golden Weather* about it.

Felix seemed equally a contributor to that faintly surreal atmosphere. He told us, in his curious neighing whisper, that he was going to set Karl's bonfire alight on the night *before* Guy Fawkes. Why? There was no why about it. The idea amused him, excited him. He was just being William to Karl Morton's Hubert Lane. I thought it was probably no more than talk, like his stories of all those girls, his violin pupils, he said he 'rooted'.

Around midnight on the night of the fourth there were shouts and banging on doors. Help! A disaster! Karl Morton was calling to us – and to Felix and Hazel. So was his mother, in her strangled baritone. The bonfire was alight! Spades and shovels were handed around and we rushed down on to the sand in pyjamas to put it out. The landlady, who dragged one foot and couldn't get down to the beach, watched from the veranda, barking and croaking at us. There was a brisk breeze off the sea, fanning the blaze. Felix, positioning himself between fire and water, contrived to throw spade-fulls of sand too high, so the wind caught them and blew them in our faces. It was only now I wondered about the burning down of the restaurant, said to have been an accident, but somehow connected with the drama of Hazel and the cook. Was our neighbour across the yard a secret pyromaniac? Had Felix fiddled while his restaurant burned?

By now Karl had run a hose down from the house, and soon the bonfire was a nonfire. Some of it survived, hissing, collapsed and black, though the landlady look-alike had been cremated. Kay and I were sorry for Hubert Lane, defeated by the irrepressible William. We told him he should build it up again tomorrow. It would be smaller, but still a very nice bonfire. I don't remember whether he did. My mind was on exams.

WHEN I WAS A CHILD I WAS BOTHERED by space. The idea that it went on for ever in all directions was so disconcerting I felt I had to imagine it enclosed by a wall, or some kind of infinite envelope. It would go thus far and no further. But then came the thought, what was beyond the wall, outside the enclosure? Logically it had to go on, and conceptually that was beyond my grasp. If I had been a young Einstein I might have developed a theory; since I was not, I had to live with the contradiction. Christianity spoke of 'the mystery' – and then offered to resolve it, like the Fun Doctor pulling a weary white rabbit out of his weary black hat. But this was the real mystery, the unresolvable one: consciousness extending beyond the limits of comprehension.

Later there were thoughts about 'life after death'. Heaven was supposed to be eternal and continuous bliss, but that (and equally its infernal opposite) was not just inconceivable; it was a nonsense. I didn't know, of course, that great minds in the Christian tradition

– St Augustine for example – had wrestled with this problem; that Blake had tried to resolve it by conceiving of Heaven as 'war and hunting'. Dante had made Heaven sound like a nice school, with pretty ever smiling Beatrice the teacher, and a lot of white light. I think I was at MAGS when I came up with the formula 'consciousness is contrast'. There could be no positives unless there were counterbalancing negatives. Light and dark, heat and cold, soft and hard, swift and slow – without a clear sense of one there could be none of the other. 'Heaven' logically was no different from being dead as an atheist believed – gone, absent, non-existent.

These existential puzzles (there was no angst, that I can recall, or very little) were, like my wrestling with the notion of a 'free' will, and the mind/body conundrum that would resurface much later in my novel *The Death of the Body*, the ground of my intellectual development. Life was full of contradictions, and consequent ironies, which were not only unresolvable: their recognition was the necessary adjunct of full consciousness.

This view in turn governed my reading of literature. I saw a poem as a map of life, of the living mind, of consciousness – the more complex the better, and truer: and if it could make you feel those contradictions, could make complexity seem present, there, in your face, then that was major poetry; that was poetic greatness. Shakespeare, for example:

> It hath been taught us from the primal state
> That he which is was wish'd until he were;
> And the ebb'd man, ne'er lov'd till ne'er worth love,
> Comes dear'd by being lack'd. This common body
> Like to a vagabond flag upon the stream
> Goes to and back, lackeying the varying tide
> To rot itself with motion.

Or Hopkins:

Wert Thou my enemy, O Thou my friend,
How wouldst Thou worse, I wonder, than Thou dost
Defeat, thwart me?

So I was ready, more than ready, for the American New Critics (as Allen Tate, John Crowe Ransom, and their cohort were then called) when I came to them as part of that history of criticism paper in my MA year. They looked for ironies, ambiguities, paradoxes as the mark of maturity in a work of literature. Like every critical movement and method, theirs was not faultless, and only as good as the individual practitioner who applied it. It was not for me a doctrine, and I was never going to be a proselytiser. But I think it must have given a unity to everything I wrote that year, and particularly to my seven examination papers.

By that night before Guy Fawkes I knew the exams were going well. I had a clear sense of what was wanted, and a feeling afterwards that I could predict the outcome within a few marks. Marks in the arts faculty were less liberally assigned than they have become in recent years. Averaged over the seven papers, you needed 50 per cent to pass, 60 per cent for lower second-class honours, 70 per cent for upper seconds and 75 per cent for a first. I had done three papers by the night of the fire. Four to go, and I was feeling increasingly confident.

Charles Brasch had written to say he was coming to Auckland and would like to see me, and to meet Kay. We invited him for the evening after my last paper, 11 November. Between Guy Fawkes and Armistice Day I had completed the remainder of my papers and estimated my marks. No matter how I did the arithmetic, however conservatively, I couldn't see myself getting less than that magical average of 75 per cent. I didn't tell Charles, but I told Kay. If I was right it meant first-class honours and (though there were few of them in those days) the possibility of a scholarship that would take us overseas.

But Charles Brasch – New Zealand's Maecenas – and for dinner!

It would have to be pan-fried rice and oysters, surely – preceded by a mighty salad, and followed by a tart (from a shop – a good one) and fruit. And to drink?

Kay and I were children of our time and place, 1950s New Zealand, where the pubs were for men only and shut at 6 p.m., and where restaurants that attempted to serve wine with meals were fined and closed down. Alcohol, when we drank it (not very often) was beer, occasionally cider. On party occasions there might also be whisky or gin, if the party-giver could afford it; and there were other strange drinks, with names like Pimm's No. 1 Cup, and Honeymoon Cocktail, mainly for the women, who might also drink 'shandies' – a mixture of beer and lemonade. Kay had grown up at Henderson where New Zealand's wine industry was born. But in those days the product was referred to, with an emphasis somewhere between indifference and contempt, as 'Dally plonk' (Dalmatian blanc, I imagine, though the term referred to wine of any colour), and was sold only in bulk. The signs she remembers from childhood, LICENSED TO SELL TWO GALS, meant, not 'up to two gallons', but 'not less than two gallons'.

But we were also children of good literature, including modern novels, and so knew that the right thing to do, the *refeened*, the sophisticated thing, was to serve wine with a meal. Frank used to give us Lemora, a citrus wine which he poured out of a flagon into the peanut-butter jars that served as glasses – thus managing to be at once 'European' but not 'bourgeois' (a word he used a lot, always with negative emphasis, and mispronounced boogeois). But neither of us, nor anyone I have spoken to since who tasted the stuff, liked Lemora, and we wanted to do better than that for Charles. We both knew, again from reading (ah, how good books can lead you astray!) that port was posh. It was expensive, but I decided I would buy a bottle for Charles's visit. Our pan-fried rice would be served with port!

Many years later, when I was Senior Visiting Fellow at St John's College, Oxford, and used to withdraw after dinner at high table to sit with the fellows at another table in a small ancient panelled room where dessert was eaten under a hundred-candle chandelier, while the port, the sherry and the sauterne circulated, and snuff was taken, I often thought of telling this story and never did, either because I lacked the courage, or because I sensed it would not be believed, or perhaps (even) that it was so foreign in this place it might have seemed in some way ostentatious.

Charles arrived and we all did our best. The flat had been cleaned and tidied within an inch of its life. He and I sat on the divan among cushions under the island matting and the Louise Henderson, swivelling our knees, one right the other left, so we could seem to face one another, and talked and nibbled (cashew nuts, almost certainly) while Kay made final preparations. Charles had an almost paralysing effect on me – not a physical or vocal paralysis, but an interior one, in which five out of six things I thought to say were instantly struck out by a frantic inner editor, leaving something safe and acceptable, boring and obvious. Perhaps I had a sense of being too closely observed. But I think it was more that he flinched so visibly at the mention of anything he considered bad taste, bad writing, bad art; and there was a confidence went with that sensitivity – if something made him flinch then it could not be good, must not be defended – and so a flavour of priggishness. I always felt this with Charles; but at the time of that visit, when I was a Young Aspirant and he an Important Editor, I tried too hard to please, felt afterwards I had behaved falsely, and half resented it, as if the fault had been his and not my own.

Kay summoned us to the tiny table with the splendid view out to Rangitoto. The salad (much of it no doubt fresh from Frank's garden) came first. It was delicious, served with aioli made to Frank's recipe, the oil mixed drop by drop with the beaten egg-yolk, some small pieces of bread dropped into the mix to prevent curdling. The pan-fried rice followed. It looked very good. At this point Charles was offered port. He hesitated, and declined. He hesitated again, and then told us the facts of culinary life. Port was not drunk with the meal. It was served afterwards, with dessert (which was not to be confused with 'pudding'), and was always passed to the right around the table.

I imagine his hesitation had been to deal with the question of whether he should educate this young couple for the future, at the expense of their comfort now; or let them discover the uses of port later, and meanwhile enjoy the social occasion in unembarrassed ignorance. Being Charles, he chose the former.

I remember a story, probably apocryphal, of the Queen giving dinner at the palace for an African dignitary who, feeling thirsty, looked around for water, saw what he did not know was his finger bowl, and drank from it. While the lackeys looked at one another and wondered what to do next, her Majesty casually took a sip or two from her own finger bowl. Brasch might have been wealthy and civilised, but he was clearly not royal. For myself I was glad of the lesson, but not grateful for the embarrassment.

Back in Dunedin he wrote thanking us for the good evening we had given him and regretting that we could not meet more often. To Frank he wrote, 'I felt a bit concerned that Karl was not looking very strong, but perhaps he was simply exhausted after exams – a year ago I had put him down as fairly tough.' Of course I was not looking as strong, or as tough, as I had looked at our first meeting, when I had packed on extra clothes and talked bullishly about playing centre forward for Varsity. In fact his journal entry written just two days after our dinner, shows he was 'startled' by the degree to which I had shrunk. He records some of our conversation – about my play, that Frank had suggested he and I write one together, that I wanted to write a novel, that Kay and I wanted to go to England but were 'not quite sure of the reason for going'. He makes no mention of the meal, the flat with its Polynesian matting, the view across the gulf (despite the fact that one of his best-known poems was called 'A View of Rangitoto'), or even the culinary solecism of port wine offered with pan-fried rice and oysters. By far the largest part of the entry is devoted to personal appearance, which seems to

337

have been an obsession – as if he saw more than his sensibility could accommodate, or, indeed, interpret. Previously, he writes, I had struck him as 'loosely built but wiry with a long strong jaw [. . .] an out-of-doors young man well able to meet the world'. Now,

> . . . I was startled to meet a tallish but very slight figure with small well-kept dark-red beard on a long head, the skin very pale, grey pensive noticeable eyes & a delicately formed high thin birdlike nose, hair pale and rather thin; the whole head suggesting both a very refined Viking figurehead on a ship's prow, & a hollow-cheeked fasting Christ from some rococo Italian or Spanish painting or majolica statue, too pure & sensitive and melting-eyed.

If I had seen either of these two entries, written sixteen months apart, the first with its ugly jaw would have upset me; but I think the 'hollow-cheeked . . . melting-eyed' Christ might have troubled me even more. He mentions that I have just finished my exams and that a few weeks of sun might restore me; 'but I thought his want of robustness disquieting.'

Kay gave him no such anxiety:

> His wife by contrast looked warm-blooded & rich with life – dark skin, full bright eyes, & generous mouth; quiet, but alert and responsive. For me it was a happy evening; we talked freely, constraint evaporated, & I felt there was confidence on both sides.

A day or so later Kay and I went off by bus on a camping holiday at Tairua, a wonderful wild haven nothing like the resort-suburb it has since become, where we met up with her sister and husband who arrived by car. Around the campfire the two sisters argued fiercely about the Masons, Olwen loyal to the memory of their father, who had been some kind of grand master, Kay sharply critical of the order as an absurd, secretive and outdated male preserve. I defended Kay. Olwen wept. We swam in the lagoon and in the open sea, climbed the sombrero-shaped hill, explored an old graveyard with carved wooden 'headstones' that seemed to record the deaths of fishermen with Portuguese names. It rained and Kay and I lay in our pup-tent and felt weightless and witless, happy, companionable and in love, with a future yet to be deciphered, but full of excitement and promise.

Just before Christmas Charles wrote, having heard 'some thunderous growling from Frank', to ask what had happened about my degree. I replied attempting to explain why Frank was upset on my behalf. I had my MA with first-class honours, top aggregate in a good class in which there were two others with 'firsts'. Musgrove had seemed to offer me a junior lectureship, and then, while I was away camping, had given it to Don Smith, whose name had also gone forward as the department's nomination for a scholarship, since my own application for one had been technically 'late'. Curnow, Pearson and Tom Scott were not pleased; Reid and Joseph were neutral. To Brasch I wrote, 'I don't know Musgrove well enough for it to be personal. Probably he had everything worked out for Smith and I upset all the plans by getting higher marks. Anyway it's not frightfully important – I have my "first".' I was also to receive the College Prize in English for that year, and the Fowlds Memorial Prize for the top graduate in the Faculty of Arts. Dr West's wound on my record was still there, but as a fading scar. I had begun to 'peak', and not 'too early'.

I FELT WONDERFULLY FREE, ACCEPTED some reviewing work for a Radio New Zealand books programme, and took a job as a postman. It was a role for a poet sanctioned by James K. Baxter, who did it for a number of years, and to be ratified years later by Ian Wedde. The postman (I think as yet there were no postwomen) started early, sorting his day's lot into whatever order he had chosen for his streets. He was on the road before nine, and finished often by early to middle afternoon, after which he had the rest of the day to work at writing, or to think about it, or to walk on the beach and play chess with Felix. As most people still did then, I went to and from work by public transport – bus, then ferry, then bus. My sorting centre was in Upper Symonds Street, and my delivery run was somewhere between Dominion and Sandringham Roads.

I carried a whistle around my neck, and was supposed to blow it each time I dropped letters into a box. So my approach was heralded, and housewives came out to their gates to see if there was anything for them today 'apart from bills'. There were endless jokes about the bills I brought, and what I could do with them. Sometimes I was invited to shelter on a veranda or in a garage from a heavy shower; now and then offered a cool drink or tea. I began to see novels lurking behind these gates, in these suburban gardens, behind those windows open to the summer. There were encounters to be welcomed, others to be avoided; people hungry for talk, for human contact, who could tell you things you were interested to hear, and other things you would prefer not to know. If you were too obliging your run would never be finished; if you were unobliging, you would be made to feel unwelcome and the street would turn its back on you.

I enjoyed the work. I don't remember that I wrote anything; but this suburb, the flatlands between Mt Eden/Maungawhau and Mt Albert/Owairaka, was like home base for me. It connected with my roots. I felt as if my tanks were being replenished.

One day, packing sorted letters into my bag, I somehow missed one large bundle and left it behind. When I came to those streets I felt like the Pied Piper without his pipe. I had no choice but to walk a gauntlet of increasingly questioning, disbelieving and finally displeased women as I said repeatedly, 'Nothing for you today. Sorry. Better luck tomorrow.' By the time I got back to the centre phone calls had been made and it was known I had left mail behind. Reprimands were delivered, but with no great ferocity. I was new to the job. It had happened before. Just be careful in future.

340

Next Saturday it was raining heavily when I left Takapuna. The harbour water was subdued and pitted with it. It rained all through the morning, as it does sometimes in Auckland – heavy, heavier, heaviest, blown down from the islands of the warm north-east, straight in off the sea, and down, drumming on corrugated-iron roofs, beating flowers flat, causing birds to roost, hunched, ruffled and disconsolate, on drainpipes under eaves and among sheltering branches. The gutters rushed and spilled, cars in the streets sent out showers left and right, gardens flooded and footpaths streamed. When I got home, all my clothes dripping, my shoes full of water, there was a very wet letter waiting for me. I dried it in the toaster. Professor Ian Gordon of Victoria University, external assessor for the Auckland English Department that year, had suggested my name to Professor Piper at the University of New England in New South Wales who was offering me a lectureship, for one year but with the possibility of renewal, and at full lecturer salary, £1200 per annum.

I don't think we hesitated long. With that kind of money (I would be a 'thousand-a-year man'!), and with Kay working, we could save and go on from there to England with or without the scholarship. We stared out through the streaming windows towards that distant gap on the horizon I had named the Gateway to the World.

Everything followed fast – resignations from Post Office and university library, passports, tax clearances, travel bookings, goodbyes to family and friends. With Frank and Janet there was (as Frank described it in a letter to Charles) 'a farewell expedition [by bus] with the Steads, swimming under the cliffs away up the coast on a perfect day, with nobody about'. It was something I remembered long afterwards, an idyll that got incorporated into my nostalgia, to be carried about like a talisman, one of the recurrent images that would call me home. Years afterwards I even borrowed, and put into a novel, the moment when Frank, that antic icon of our literature, wreathed himself in seaweed, picked up a piece of driftwood, and did a pan dance in the shallows, lifting his knees high and playing on his pretend pipe. There were naval gun emplacements above us on the cliffs; and there was a moment of shock, and for Janet of panic, when they began firing over our heads and out to sea – blanks, possibly, but they thundered as if real, and Janet had to be comforted and reassured.

I was to carry that memory more than half a century, without the least shadow on it, until 2007 when I read Frank's account written just afterwards in his letter to Charles. The day, he said, had been 'perfect'. 'But Janet, apparently enjoying herself, was collecting misinterpretations and minor traumas to last her for several days afterwards. There is nothing I can do.'

He was working already to get her away to Europe, and we would meet up with her there. In fact our interactions with Frank and with Janet were to continue on and off until their deaths, his in 1981, hers in 2006. In all that time the only really dark patch occurred when Janet wrote a story which seemed to be about us at Takapuna. There was a poet and his wife, a pregnancy, an abortion, consequent lifetime sterility for her, the loss of poetic powers (and of hair) for him . . . It was called 'The Progress of Poetry', not a good or successful piece of writing, and so blackly targeted it felt like a malediction. This was something that came later and is, therefore, outside the frame (or Frame) of the present book; but I refer to it now because, in apologising, and trying to explain (this was in 1964), Janet wrote me a letter in which she referred back to our days at Takapuna:

> Some years ago when I was living at Esmonde Road I met the very first poet I had ever known. He was a very young man with a very young wife. He was (and is) a brilliant scholar. He looked and talked like a 'real' poet. I spent some of the happiest evenings of my life listening to him talking about poetry. I remember vividly the time he read 'Sailing to Byzantium'. When I was *Underseas** I often

---

* A reference to my poem 'Pictures in a Gallery Undersea'.

thought of the young man and his wife for they had both been a treasured part of my Takapuna days. I thought I hope he still writes poetry. What if he has stopped writing? He must never stop.

New Zealand seemed so far away when I wrote that story. I wondered about people I had known, what they were doing, how they were living. Perhaps I voiced my fears, perhaps I tinged them with feminine jealousies and hopes. But I want you and Kay to understand that I've never felt any malice towards you.

WE WERE FAMILIAR WITH THE WHOLE business of getting ready to go 'overseas' – had been through it with friends, had helped Patsy and John pack. You took everything you owned, including sheets and towels, cutlery and kitchen things. There were three categories of luggage – 'cabin baggage', 'wanted on voyage' and 'hold'. 'Wanted on voyage' went into baggage rooms which were accessible once a day. 'Hold' vanished into the hold until you reached your destination. Carriers were involved at each end of the journey.

We had also become accustomed to the ritual of farewells down at Auckland's wharves. They were so significant in those days. Only the rich travelled 'overseas', or soldiers going to a war, or a few young people unshackled by personal daring or academic prospects from the social pressure to buy quickly into the suburbs and 'settle down'. Friends of the travellers were given a pass allowing them on board. While the engines throbbed and rumbled, working up a head of steam, the visitors were permitted to inspect your cabin, sample the lounges, walk on the deck, look over the rail where you would soon stand waving, and from where you would watch the world's oceans, calm or turbulent, swish by, see the desert sands of Suez or the jungles of Panama (or, as in our case, both, once each way), and in the middle latitudes watch flying fish sprinting from the bow-wave. Soon there came the call over loud-speakers, 'All visitors ashore.' The stay-at-homes returned to the wharf and stood in a crowd, craning up to identify their friends among the departing ones lining the rail. Streamers were thrown back and forth. Cranes were rolled back, gangways pulled up, ropes released from bollards. The fog-horns blasted three times so the air, and even the wharf underfoot, shuddered, and slowly the ship was guided by tugs out into the channel, streamers stretching and breaking and falling into the water, faces at the rail blurring into a mass, everybody waving, and calling back and forth, and singing 'Now is the hour . . .' – and weeping.

After which there was the trudge down the wharf to bus or tram or ferry, and the leaden feeling that the travellers were going out into the unknown, into danger and adventure, and you were stuck here at 'the world's end where wonders cease' – a line of Allen Curnow's, who had also written

> O I could go down to harbours
> And mourn with a hundred years
> Of hunger, what slips away there.

Yes, we were still a colony, and we were remote. In the next half century cheap air travel, phone and fax links, then e-mail and internet, satellite positioning and Google Earth – technology of every kind – would shrink the world, close the gaps. To fly economy class to London would be hardly worse than the old overnighter, by rail second class to Wellington, though now you would arrive, not with a passport that said 'British Subject and New Zealand Citizen', but with an Uruwhenua saying your country was New Zealand/Aotearoa and that you were this document's 'holder', one required to answer the question, 'What is the purpose of your visit?' World travel was to become commonplace, but the welcome less warm, your foothold abroad less secure. To leave our own shores would never again be so significant, so magical, so full of yearning and apprehension, excitement and regret.

Patsy and John were the most recent we had waved away. Now friends and family were there to wave, to fade into a blur on the wharf as they watched us diminish at the rail. The tugs turned our ship, the P&O liner *Orsova*, about, set it on its way out in the stream, released it, and we sailed slowly, grandly, down the harbour, past the white museum on the hill with its portentous Doric columns, around Mt Victoria and North Head, and down the gulf past, on one side, Rangitoto with its pepperpot lighthouse, on the other the pale orange-yellow stretch of Takapuna Beach, backed by its white weatherboard houses and red iron roofs. We could pick out the Mortons' house, and imagine that figure on the beach was Hazel walking Fifi before giving her 'tea'.

And then on we sailed, out into the gap, my 'Gateway to the World', where our white ship must have seemed to sit on the horizon in the evening light, as so many I had watched had done, fading, sinking over the rim of the world into that other place, and another life.